Programming Languages for MIS

Concepts and Practice

Programming Languages for MIS

Concepts and Practice

Hai Wang
Shouhong Wang

CRC Press
Taylor & Francis Group
Boca Raton London New York

CRC Press is an imprint of the
Taylor & Francis Group, an **informa** business

AN AUERBACH BOOK

CRC Press
Taylor & Francis Group
6000 Broken Sound Parkway NW, Suite 300
Boca Raton, FL 33487-2742

© 2014 by Taylor & Francis Group, LLC
CRC Press is an imprint of Taylor & Francis Group, an Informa business

Version Date: 20130925

International Standard Book Number-13: 978-1-4822-2266-1 (Hardback)

Library of Congress Cataloging-in-Publication Data

Wang, Hai, 1973-
   Programming languages for MIS : concepts and practice / authors, Hai Wang, Shouhong Wang.
      pages cm
   Includes index.
   ISBN 978-1-4822-2266-1 (alk. paper)
   1. Management information systems. 2. Programming languages (Electronic computers) I. Wang, Shouhong. II. Title.

T58.6.W347 2014
658.4'0380285513--dc23   2013031596

Visit the Taylor & Francis Web site at
http://www.taylorandfrancis.com

and the CRC Press Web site at
http://www.crcpress.com

Contents

Preface

There have been critical discussions on the management information systems (MIS) curriculum design during the last several years. The most notable trend in the MIS curriculum renewal movement is to develop more new MIS courses to meet the needs of the job market of MIS graduates. The needs of the job market have considerable implications for the design of MIS courses to educate the next generation of MIS professionals. MIS students must acquire the fundamental theories of MIS as well as the essential practical skills of computer applications to develop the lifelong learning ability in information technology. Technical skills should focus more on problem solving and practical applications. Regardless of changes in the MIS curricula over the past years to meet the requirements of the job market, as well as the requirements of accreditation organizations such as AACSB and ABET, programming remains a core requirement in most MIS programs.

In the modern service-oriented age, development and maintenance of web-based applications still rely heavily on applications of computer languages regardless of the advances of a variety of software packages. To meet the challenges of the ever changing information technologies, educators need to offer courses in important programming languages for their MIS majors. On the other hand, MIS majors cannot afford to learn multiple computer languages on the one-language/one-course basis. The key to the solution to this problem is to make a pedagogical paradigm shift and to develop courses in multiple computer languages.

Few guidelines for MIS courses of computer programming can be found in the literature or on the Internet. The selection of computer languages for programming courses is a crucial task for the pedagogy design. The design components of such courses are based on four considerations. First, the selected computer languages must be representative and should cover essential concepts and features of all kinds of computer languages that are used in business organizations. Second, the selected computer languages must be commonly used in the industry. Third, the selected computer languages should not require additional computing resources in the ordinary computing labs of the MIS programs. Fourth, the scope and the workload for MIS students to learn these computer languages should be manageable.

Considering these factors, we selected the following computer programming languages for this book: C++, HTML, JavaScript, CSS, VB.NET, C#.NET, ASP.NET, PHP (with MySQL), XML (with XSLT, DTD, and XML Schema), and SQL. Java is a full-scale computer programming language and has been widely used in the industry. This book does not include Java because it requires the Java platform and installation of the Java computing environment on computers with the Windows platform, which could be demanding. In addition, .NET and Java, the two major computer language platforms, share a great similarity of language characteristics. The interested reader who wants to learn Java is referred to our book *Programming Languages for Business Problem Solving,* published by Taylor & Francis, 2007 (ISBN 1-4200-6264-6), for its chapter on Java.

Due to time constraints, it is impossible for students to learn all these languages in great detail. Nevertheless, students are expected to have general knowledge of commonly used computer languages and to be able to develop basic skills of programming. Our methodology applied to the programming courses is to learn languages through typical examples. Specifically, we teach typical problems of MIS applications and their solutions through the use of these computer languages.

A course that uses this book usually consists of two distinct modules: the teaching module and the project module. The teaching module provides an overview of representative computer languages. The project module provides an opportunity for students to practice the computer languages involving hands-on projects. The interested instructor is referred to our pedagogical research papers for the relevant discussions on teaching and learning multiple computer languages in a single course: "An Approach to Teaching Multiple Computer Languages," *Journal of Information Systems Education,* 12(4), 2002, 201–211; and "Design and Delivery of Multiple Server-Side Computer Languages Course," *Journal of Information Systems Education,* 22(2), 2011, 159–168.

The book includes an introduction and eight chapters. The introduction discusses basics of computer languages and the key characteristics of all procedural computer languages. Chapter 2 introduces C++ and explains the fundamental concepts of the two programming paradigms: function oriented and object oriented. Chapter 3 includes HTML, JavaScript, and CSS for web page development. Chapter 4 introduces VB.NET for graphical user interface development. Chapter 5 introduces C#.NET, which is similar to Java. Chapter 6 explains ASP.NET, an important server-side programming language for the Windows platform. ASP.NET incorporates VB.NET, C#.NET, and ADO.NET. Chapter 7 introduces PHP, a popular open source programming language, and explains the use of the MySQL database in PHP. Chapter 8 discusses XML and its companion languages, including XSTL, DTD, and

XML Schema. Finally, Chapter 9 discusses SQL, which is a part of application of server-side programming for database processing.

MIS students will be able to use the concepts and practices in this book as the starting point in their journey to become successful information technology professionals.

Shouhong Wang, PhD
University of Massachusetts, Dartmouth

Hai Wang, PhD
Saint Mary's University, Halifax, Nova Scotia, Canada

The Authors

Hai Wang is an associate professor at the Sobey School of Business at Saint Mary's University, Halifax, Nova Scotia, Canada. He received his BSc in computer science from the University of New Brunswick, and his MSc and PhD in computer science from the University of Toronto. He has published more than 50 research articles in the areas of MIS, big data, data mining, database management, knowledge management, and e-business. His research has continuously been funded by the Natural Sciences and Engineering Research Council of Canada in the past years.

Shouhong Wang is a professor at University of Massachusetts, Dartmouth. He received his PhD in information systems from McMaster University. He has over 30 years' experience of higher education in the MIS field. He has published more than 100 research papers in academic journals and several books on the subject of MIS.

Acknowledgments

Windows, Notepad, WordPad, Windows Explorer, Internet Explorer, Visual Basic, Excel, Access, VB.NET, C#, ASP.NET, Visual Studio.NET, and SQL Server are trademarks of Microsoft Corporation.

Mozilla Firefox is copyrighted by Mozilla Corporation and Mozilla Foundation.

MySQL, Java, and JavaScript are trademarks of Oracle Corporation.

PHP is copyrighted by the PHP Group.

Apache is copyrighted by The Apache Software Foundation.

EasyPHP is copyrighted by EasyPHP and distributed under the general public license.

CSS and XML are trademarks of World Wide Web Consortium (W3C).

Notepad++ is distributed as free software under the GNU general public license.

Dev-C++ is a free integrated development environment developed by Bloodshed Software and distributed under the GNU general public license.

1

INTRODUCTION

1.1 Computers

A computer is a general purpose machine that can be programmed to carry out computation and data processing operations. Since programs can be readily changed by humans through programming, the computer can solve a variety of problems. A computer has a central processing unit (CPU), which interprets and executes programs, and primary memory, which stores programs and data. The components of a computer system also include secondary memory, input device, and output device, as shown in Figure 1.1. An input device converts human signals and data into the signals that can be processed by the CPU. The keyboard and mouse are examples of input devices. An output device converts the signals from the CPU into a form understandable to a human. The monitor and printer are examples of output devices. A device, such as the touch screen or network communication device, can be both an input and output device. Similar to a primary memory, a secondary memory can also be used to store programs and data. There are two main differences between primary memory and second memory. First, primary memory is volatile in nature, while secondary memory is nonvolatile. The programs and data that are stored in the primary memory cannot be retained when the power is turned off. A secondary memory can retain the stored programs and data even if the power is turned off. Second, it is much faster for the CPU to access programs and data in the primary memory than in the second memory. The programs or data stored in the secondary memory are read in batches into the primary memory before they are used by the CPU.

1.2 Computer Programming Languages

1.2.1 Role of Computer Programming Language

A computer programming language is an artificial language designed to communicate instructions to a computer. Programming languages are used to create programs that control a computer to perform the tasks as designed. The tasks a computer can carry out include:

- Manipulating data and information
- Reading data from and/or writing data to the secondary memory or other input/output devices
- Presenting data for a human through the user–computer interface

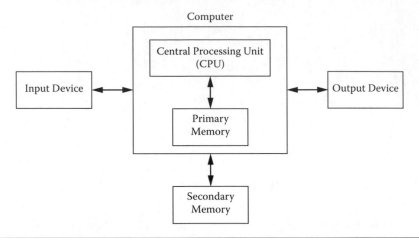

Figure 1.1   A computer system.

There are many computer programming languages. Each computer programming language has its syntax. There is no single computer programming language that can fit all types of applications.

1.2.2 Software Systems

The software systems in a computer are structured in layers, as illustrated in Figure 1.2. As shown in the figure, application software is built by the software developer using high-level programming languages that programmers can easily understand and use. However, the programs in high-level programming languages cannot be executed by the computer unless the programs are translated into the machine executable code (i.e., specific strings of binary digits). To translate a program in a high-level programming language into the machine executable code, a special program, called the compiler or interpreter for that high-level language, must be applied, as shown in Figure 1.3. Once a program in a high-level programming language is translated into the machine-executable code, it can be used an infinite number of times.

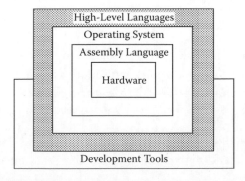

Figure 1.2   The role of computer programming language.

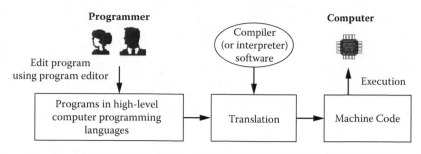

Figure 1.3 Translation of computer programs.

If a program in a high-level programming language has a syntax error, the translation will fail and machine-executable code will not be generated. On the other hand, a program without a syntax error could have a logical error, or semantic error, and the final execution result could be incorrect. To ensure that a program is executed correctly, the computer programmer must do the following three tasks.

1. Understand the application to be developed.
2. Design the program for the application.
3. Debug to fix all syntax errors as well as logical errors.

1.2.3 Taxonomies of Computer Programming Languages

There is no overarching classification scheme for programming languages. In this book, we introduce three major classifications.

1. *Procedural language versus markup language.* A procedural language is capable of commanding a computer to carry out arithmetic or logical operations. All programming languages except for HTML and XML are procedural languages. A markup language is used for annotating a document (or a data set) in a way that is syntactically distinguishable from the text. HTML and XML are markup languages.
2. *Function-oriented language versus object-oriented language.* A function-oriented language uses functions as modules. C is a typical function-oriented language. An object-oriented language uses objects as modules. C++ is a typical object-oriented language. A computer language can be a blended language of function-oriented and object-oriented languages, such as JavaScript and VB.NET.
3. *Client–side language versus server-side language.* A client-side language is used to create the computer programs that are executed on the client side on the web. JavaScript and HTML are typical client-side languages. In contrast, programs in server-side languages such as PHP and ASP.NET are executed by the Web server and have greater access to the information and functional resources available on the server in response to the client's request.

1.3 Computing Architecture in the Internet Environment

Massive client–server networks are connected to build the Internet (or World Wide Web). A general computing architecture in the Internet environment is illustrated in Figure 1.4. Computers are linked to the Internet through the Internet providers.

Client is a computer that accesses a service made available by a server. It is equipped with client-side programs.

Firewall is a computer with special software to protect the Web server, database server, and the database from unauthorized access, viruses, and other suspicious incoming code.

Web server stores the web portal, processes all applications (e.g., order process and payment), and makes all responses to the Internet users' requests. To support applications, a web server has three important software components: API, middleware, and ODBC:

API (application program interface) is a set of functions that allow data exchange between the application software and the database.

Middleware is specialized software of server-side programs to access the database.

ODBC (open database connectivity) is a software interface to relational databases. On a computer of the Windows platform, you can set ODBC for a particular relational database (e.g., structured query language server) or tabular data (e.g., Excel) through [Administrative Tools] in the [Control Panel] of [Settings] in the Windows operating systems. In the Java platform, JDBC (Java database connectivity) plays a similar role.

Database server is the dedicated server for the data retrieval and maintenance of the database.

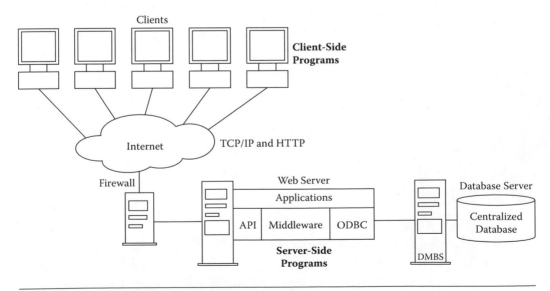

Figure 1.4   Computing architecture in the Internet environment.

1.4 Key Characteristics Shared by All Procedural Programming Languages

As discussed in the previous sections, a procedural programming language is used to carry out arithmetic or logical operations. All procedural programming languages share key characteristics, although individual procedural programming language can have its unique features. Thus, the knowledge of the key characteristics learned from one procedural programming language can be applied to other procedural programming languages.

1.4.1 Syntax, Sentence, and Word

A computer programming language has its syntax—the rules that govern the structure of sentences of the programs written in the language. In a procedural programming language, a sentence consists of words, numbers, and punctuation. There are two types of words in a procedural programming language: keyword (or reserved word) and user-defined word. A keyword represents a specific meaning of the language (e.g., a specific instruction). A user-defined word is defined by the programmer to name a variable or a module. A word used in a procedural programming language must not contain a space and is usually case sensitive.

1.4.2 Variable

A variable is the name of a piece of CPU memory that holds data. A variable name is defined by the programmer and must be a user-defined word. Clearly, variable names are case sensitive; that is, `AVariable` is different from `avariable`. In addition, a name of a variable must be a single user-defined word without a space. A variable has its data type, such as integer, character, etc. The data held by the variable are called the value of the variable. The original value of a variable could be a default value depending on its data type (such as 0 for an integer and space for a character). The value of a variable can be changed through operations, but can never be lost unless the computer program is terminated. Figure 1.5 shows examples of the basic property of variables.

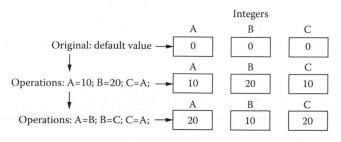

Figure 1.5 Examples of the basic property of variables.

1.4.3 Arithmetic Operation

Arithmetic operations in procedural programming are similar to day-to-day arithmetic calculations, but use reverse expression. For instance, instead of A+B=C, C=A+B is used in programming; this means: "Let C equal A plus B." Multiplication is denoted by the asterisk symbol "*", and division is denoted by the slash symbol "/". The following are several examples of arithmetic operations:

`A=10`	Let A equal 10.
`C=A+B`	Let C equal A plus B.
`B=A*10+(B/10)`	Let B equal 10 times A plus 1/10 of the original value of B.

1.4.4 Execution Sequence

A computer program consists of a set of instructions. During the execution of the procedure of a program, instructions are executed one after another in a sequence (so-called execution sequence) in which they are encountered, but not in the order in which they are listed in the program. Logical instructions (e.g., if-statement and loops) can control the execution sequence of the program, as explained next.

1.4.5 If-Then-Else Logic

An if-then-else statement controls the computer execution sequence based on a condition that is defined by the current value of a particular variable(s). The if-then-else logic is illustrated in Figure 1.6.

1.4.6 Loop

A loop is a group of instructions that are specified once but are executed several times in succession. A loop statement defines such an iteration procedure, as illustrated

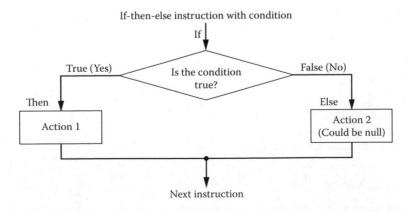

Figure 1.6   If-then-else logic.

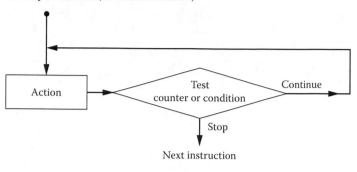

Figure 1.7   Loop.

in Figure 1.7. Loop is actually a variation of if-then-else logic. The common loops include for-loop and do-loop. The variable used in a loop to control the execution of the loop is called a counter.

1.4.7 Module

A large program must be divided into modules to make the program easy to debug. Also, a module can be reused. Here, a module could be a paragraph of instructions, an independent function, or a class, depending upon the specific language in discussion. An instruction in a module can call another module to accomplish a specific task carried out by the called module, as illustrated in Figure 1.8. A module has its name, which is a single user-defined word. The communication between the calling module and the called module can be implemented by passing the values of special variables termed arguments or parameters. Argument and parameter are exchangeable terms in this book.

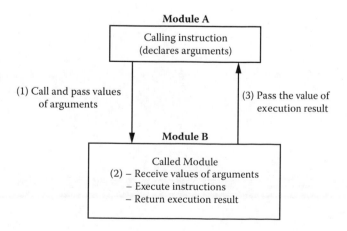

Figure 1.8   Module.

Chapter 1 Exercises

1. Discuss the general model of a computer system. Why does it include secondary memory?
2. Discuss the role of computer programming languages.
3. Discuss how a computer program in a high-level language can be executed by the computer.
4. Discuss the taxonomies of computer programming languages.
5. Discuss the components of computing architecture in the Internet environment.
6. Provide examples of user-defined words that can be used for programs written in a procedural programming language.
7. Suppose that there are two variables: x and y. x stores "Beer" and y stores "Water." How can you swap the values of the two variables to let x store "Water" and y store "Beer"?
8. Suppose that there are three variables: Purchase, TaxRate, and Payment. Purchase stores the money value of the purchased merchandise, and TaxRate stores the state sales tax rate. Write an arithmetic operation to let Payment store the payment amount after tax.
9. Write an if-then-else statement using structured English for the GPA scheme: Grade "A" = 4.0 points, grade "B" = 3.0 points, grade "C" = 2.0 points, grade "D" = 1.0 point, and grade "F" = 0 points.
10. Write a loop statement using structured English to let the computer list 0.3, 0.6, 0.9, 1.2, 1.5, ..., 30.
11. Discuss the advantages of the use of modules in programming.

2
C++

2.1 Introduction to Function-Oriented and Object-Oriented Programming

In the 1960s and 1970s, the structured program theorem was the main stream of programming methodology. In structured programming, a computer program can be expressed by a computable function or a combination of functions. In this book, the structured program theorem is called function-oriented programming. C is a typical function-oriented programming language.

Object-oriented programming (OOP) was first discussed in the late 1960s by people who were working on the SIMULA language. OOP did not become a popular method until the 1980s. Recently, the object-oriented philosophy has been extended to systems development. The computational environments for networking, multimedia, cloud computing, and mobile computing all require object-oriented systems. C++ is a typical OOP language.

This chapter will explain the basic concepts of function-oriented and object-oriented approaches and provide necessary knowledge of both programming paradigms for students. We will use examples to describe the characteristics of the two programming theorems. Traditionally, C and C++ are two languages, although C++ was migrated from C. Actually, C and C++ share many syntax features. Recently, C++ has become nearly a superset of C. In this chapter of C++, we call a typical function-oriented program a "C program" and a typical objected-oriented program a "C++ program." Since C and C++ languages have been the fundamental computer languages, we believe that the benefit of knowing C and C++ languages would be far beyond what we initially desired. Learning C and C++ together is the best way to gain a comparative view of the two programming theorems. In fact, many commonly used computer programming languages adhere to the concept and the characteristics of C and C++. Many procedural programming languages have blended features of function-oriented and object-oriented programs.

2.2 A Tour of C Language

C is a "mid-level" language. Compared to low-level languages (assembly languages), C programs are easier to write and take fewer instructions. They allow the programmer to take full advantage of the built-in capacities of the computer. Compared to high-level languages (e.g., VB.NET), C programs are more compact and efficient; they provide the programmer with flexibility in writing a set of programmed instructions at a low level.

Let us examine the style of C program. Suppose we want to display the string "Hello, World !" on the screen. The C program could be written as follows:

Listing 2.1: An Example of C Program (`HelloWorld.cpp`)

```
/* C Programming Example */
#include<iostream>
using namespace std;
void main()
{
    printf("Hello, world ! \n");
}
```

We use a Microsoft Visual Studio computing environment to run this program. Start Microsoft Visual Studio. After the start page has been loaded, you may simply close it and start to edit your own program (see Figure 2.1).

Click on [File] on the top menu and then [New Project]; you will be allowed to create a project. In the New Project window, select [Win32] on the left pane in [Visual C++] and [Win32 Console Application] on the right pane. It would be a good practice to choose your own folder (e.g., F:\Wang), which will hold your project and the project name (e.g., C-Project), which will keep your programs (see Figure 2.2).

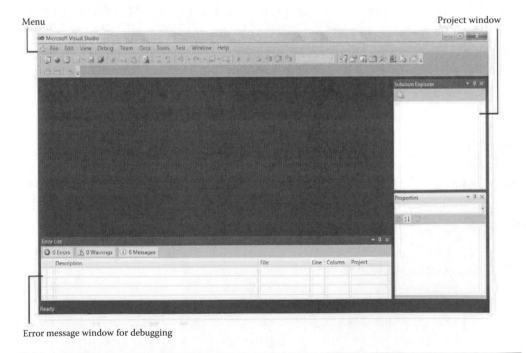

Figure 2.1   Microsoft visual studio environment.

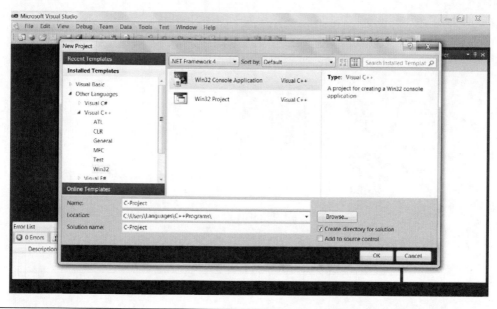

Figure 2.2 Create your project.

Figure 2.3 Set your project.

Click on [OK] and you will see the Win32 Console Application Wizard window. You choose [Application Setting] on the left pane and select [Empty Project] (see Figure 2.3). Click on [Finish] and the environment creates your project in your folder. Right-click on your project name in the [Solution Explore] pane; you will see a pop-up menu. Select [Add] on the menu and then [New Item] on the second pop-up menu (see Figure 2.4).

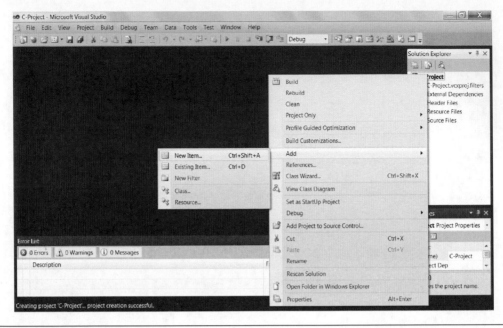

Figure 2.4 Add your program.

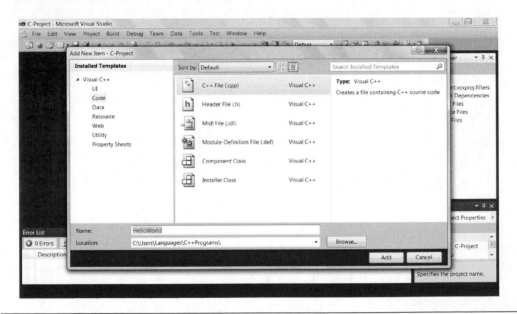

Figure 2.5 Add `HelloWorld.cpp` to the project.

Once the [Add New Item] window shows up, you choose [Code] on the left pane, choose [C++ File (.cpp)] on the central pane, and type the program name, say, HelloWorld (see Figure 2.5). It is a good practice of programming that you do not put space in any name of a program and variable. Click on the [Add] button after entering the program name; you are allowed to edit the program now.

After you edit the program, click on the [Save] icon on the top menu to save the program. Click on [Build] on the top menu and then click on [Build *Project*]

Save   Build project

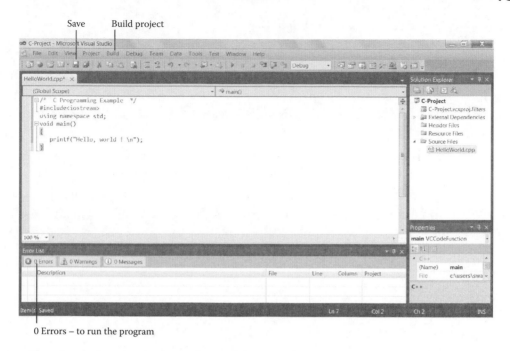

0 Errors – to run the program

Figure 2.6 Edit and compile `HelloWorld.cpp`.

Figure 2.7 Execution result of `HelloWorld.cpp`.

on the pop-up menu to compile the program. If your program is correct, you should have [0 Errors] on the Error List (see Figure 2.6). Now the program is ready to execute. You press [Ctrl] and [F5] keys simultaneously, and you will see the execution window (see Figure 2.7). This environment allows the execution result to stay on the screen until you press any key to close it.

Note that Microsoft Visual Studio is a project-based environment, and a project can have only one `.cpp` program with the `main()` function.

Strictly speaking, C and C++ are two different programming languages: C is function oriented and C++ is object oriented. The extension used for the file name of a C program should be `.c`, and `.cpp` is used for C++. Recently, however, many compilers (such as Microsoft Visual Studio, used in this book) do not differentiate the two, and `.cpp` can be used for C++ program files as well as C program files.

2.2.1 C and C++ Keyword and User-Defined Word

A C or C++ program is a set of C or C++ words and symbols. C and C++ are case sensitive. For instance, "Word" and "word" are two different words in C and C++. C and C++ have their reserved words, called keywords, that implement specific features and may not be used as user-defined words such as variable names and function names. Commonly used keywords in C and C++ are listed in Appendix 2.1.

To define variables and functions, the programmer must use user-defined words for those variable names and function names. The programmer can use any words other than keywords for the user-defined words. However, professional programmers usually use meaningful user-defined words to make the program easy to read and easy to maintain. For example, `CustomerPayment` for a variable of a customer's payment seems to be much sounder than `xyz` for self-documentation.

2.2.2 Comment Statements

A comment statement is delimited by `/*` and `*/` or is placed after `//` (for C++) to explain the logic of the program for human reading. Comment statements are not translated by the compiler, and the program editor simply prints the comments for the programmer.

2.2.3 Preprocessor

A `#include` statement is a preprocessor, which tells the C or C++ compiler to look for a header file before processing the program. A header file is a file that allows the program to use the resources stored in the C and C++ standard library. The `#include` statement places the contents of the header file in the program. In the `HelloWorld.cpp` example (Listing 2.1), the C++ compiler looks for the header file named `<iostream>` for the input/output purpose. You may read manuals to determine which header files of the standard library should be included in your program. As beginners, you may simply include `<iostream>`, `<cstring>`, and `<cmath>` in any cases. Including unnecessary header files does not cause any problems other than wasting the CPU memory.

2.2.4 Namespace

A large program can be assembled by many pieces of small programs written by many programmers. Thus, it is inevitable that the same name of a module is used in different small programs but represents different identifiers. Namespace is applied to avoid confusion. A namespace is an abstract container created to hold a logical grouping of names. Beginners may learn more about namespace later, but simply place the statement `using namespace std;` right after the preprocessors, as shown in Listing 2.1.

2.2.5 *Structure of a C Program, Functions, and Arguments*

The elemental module of a C program is a function. Listing 2.1 (`HelloWorld.cpp`) shows a function named `void main()`. The function `void main()` is special. Execution begins with the function `void main()`. As explained later in this chapter, a function has its type depending upon the type of return data. In this example, the `main` function does not return any data, and the type is `void`. Note that this book uses the Microsoft Visual Studio environment for C and C++ in which the `main` function could be of `void` type. However, in some development environments, `int main()` is used for the main function, which must include a return statement such as `return(0);` at the end of the `int main()` program, although it does not seem to make much sense.

Every C or C++ program has one and only one main function. A function specifies the operations the program will perform and its argument (or parameter). The argument is placed within the pair of parentheses after the function name and indicates the data to be passed to the function from another function for processing. In this case, there is no argument in the `void main()` function.

There are two types of functions in C. One type is the user-defined function. The name of a user-defined function must be a user-defined word, except for the `main()` function, which is a special user-defined function. We will explain more about user-defined functions in general later in this chapter. The other type of function is C standard function. The procedures of those standard functions have been built in the C and C++ libraries, and the programmer is allowed to use them as instructions. Clearly, the name of a standard function is a C and C++ keyword. In Listing 2.1, `printf()` is a standard function, or an instruction. Note that the concepts of function and argument (or parameter) presented in this chapter are universally applicable to all procedural computer languages.

A pair of braces indicates a functional body, a group of instructions. "{" is used to begin the functional body, while "}" marks the end of the functional body. A functional body (e.g., a loop) can be nested within another functional body. Braces must be balanced to make a correct structure of the program (see Figure 2.8). The location of a brace in a line is not important. If a function body is so simple that it has only one statement, the pair of braces may be omitted.

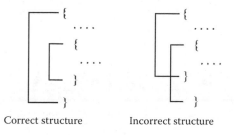

Correct structure   Incorrect structure

Figure 2.8 Structure of C and C++ programs.

2.2.6 Statements and Semicolon

A complete C or C++ statement (instruction) ends in a semicolon ";". However, a semicolon after an end brace "}" might be omitted if the omission causes no ambiguity.

2.2.7 Data Type

The data type must be declared before a variable is used in the program. Important types of data include int for integers (e.g., 1, 2, 3), float for floating point numbers (e.g., 1.0, 3.14, 0.699), double for double precision floating point numbers, and char for characters (e.g., "a," "b," "D") or strings (e.g., "John Smith"). For example,

`int a, b, c;`	defines the three variables a, b, c as integers
`float x;`	defines variable x as a floating point number
`double y;`	defines variable y as a double precision floating point number
`char k;`	defines variable k as a character
`char CustomerName[32];`	defines `CustomerName` as a string variable that can hold up to 31 characters

We will learn more about strings later in this chapter.

The data type for a variable can be declared anywhere in the program before the variable is used for the first time.

2.2.8 Arithmetic Operations

The symbols of arithmetic operations are similar to those in most other languages—for example,

`x=5;`	let x equal 5
`x=a+b;`	let x equal the value of a plus b
`x=a-b;`	let x equal the value of a minus b
`x=a*b;`	let x equal the value of a times b
`x=a/b;`	let x equal the value of a divided by b
`x=pow(a,b);`	let x equal the value of a^b (power)

There are some special operations in C and C++—for example,

`y=x++;`	means y=x+1
`y=x--;`	means y=x-1

When making a user-defined word, avoid confusion with the minus sign and a hyphen. For example, the word `Customer-Payment` could be interpreted as "`Customer` minus `Payment`." In this book, we use the so-called camel style for user-defined words, such as `CustomerPayment`.

2.2.9 for-*Loop*

The for-loop provides a repetition structure handling the details of counter-controlled repetition. A typical for-loop structure is

```
for(int [counter]=1; [counter]<=[final value]; [counter]++)
{ [repetition actions] };
```

The following is an example of a for-loop. Note that the line numbers are used for annotation and are not a part of the program:

Listing 2.2: An Example of a for-Loop (`ForLoop.cpp`)

```
1 #include<iostream>
2 using namespace std;
3 void main()
4 {
5   int i;
6   for (i=1; i<=10; i++)
7   printf("%4d %4d \n", i, i*i);
8 }
```

In this example, `i` is the for-loop control variable (counter). (`i=1;  i<=10;  i++`) means that the initial value of `i` is set to 1, and the for-loop increments `i` by 1 (i.e., `i++`) each time. The repetition continues as long as `i` is less than or equal to 10. In other words, the action (`printf`, in this case) repeats 10 times. The execution result is exhibited in Figure 2.9.

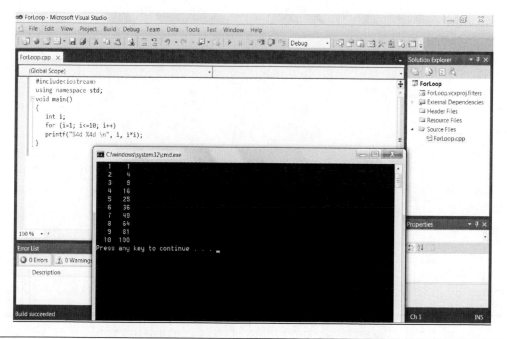

Figure 2.9　Execution result of `ForLoop.cpp`.

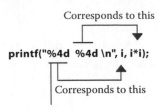

Prints a 4-digit integer number

Figure 2.10   Argument of command `printf()`.

2.2.10 `printf()` *Statement with Conversion Specifier*

In the `printf()` statement of Listing 2.2, the `%` symbol is called a conversion specifier that indicates the format of input and output data:

`%d`   print an integer number; for example, `%4d` is to print an integer number up to four digits

`%f`   print a floating point number; for example, `%4.2f` is to print four digits before the decimal point and two digits after the decimal point

`%s`   print a character string

`%u`   means free format

In the argument, `\n` means "advance the cursor to the beginning of the next line." The relationship of the argument in the `printf()` statement is briefly illustrated in Figure 2.10.

Note that simple commands `cout` (for screen output) and `cin` (for keyboard input) for free format input–output operations are available in C++, as illustrated in C++ examples later in this chapter.

2.2.11 `if`*-Statement*

The `if`-statement is used to choose among alternative courses of actions. The general syntax of the if-else structure is

```
if ( [condition] ) { [action_1] ; }
else                { [action_2] ; };
```

Note that an action in an if-statement can contain another if-statement, as shown in the example in Listing 2.3 (`IfStatement.cpp`).

Listing 2.3: An Example (C++) of if-Statement (`IfStatement.cpp`)

```
1 #include<iostream>
2 using namespace std;
```

```
3 void main()
4 {
5     double GrossIncome, StateTax, FederalTax;

6     cout << "Input a number for gross income ...\n";
7     cin >> GrossIncome;

8     if( GrossIncome==0.0 )
9             FederalTax=StateTax=0.0;
10    else
11        {
12          if( GrossIncome<=10000.0 )
13          {
14          FederalTax=GrossIncome*0.15;
15          StateTax=(GrossIncome-FederalTax)*0.05;
16          }
17          else
18          {
19          FederalTax=GrossIncome*0.25;
20          if((GrossIncome<=25000.0) && (GrossIncome>10000.0))
21                    StateTax=(GrossIncome-FederalTax)*0.08;
22                  else
23                    StateTax=(GrossIncome-FederalTax)*0.10;
24          }
25        };
26    printf("Federal tax is %5.2f \n", FederalTax);
27    printf("State tax is %5.2f \n", StateTax);
28 }
```

The complex if-statements in Listing 2.3 implement the following decision logic:

	CONDITIONS			
	GROSS INCOME = 0	GROSS INCOME = (0,10K]	GROSS INCOME = (10K,25K]	GROSS INCOME > 25K
Federal tax rate	0	15%	25%	25%
State tax rate	0	5%	8%	10%

Note that, in the if-statement, the double equality (==) is used for testing the equality condition (see line **8** of Listing 2.3). In the condition expression, operator && stands for logical AND of two conditions (see line **20** of Listing 2.3). Logical OR is represented by operator ||.

Figure 2.11 shows the execution result of IfStatement.cpp given the user's input.

Figure 2.11   Execution result of IfStatement.cpp.

2.2.12 String and String Processing

Data processing more often involves string (a set of characters) processing. A string is stored as an array of data type `char`. Suppose we use a 15-character string; we need to declare an array

```
char mystring[16];
```

because one space of the array is reserved for the null character in C and C++ to be used for "pointer"—a unique feature of C++. Also, since the index of an array begins with zero, which often causes confusion, one may declare an array two spaces longer than what is needed. Two major operations are commonly used in string processing. One is the string copy (`strcpy`) operation, and the other is the string comparison (`strcmp`) operation. The syntax of `strcpy` is

```
strcpy([destination string], [source string]);
```

This means to copy the source string to the destination string. Instead of `strcpy`, `strcpy_s` is commonly used to avoid buffer overflow, or a warning message will appear after compiling. The `strcmp` operation returns a value, which is explained as follows:

```
strcmp([string-1], [string-2]);
```

It returns 0 if the two strings are identical, 1 if string-1 is greater than string-2, and -1 if string-1 is less than string-2.

A string can be passed to a function for processing or can be returned from a function. C and C++ have a unique feature of "pointer," which is associated with a `char` type variable. In this book, we do not discuss pointer in any detail, but use the * symbol before the string argument of the returning function. You will see more examples of string processing in the program examples later in this chapter.

2.3 Functional Approach

2.3.1 Functional Decomposition

A large complex program must be decomposed into modules for better program design, easy maintenance, and reuse. There are two major types of decomposition approaches: the functional approach and the object-oriented approach. Traditional structured analysis and structured programming follow the functional decomposition approach, which is adopted in C. In C programming, a module is defined as a function. Functional decomposition can be illustrated by the diagram shown in Figure 2.12. The size of a function is usually small (e.g., about 20 lines) to maintain readability of the program. A good programming practice never produces a large program (e.g., hundreds of lines) without dividing it into readable functions.

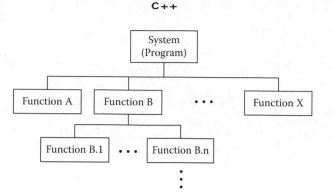

Figure 2.12 Functional decomposition.

2.3.2 A Simple Example of User-Defined Function

To explain how to write user-defined functions in C, we give a simple example in Listing 2.4. In this program, the main program calls the function that calculates the average value of two numbers and then prints the result.

Listing 2.4: A Simple Example of Function (`SimpleFunction.cpp`)

```
 1 #include<iostream>
 2 using namespace std;

 3 /* function CalculateAvg is double type, and has two arguments */

 4 double CalculateAvg(double, double);

 5 void main()
 6 {
 7  double FirstNumber, SecondNumber;
 8  double Average;

 9  FirstNumber=10;
10  SecondNumber=15;

11 /* call function CalculateAvg using two arguments */

12  Average=CalculateAvg(FirstNumber, SecondNumber);
13  printf("The average of the two numbers is : %f . \n", Average);
14 }

15 /* function CalculateAvg() */

16 double CalculateAvg(double Number1, double Number2)
17 {
18  double Answer; /* Local variable */
19  Answer=(Number1 + Number2) / 2;
20  return(Answer);
21 }
```

We examine how the program in Listing 2.4 works. Line **4** defines the prototype of the function, named `CalculateAvg`, used by the `main` function. `CalculateAvg` is the user-defined function name. Lines **5–14** are the `main` function. Lines **7** and **8**

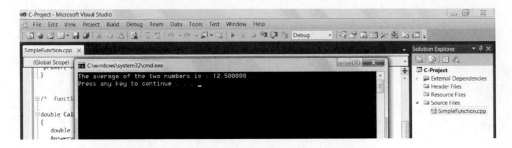

Figure 2.13   Execution result of `SimpleFunction.cpp`.

define the types of three variables, named `FirstNumber`, `SecondNumber`, and `Average`, used in this `main` function. Lines **9** and **10** assign values to `FirstNumber` and `SecondNumber`. Line **12** calls function `CalculateAvg`, bringing the values of `FirstNumber` and `SecondNumber` to the called function. This line also lets the value received from `CalculateAvg` pass back to `Average`.

Upon the calling, the computer execution sequence turns to line **16,** the starting point of the `CalculateAvg` function. The computer passes values of `FirstNumber` to `Number1` and `SecondNumber` to `Number2` and executes lines **17** through **21**. Line **18** defines a local variable for this function. A local variable is only valid within the function and is not accessible from an external module. Line **19** makes calculations. Line **20** returns the result value back to the calling function. The computer execution sequence returns to line **12** (the `main` function) and passes the result back to `Average` in the `main` function. Line **13** prints the value of `Average`. The execution result of this program is shown in Figure 2.13.

2.3.3 Declaration of User-Defined Function

The declaration statement indicates the prototype of the function that is used in the present function right after the preprocessor and before the `main` function. The general syntax of declaration statement is

```
[function type] [function name] (data types of arguments);
```

The type of the function must be the type of the data returned by the function. For example, in Listing 2.4 (`SimpleFunction.cpp`), line **18** defines the data type of `Answer` to be `double`. `Answer` is returned by the function (line **20**). Hence, the type of this function is `double`. If there is no return data from the function, the type of the function is `void`. Each function can have arguments to receive data passed from the calling-function.

2.3.4 Calling-Function and Called-Function

The statement that uses a function is termed the calling-function. In the example of Listing 2.4, the statement `CalculateAvg(FirstNumber, SecondNumber)`

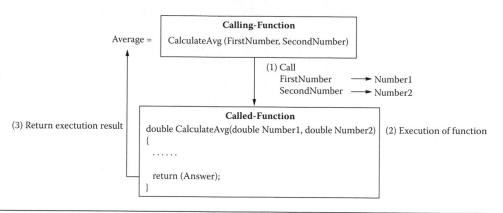

Figure 2.14 Function operations.

(line **12**) in the `main()` function is the calling-function. The function used by the calling-function is termed the called-function. In the example of Listing 2.4, the `CalculateAvg(double Number1, double Number2)` function is the called-function. If a C program has two or more called-functions, the order of the called-functions in the program is not important because the function names as their identifiers are used in the program. The calling-function passes the corresponding value for each of the arguments (or parameters) to the called-function for processing. If the called-function returns a result to the calling-function, the type of the return value is the type of the called-function. If there is no return value, the return type (and thus the type of the function) is `void`. Note that the order of the arguments in the calling-function must be the same as the order of the arguments in the called-function, and the data type of the argument in the calling-function must match the data type of the corresponding argument in the called-function. Figure 2.14 shows how a user-defined function operates using this example.

2.3.5 Structure Diagram

There are many tools available to assist computer programmers in designing and documenting programs. One of the tools for function-oriented (or structured) programming is structure diagram. A structure diagram is a hierarchy chart on which the functions are represented as modules and the sequence of the execution of these modules can be traced from top to bottom and from left to right. The program in Listing 2.4 can be represented by the structure diagram in Figure 2.15. This example is simple, and only one function is used by the `main` function.

2.3.6 An Example of Two Functions

Practically, the programmer must design the program by drawing a diagram first, and then do programming based on the design "blueprint." It is not a good practice to write a program without a clear design of the program.

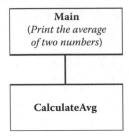

Figure 2.15 Structure diagram of `SimpleFunction.cpp`.

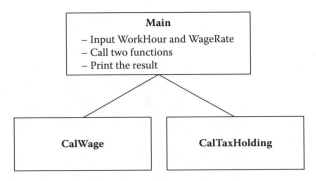

Figure 2.16 Structure diagram of `TwoFunctions.cpp`.

This subsection presents an example of two functions. This program calculates the payroll based on the employee's work hours, the wage rate, and the tax withholding formula. One function calculates the wage, and the other function calculates the tax withholding. The main function allows the user to input the employee's work hours and the wage rate. It then calls the two functions and prints out the result. Figure 2.16 shows the structure of the program. The order of execution of the functions in a structure diagram is "top to bottom, left to right."

Listing 2.5 exhibits the program. The program is rather straightforward. As demonstrated by the example, the function-oriented program has advantages. For example, if the tax withholding formula needs to change, only the function named `CalTaxHolding` is relevant to the change. Such a property of a function-oriented program makes programs easy to debug, easy to maintain, and easy to reuse. Figure 2.17 shows the execution result.

Figure 2.17 Execution result of `TwoFunctions.cpp`.

Listing 2.5: An Example of Two Functions (`TwoFunctions.cpp`)

```
 1 #include<iostream>
 2 using namespace std;

 3 double CalWage(double, double); /* Calculate Wage */
 4 double CalTaxHolding(double); /* Calculate tax holding */

 5 void main()
 6 {
 7 double WorkHour, WageRate, TotalWage;
 8 double TaxHolding;

 9 cout << "Please input weekly work hours: \n";
10 cin >> WorkHour;
11 cout << "Please input wage rate: \n";
12 cin >> WageRate;

13 TotalWage=CalWage(WorkHour, WageRate);
14 TaxHolding=CalTaxHolding(TotalWage);
15 printf("The total wage before tax holding is: $ %4.2f \n", TotalWage);
16 printf("Payment after tax holding is: $ %4.2f \n",
            TotalWage-TaxHolding);
17 }

18 /* function CalWage() */
19 double CalWage(double Hours, double Rate)
20 {
21  double Total; /* Local variable */
22  Total= Hours * Rate;
23  return(Total);
24 }

25 /* function CalTaxHolding() */
26 double CalTaxHolding(double Wage)
27 {
28  double Holding; /* Local variable */
29  if (Wage < 200) { Holding = Wage * 0.1; }
30  else
31  {if (Wage < 300) { Holding = Wage * 0.15; }
32   else { Holding = Wage * 0.2; }
33  };
34  return(Holding);
35 }
```

2.3.7 *An Example of Multiple Functions*

This subsection presents a C program with multiple functions that prints out a table of monthly payments given the loan terms and the interest rates. It uses for-loop, if-statement, and multiple function calls. The structure of the program is shown in Figure 2.18. The main function calls the four functions from left to right in sequence. The two loops indicate the repetition of the execution of the four functions. The outer loop repeats the entire procedure for a 3-year horizon, and the inner loop repeats the procedure for the five interest levels. The program is listed in Listing 2.6.

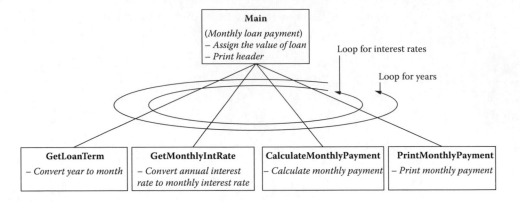

Figure 2.18 Structure diagram of `LoanPayment.cpp`.

Listing 2.6: C Program with Multiple Functions (`LoanPayment.cpp`)

```
1  /*  This is a C program to printout the monthly payment  */
2  /*  given a term loan and annual interest rates          */

3  #include<iostream>
4  using namespace std;

5  int GetLoanTerm(int);    /*  These four are functions  */
6  double GetMonthlyIntRate(double);
7  double CalculateMonthlyPayment(double, int, double);
8  void PrintMonthlyPayment(int, double, double, int);

9  void main()
10 {
11   int i, j;                    /* for loop counters */
12   int LoanTermYears;
13   int LoanTermMonths;
14   double LoanAmount;
15   double AnnualIntRate;
16   double MonthlyIntRate;
17   double MonthlyPayment;

18   /* Define the loan amount     */
19   LoanAmount=1000;

20   /* Print out a heading        */
21   printf("** MONTHLY PAYMENT FOR $%5.0f LOAN ** \n", LoanAmount);

22   /*  The main function uses two for loops     */

23   for (i=1; i<4; i++) {    /* generates 3 years of loan term */
24     LoanTermYears=i;

25     for (j=1; j<6; j++) { /* generates 5 annual interest rate */
26     AnnualIntRate=0.045+0.005*j;

27     /* Change years to months   */
28     LoanTermMonths = GetLoanTerm(LoanTermYears);
```

```
29    /* Change annual interest rate to monthly interest rate */
30    MonthlyIntRate = GetMonthlyIntRate(AnnualIntRate);

31 /* Calculate monthly payment    */
32   MonthlyPayment =
33   CalculateMonthlyPayment(LoanAmount,LoanTermMonths,MonthlyIntRate);

34 /* Printout the table, a line each time        */
35 /* j is used as a flag to control the format  */

36   PrintMonthlyPayment(LoanTermYears,AnnualIntRate,MonthlyPayment,j);
37   }
38 }
39 }

40 /*  Four functions are defined below   */
41 /* (1) Change years to months  */
42 int GetLoanTerm(int Years)
43 {
44  int Months;
45  Months = 12 * Years;
46  return(Months);
47 }

48 /* (2) Change annual interest rate to monthly interest rate  */
49 double GetMonthlyIntRate(double AnnualRate)
50 {
51   double MonthlyRate;
52   MonthlyRate = AnnualRate / 12;
53   return(MonthlyRate);
54 }

55 /* (3) Formula of the calculation of monthly payment  */
56 double CalculateMonthlyPayment(double Loan,
57                                    int Term, double InterestRate)
58 {
59  double Payment;
60  Payment =
61  (Loan*pow((1+InterestRate),Term)*InterestRate)/
62                          (pow((1+InterestRate),Term)-1);
63  return(Payment);
64 }

65 /* (4) printout an item, the Flag controls the format  */
66 void PrintMonthlyPayment(int Term, double InterestRate,
67                                    double Pay, int Flag)
68 {

69  if(Flag==1)
70  {printf("  %2d YEAR %1.4f %5.2f \n", Term, InterestRate, Pay);}
71   else
72    {printf("        %1.4f %5.2f \n", InterestRate, Pay);};
73 }
74 /*  END of the program  */
```

We examine how the program in Listing 2.6 works. Lines **5–8** define the prototypes of the four functions used in this program. Lines **9–39** are the main function.

Lines **11–17** define the types of all variables used in this main function. Line **19** assigns a value to LoanAmount. Line **21** prints a heading for the printout on the screen. Lines **23–38** are a for-loop. It generates data for the loan terms up to 3 years. Lines **25–37** are another for-loop embedded in the first for-loop. This for-loop generates data for five different interest rate levels. Within this loop, line **26** generates the annual interest rate. Since this program is to display the monthly payment for a loan and the loan term is usually expressed in years, we must change the number of years to the number of months. Line **28** calls the function GetLoanTerm to make a conversion. The computer execution sequence turns to line **42**. After lines **43–47,** the loan term has been changed to months, and the execution sequence returns to line **30.** Line **31** calls the function GetMonthlyInRate to convert the annual interest rate to the monthly interest rate. The execution sequence turns to line **49**. After lines **50–54,** the interest rate has been converted into the monthly interest rate, and the execution sequence returns to line **32** (line **33** continues the instruction). The instruction of lines **32** and **33** obtains the monthly payment by calling the function CalculateMonthlyPayment, and the execution sequence jumps to line **56** (line **57** continues the instruction). Lines **58–64** complete the calculation and return the result to MonthlyPayment (line **32**). The execution sequence then turns back to line **36,** which calls the PrintMonthlyPayment function to print the monthly payment. The execution sequence turns to line **66** (line **67** continues the instruction). Note that this function does not return any value and is of the void type. The logic defined in lines **69–72** is to make the printout formatted, corresponding to the for-loops in the main function. For beginners, it might not be straightforward.

Remember that the computer is under the control of the two embedded loops. The computer repeats the calculations and printing 15 times. After each time of the iteration, the computer updates the values of the control counters, and new data are generated and printed on the screen. The order of these functions in the program is not important. As long as a necessary function is included in the program, the computer can find it anywhere by searching the function name in accordance with the program logic. The execution result of this program is shown in Figure 2.19.

Using function-oriented programming languages, one is able to implement a large software system through functional decomposition. Function-oriented programming has been widely used in the stand-alone computer environment for calculations. However, in the software engineering field, people have found that the functional decomposition approach has disadvantages, including:

1. Interfaces between functions are often too complicated.
2. Modules are often difficult to reuse because the partition of functions is very much an arbitrary one.
3. The separation of data from the processing makes the computation in the networking environment inefficient.

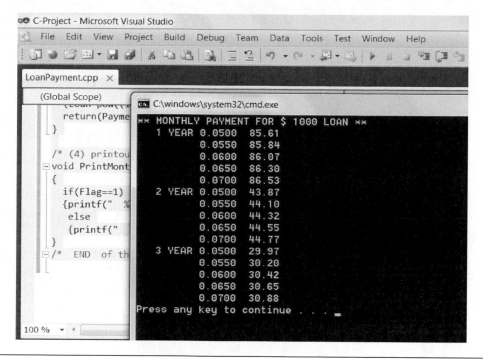

Figure 2.19 Execution result of `LoanPayment.cpp`.

2.4 Object-Oriented Approach

2.4.1 Object and Class

The elementary unit in the object-oriented programming theorem is object. People found that decomposition of a system based on objects is more natural than functional decomposition. Object-oriented programming is effective in the Internet computing environment or user interface development. Examples of object include:

- A customer—physically existing body
- An inventory item—physically existing good
- A ticket—a document
- A game—an event
- A button on a screen—a widget representing a program

A set of objects that have common characteristics is defined as a class. Follow the above examples of object:

- CUSTOMER—class of customers
- INVENTORY—class of inventory items
- TICKET—class of tickets
- GAME—class of games
- BUTTON—class of buttons

Actually, OOP is about programming for classes. Precisely, OOP is class-based programming. Object and class are often used interchangeably when talking about OOP, but they are different: An object is an individual entity of its class.

An object encapsulates its data descriptions (or attributes) and the operations that apply to it. There are two types of operations in the object. An operation that manipulates the encapsulated data in the object is called a method. The operation procedure that sends messages to other object(s) is called a request for service. Conceptually, method in OOP is not much different from function in function-oriented programming, and message sending in OOP is not much different from calling-function in function-oriented programming. However, people use different terminology to differentiate the programming paradigms. In OOP, the module unit is class, which represents the set of objects encapsulating the attributes and the operations.

Classes can be organized into hierarchies in which the subclasses inherit the properties of their superclass(es). For example, the INVENTORY class can have its subclasses—say, COMPUTER, PRINTER, PAPER, etc. Inheritance provides an explicit method for identifying and representing common attributes. Suppose we have already written some programs for the parent class (e.g., INVENTORY); then we do not need to write similar programs for the child class (subclass) (e.g., COMPUTER) for the same manipulations (e.g., order processing). This is the importance of inheritance.

To analyze, design, and make documentation of the organizations of object-oriented programs, system specialists need diagrammatic tools for OOP similar to structure diagrams for function-oriented programs. The universal modeling language (UML) is promoted to become a "standard" tool for object-oriented analysis and design. However, the complete version of UML is hard for beginners to learn. In this book, we use a simplified version of OOP design diagram symbols, as shown in Figure 2.20. The figure shows the elementary constructs representing object class, attributes, method, message sending, and inheritance.

C++ is one of the first OOP languages that have been widely used for software development. It is typical and standardized, although it is not perfect.

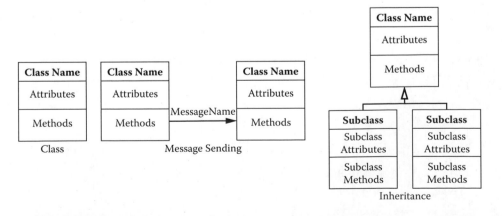

Figure 2.20 OOP diagram constructs.

2.4.2 Descriptions of Class

In C++, the general description of class construction is shown in Listing 2.7 (it is not a program).

Listing 2.7: A Class Description Format in C++

```
class ClassNameIdentifier
{
private: // Data and methods cannot be accessed directly from outside

        Data;
        Methods;

public: // Data and methods can be accessed directly from outside

        Data;
        Methods;

};
```

Listing 2.8 is an example of a C++ program that describes the class named INVENTORY. A class is saved as a header file with extension .h, which means a part of library.

Listing 2.8: The INVENTORY Class Description (inventory.h)

```
 1 // This code defines the class named INVENTORY
 2 // File inventory.h
 3 class INVENTORY
 4 {
 5 private:
 6 // Attributes of the class
 7 unsigned int InventoryValue;

 8 public:
 9 // A constructor initializes the value to 4
10 INVENTORY() { InventoryValue=4; };

11 // Methods of class
12 void Increment()  { InventoryValue++; };
13 void Decrement()  { InventoryValue--; };
14 unsigned int AccessValue() { return InventoryValue;};
15 };
```

In the simple example of Listing 2.8, line **3** defines the name of the class. This class has only one attribute, InventoryValue. In the public section, the class is initialized by the constructor, and InventoryValue is assigned 4 in this example (line **10**). There are three methods in this class. The first method is named Increment (line **12**) for stocking up. Its process is to increase the value of the object by 1. The second method is named Decrement (line **13**) for selling. Its process is to decrease the value by 1. The third method simply returns the value of InventoryValue. Note that a class is ended with "};"—a close bracket plus a semicolon. Several new concepts are discussed further.

2.4.3 public *and* private *Statements*

public means that the attributes (data) or methods in this part are accessible to objects of any other class, and private means that the attributes (data) or method in this part is accessible only to objects created from the current class. Commonly, attributes (data) are placed in private, and methods are placed in public.

2.4.4 Constructor

Constructor is a specific method that always has the same name as the class. A constructor can have its own operation, as shown in Listing 2.8, or can turn to an independent method as shown later in other examples. The constructor initializes the values of the attributes of the object declared. Generally, there are three ways to implement a constructor:

1. Assign values directly by using assign statements in the program.
2. Accept values from the users (keyboard).
3. Read disk files/database.

To focus on the major features of C++, we do not discuss disk files/database in this chapter.

2.4.5 Use of Class—Declare Object and Message Sending

Once a class has been defined in a header file, a program (the main program or other classes) can declare an object of this class using a statement

```
CLASSNAME ObjectName;
```

for example,

```
INVENTORY Item1;
```

A class module allows another module to use its individual methods (i.e., not necessarily all of the methods) through the message sending defined by a statement

```
ObjectName.MethodName;
```

for example,

```
Item1.Increment();
```

Note that the private data and method of an object cannot be accessed or modified by another object without sending a message.

The program in Listing 2.9 shows how to declare objects and how a program sends a message to an object and acquires information from the object. Remember that a C++ program has one and only one `main` program. The `main` program is stored in a program file with extension `.cpp`.

Listing 2.9: Program Uses the `INVENTORY` Class (`InventoryProcess.cpp`)

```
 1 // C++ program that uses the class INVENTORY
 2 #include<iostream>
 3 #include"inventory.h"
 4 using namespace std;

 5 void main()
 6 {
 7 INVENTORY Item1;    // Item1 is an object of INVENTORY
 8 INVENTORY Item2;    // Item2 is another object of INVENTORY

 9 Item1.Increment();   // Messages
10 Item2.Decrement();
11 printf("Inventory item-1's value is %u \n", Item1.AccessValue() );
12 printf("Inventory item-2's value is %u \n", Item2.AccessValue() );
13 }
```

We examine how the C++ program in Listing 2.9 (`InventoryProcess.cpp`) works with the class defined in Listing 2.8 (`inventory.h`). Line **3** instructs the computer to find the header file for the class used by this program. When writing a program to use a defined class, one has to include the file that contains the class. In this example, the `inventory.h` header file of the `INVENTORY` class is included. Note that this header file is developed by the user (i.e., it is not a standard library header file), and is cited by using quotation marks. Line **7** declares an object of the class `INVENTORY`. It is named `Item1`. The computer execution sequence turns to the `INVENTORY` class (see Listing 2.8). The program creates an object of the class and names it `Item1`. Conceptually, object `Item1` has its own value of the attributes and can perform operations independently. Upon the creation of the `Item1` object, the computer executes the constructor of the class for this object. In this example, the initial value of the attribute `InventoryValue` is set to 4 (see line **10** of Listing 2.8).

The computer execution sequence returns back to line **8** in Listing 2.9. Similarly to line **7,** line **8** declares another object, named `Item2`. In this example, the initial value of the attribute `InventoryValue` of `Item2` is also set to 4. At this point, the computer holds two objects of the `INVENTORY` class.

Line **9** in Listing 2.9 is a message sent to object `Item1`, requesting to execute the method `Increment`. The computer execution sequence turns to line **12** in Listing 2.8 for this object. Remember that the attribute `InventoryValue` of `Item1` is initially set to 4. After the execution of line **12** in Listing 2.8, `InventoryValue` of `Item1` becomes 5.

The computer execution sequence returns back to line **10** in Listing 2.9. It sends a message to object `Item2`, requesting to execute the method `Decrement`. The computer execution sequence turns to line **13** in Listing 2.8 for object `Item2`. As its initial value of `InventoryValue` is 4, `InventoryValue` of `Item2` becomes 3 after the `Decrement` operation.

Line **11** in Listing 2.9 is to print data on the screen. It contains a message to object `Item1` requesting to execute `AccessValue`. The computer execution sequence turns to line **14** in Listing 2.8 and returns `InventoryValue` of object `Item1` to the message sender for printing. Line **12** in Listing 2.9 does a similar job as line **11,** but requests to execute `AccessValue` for object `Item2` and prints the returned value of `InventoryValue` of `Item2` on the screen.

The preceding execution process can be depicted in a walkthrough diagram as shown in Figure 2.21.

To run a C++ program in the Microsoft Visual Studio environment, one needs to add one `main` program (`.cpp`) and all the header files (`.h`) used by the `main` program to the project. The execution result of this example is shown in Figure 2.22.

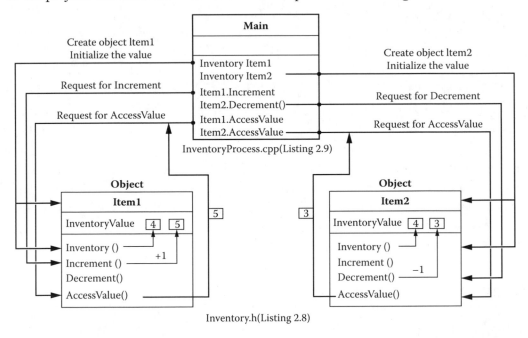

Figure 2.21 Walk through `InventoryProcess.cpp` and `inventory.h`.

Figure 2.22 Execution result of `InventoryProcess.cpp` and `inventory.h`.

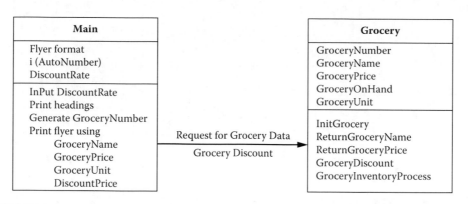

Figure 2.23 OOP design for the grocery store example.

2.5 Design of Objected-Oriented Program

This section provides an example of application of OOP. In this simple example of a grocery store, the user is supposed to input a discount rate for the grocery store and to print out a flyer. As pointed out earlier in this chapter, the programmer must design the program before working on the program. The OOP design diagram for this example is shown in Figure 2.23.

The main program for this example, named Flyer.cpp, is shown in Listing 2.10(a), and the class GROCERY (grocery.h) is shown in Listing 2.10(b).

Listing 2.10(a): Example—Flyer.cpp

```
 1 // ****   C++ program for flyers (file: Flyer.cpp) ****
 2 #include<iostream>
 3 #include<fstream>
 4 #include"grocery.h"

 5 using namespace std;

 6 // The header file of the class GROCERY used is included
 7 // The main program is to manipulate the GROCERY objects
 8 // and print a flyer based on the current discount rate

 9 void main()
10 {
11 double DiscountRate;   // for discount rate
12 // The program asks the user to input the current discount rate
13 cout<<"Please input discount rate ... in percentage. \n";
14 cin>> DiscountRate;

15 // Display the headlines of the flyer
16 printf("\n \n");
17 printf("            My Small Grocery Store      \n");
18 printf("      ****************************   \n \n");
19 printf("          Regular Price      Sale Price   \n \n");

20 // Manipulates the available Grocery objects
21 // In this case, we assume we have only 5 items
```

```
22 for (int i=1; i<=5; i++)  {
23      GROCERY Grocery;
24      Grocery.InitGrocery(i);
25 // Notice the spaces for align in the following printf statements
26      printf ("%s", Grocery.ReturnGroceryName());
27      printf("%4.2f ", Grocery.ReturnGroceryPrice());
28      printf("/ %s            ", Grocery.ReturnGroceryUnit());
29      printf("%4.2f ", Grocery.GroceryDiscount(DiscountRate));
30      printf("/ %s  \n", Grocery.ReturnGroceryUnit());
31  }
32 }
```

Listing 2.10(b): Example—grocery.h

```
 1 // ****  Class GROCERY definition  ****
 2 // File is "grocery.h"
 3 class GROCERY
 4 {
 5 private:
 6 // Attributes
 7 int        GroceryNumber;
 8 char       GroceryName[20];
 9 double     GroceryPrice;
10 double     GroceryOnHand;
11 char       GroceryUnit[5];

12 public:
13 // Constructor
14 GROCERY ()
15 {
16  // Constructor is actually implemented by method
17  // void InitGrocery(int) depending on AutoNumber
18 };

19 // The following procedure simulates the system to read a
20 // database/data file which records information of the
21 // grocery products.
22 // One may substitute this procedure by using database/files

23 void InitGrocery(int AutoNumber)  {
24       GroceryNumber=AutoNumber;

25       if (GroceryNumber==1)
26       { strcpy_s(GroceryName, "Milk        ");
27                        // Add spaces to align all grocery names
28         GroceryPrice=2.59;
29         GroceryOnHand=300;
30         strcpy_s(GroceryUnit, "Oz ");
31                        // Add spaces to align all grocery units
32       };
33       if (GroceryNumber==2)
34       { strcpy_s(GroceryName, "Egg         "); // Add spaces
35         GroceryPrice=1.89;
36         GroceryOnHand=800;
37         strcpy_s(GroceryUnit, "Dzn");
38       };
39       if (GroceryNumber==3)
40       { strcpy_s(GroceryName, "Beef        ");  // Add spaces
```

```
41          GroceryPrice=2.99;
42          GroceryOnHand=150;
43          strcpy_s(GroceryUnit, "Lb ");        // Add a space
44        };
45        if (GroceryNumber==4)
46        { strcpy_s(GroceryName, "Bean         ");     // Add spaces
47          GroceryPrice=1.09;
48          GroceryOnHand=100;
49          strcpy_s(GroceryUnit, "Lb ");               // Add a space
50        };
51        if (GroceryNumber==5)
52        { strcpy_s(GroceryName, "Melon        ");     // Add spaces
53          GroceryPrice=1.59;
54          GroceryOnHand=100;
55          strcpy_s(GroceryUnit, "Pc ");        // Add a space
56        };
57    }

58    // Next are methods of the GROCERY class ...
59    // Return Name
60    char *ReturnGroceryName() {return GroceryName;};

61    // Return Unit
62    char *ReturnGroceryUnit() {return GroceryUnit;};

63    // Return Price
64    double ReturnGroceryPrice()  {return GroceryPrice;};

65    // Calculate Price after discount
66    double GroceryDiscount(double DiscountRate) {
67       double PriceAfterDiscount;
68             PriceAfterDiscount=
69               GroceryPrice*(1-DiscountRate*0.01);
70       return(PriceAfterDiscount);
71    };

72    //  Process Inventory
73    double GroceryInventoryProcess(double InventoryChange)
74    {  GroceryOnHand=GroceryOnHand+InventoryChange;
75       return(GroceryOnHand);
76    };
77  };
```

We examine how the program of the GROCERY class in Listing 2.10(b) works first, and then we examine how the main program in Listing 2.10(a) uses the class. Lines **7–11** define attributes of the GROCERY class. Lines **15–18** are the constructor, which is empty in this example. The actual "constructor" is implemented by an independent method named InitGrocery to initialize the values of attributes for the created objects of this class. It is specified in line **23** through line **57**. As discussed earlier in this chapter, there are several ways to initialize the object. Typical business applications use disk data files or databases. In this example, we simplify the problem and use the program to assign values to these attributes based on the identification of each object created. Line **24** assigns the GroceryNumber with AutoNumber, which is brought up by the request message to the object. Lines **25–32** mean that if the value of `GroceryNumber` is 1, then a string that starts with "Milk" is assigned to `GroceryName` using `strcpy _ s`, and so on. Line **27** is a notation to explain that spaces are added to the string to make all the product names have the same length for printing. Similarly, lines **33–38** initialize the values of attributes for the object the value of `GroceryNumber`, which is 2, and so on. In this small example, the GROCERY class can have five objects.

In addition to `InitGrocery`, there are five methods in this class. Line **60** defines the method `char *ReturnGroceryName()`. As the type of returned value (`GroceryName`) is `char`, the type of `ReturnGroceryName()` is `char`. Here, the "`*`" symbol is used for the simplicity in dealing with "pointer," which is a unique feature of C and C++. In this book, we do not discuss pointer in any detail, but use the `*` symbol in any functions or methods of the `char` type. The remaining parts of these methods are all easy to follow. As explained before, the order of these methods in the program of the class is not important.

We now examine the program in Listing 2.10(a) to understand its operations. Line **4** includes the program file `grocery.h` for the GROCERY class. Line **11** defines a variable for the discount rate. Lines **13** and **14** allow the user to input the discount rate. Lines **16–19** print out the heading for the discount flyer. Lines **22–31** define a for-loop. The for-loop instructs the computer to do five times. For each time, it creates an object of `Grocery` (line **23**). When the computer encounters line **24**, the execution sequence turns to line **23** of `grocery.h` in Listing 2.10(b). Line **24** in Listing 2.10(b) means that the identification of the object (`GroceryNumber`) is assigned the value of `AutoNumber`, which is brought by `i`, the control counter of the for-loop in the `main` program (line **24** in Listing 2.10a).

Return to the `main` program in Listing 2.10(a). Within the for-loop, line **26** prints the `GroceryName`, which is obtained through the message. Line **27** prints the price before the discount. Line **28** prints the unit. Line **29** prints the price after the discount. The price after discount is obtained through the message that is sent to the object, and the object calculates the discount price and sends it back (see line **66** through line **71** in Listing 2.10b). The execution result of the program in Listing 2.10(a) and Listing 2.10(b) is shown in Figure 2.24.

Note that, in this example, method `GroceryInventoryProcess` of the GROCERY class is never used by the `main` program. In other words, a method built in a class may not be used by a particular program, but is ready for use. As an exercise, students may expand this `main` program by using this method for inventory processing.

We have learned the differences and relationships between function-oriented and object-oriented programming approaches, summarized as follows:

1. Using the object-oriented programming approach, a module is a class that encapsulates data and methods into a single software fragment. In the function-oriented approach, data and functions are separated. Definitions of object classes are natural, but definitions of functions are more or less artificial.

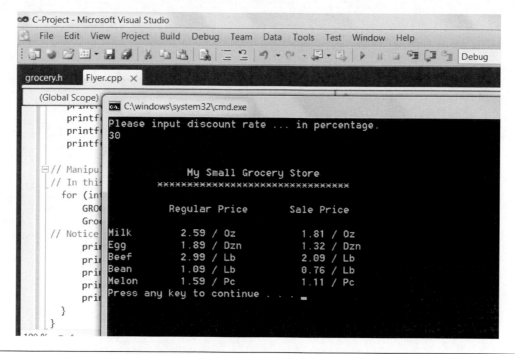

Figure 2.24   Execution result of `Flyer.cpp` and `grocery.h`.

2. In OOP, a method is actually a "function" within the class. Within a method, we still use principles of function-oriented programming. From this view, the object-oriented paradigm encompasses the function-oriented paradigm. It is not terribly wrong to set a "function" in the format of "object" for OOP, but the central concept of OOP is lost in those poor OOP programs.

3. From the view of computer execution, a called-function in function-oriented programming must be executed from beginning to end of the function module, but a message-evoked class might be used partially. In other words, in object-oriented programming, not every method built in a class must be used for a particular application. This feature makes the object-oriented programs flexible for software reuse.

2.6 Connection between Classes—An Example with Two Classes

In this section we present an example with two object classes. This example explains how classes can be related to each other through their identifiers and attributes (or keys and foreign keys in the database terminology). The example is supposed to produce an invoice of the book order upon the user types in an order number. There are two classes in this program: `order.h` and `book.h`. The two classes are related because an order must include the book number for the ordered book. Thus, the book identification (book number) plays the bond between the two classes. Using an OOP design diagram, the program is represented in Figure 2.25. Note the attributes and the methods in bold in the two classes.

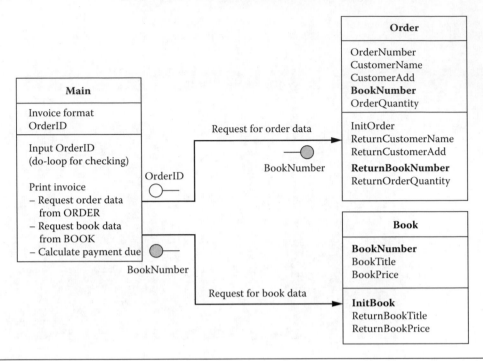

Figure 2.25　OOP design for the invoicing example.

As shown in Figure 2.25, the main program obtains information of the order to be invoiced from the ORDER class, and then it finds the book information pertinent to this order from the BOOK class. The association between the two classes is the data linkage BookNumber conveyed by the messages, as shown in the figure by the shaded data items. This linkage is implemented by the instruction of line **26** in the main program shown in Listing 2.11(a) (Invoice.cpp).

In this example, a do-loop is used to ensure that the user's input is correct (see lines **11** through **15** in Listing 2.11a). The syntax of do-loop is

```
do { Action } while ( condition );
```

Other parts of this example are rather straightforward. Figure 2.26 shows the execution result of this example.

Listing 2.11(a): Example of Two Classes—Invoice.cpp

```cpp
1 // **** Print invoices for book orders: Invoice.cpp ****
2 #include<iostream>
3 #include<cstring>
4 #include"order.h"
5 #include"book.h"
6 using namespace std;

7 void main()
8 {
9     unsigned int OrderID=0;   // for order number
```

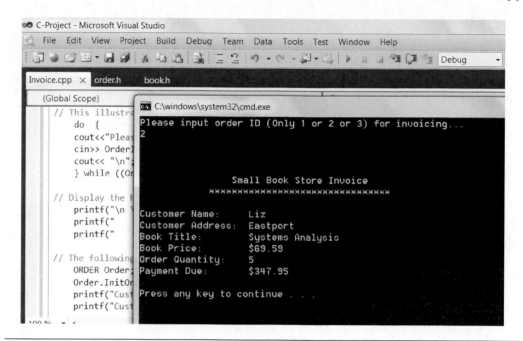

Figure 2.26   Execution result of `Invoice.cpp` with `order.h` and `book.h`.

```
10 // This illustrative example includes only 3 orders
11  do  {
12  cout<<"Please input order ID (Only 1 or 2 or 3) for invoicing... \n";
13  cin>> OrderID;
14  cout<< "\n";
15  } while ((OrderID==0) || (OrderID>3));

16 // Display the headings of the invoice
17     printf("\n \n");
18     printf("               Small Book Store Invoice       \n");
19     printf("        ****************************    \n \n");

20 // The following procedure manipulates the ORDER and BOOK objects
21     ORDER Order;
22     Order.InitOrder(OrderID);
23     printf("Customer Name:    %s \n", Order.ReturnCustomerName());
24     printf("Customer Address:  %s \n", Order.ReturnCustomerAdd());

25     BOOK Book;
26     Book.InitBook(Order.ReturnBookNumber());
27     printf("Book Title:       %s \n", Book.ReturnBookTitle());
28     printf("Book Price:       $%4.2f \n", Book.ReturnBookPrice());
29     printf("Order Quantity:   %u \n", Order.ReturnOrderQuantity());
30     printf("Payment Due:      $%4.2f \n \n",
31          Order.ReturnOrderQuantity()*Book.ReturnBookPrice());
32 }
```

Listing 2.11(b): Example of Class—`order.h`

```
1 // ****  Class ORDER definition: File is "order.h" ****
2 class ORDER
3 {
```

```
 4 private:
 5   int        OrderNumber;
 6   char       CustomerName[20];
 7   char       CustomerAdd[20];
 8   int        BookNumber;
 9   int        OrderQuantity;

10 public:
11   ORDER()
12   { // Constructor is void InitOrder(int)
13   };

14 // The following procedure simulates the system to read a
15 // database/data file which records data of the orders.
16   void InitOrder(int OrderNo)   {
17     OrderNumber=OrderNo;
18     if (OrderNumber==1)
19     { strcpy_s(CustomerName, "John       ");
20       strcpy_s(CustomerAdd, "Westport    ");
21       BookNumber=1234;
22       OrderQuantity=10;
23     }
24     if (OrderNumber==2)
25     { strcpy_s(CustomerName, "Liz        ");
26       strcpy_s(CustomerAdd, "Eastport    ");
27       BookNumber=3456;
28       OrderQuantity=5;
29     }
30     if (OrderNumber==3)
31     { strcpy_s(CustomerName, "Bill       ");
32       strcpy_s(CustomerAdd, "Southport   ");
33       BookNumber=2345;
34       OrderQuantity=20;
35     }
36   }

37 // Return data
38   char *ReturnCustomerName() {return CustomerName;};
39   char *ReturnCustomerAdd() {return CustomerAdd;};
40   int ReturnBookNumber() {return BookNumber;};
41   int ReturnOrderQuantity() {return OrderQuantity;};
42 };
```

Listing 2.11(c): Example of Class—book.h

```
 1 // **** Class BOOK definition: File is "book.h" ****
 2 class BOOK
 3 {
 4 private:
 5   int        BookNumber;
 6   char       BookTitle[30];
 7   double     BookPrice;

 8 public:
 9   BOOK()
10   { // Constructor is void InitBook(int)
11   };
```

```
12 // The following procedure simulates the system to read a
13 // database/data file which records data of the books.
14 void InitBook(int ANumber)  {
15   BookNumber=ANumber;
16   if (BookNumber==1234)
17   { strcpy_s(BookTitle, "Programming ");
18     BookPrice=49.59;
19   }
20   if (BookNumber==2345)
21   { strcpy_s(BookTitle, "Computers ");
22     BookPrice=39.59;
23   }
24   if (BookNumber==3456)
25   { strcpy_s(BookTitle, "Systems Analysis ");
26     BookPrice=69.59;
27   }
28   if (BookNumber==4567)
29   { strcpy_s(BookTitle, "Databases ");
30     BookPrice=59.59;
31   }
32 }

33 //  Return data
34 char *ReturnBookTitle() {return BookTitle;};
35 double ReturnBookPrice() {return BookPrice;};
36 };
```

2.7 An Example of Inheritance

In this section, we present an example of inheritance. This example is a payroll system. The system is supposed to produce a payroll advice note. There are two types of employee: full time and part time. The system determines the wages based on the work hours for the part-time employees, but based on the flat pay rates for the full-time employees. Using the OOP design method, the diagram of the payroll example is shown in Figure 2.27. Listing 2.12(a) is the main program Payroll.cpp, and Listing 2.12(b) is the class EMPLOYEE (in employee.h), which has two subclasses named FULLTIMEEMPLOYEE and PARTTIMEEMPLOYEE.

Listing 2.12(a): Example of Inheritance—Payroll.cpp

```
1 // ****  Payroll advice note  (file: Payroll.cpp) ****
2 #include<iostream>
3 #include<cstring>
4 #include"employee.h"
5 using namespace std;
6 void main()
7 {
8   char EmployeeNumber[5];
9   double GrossPay, TaxHolding, NetPay;

10  // Ensure a legal employee number
11  do {
```

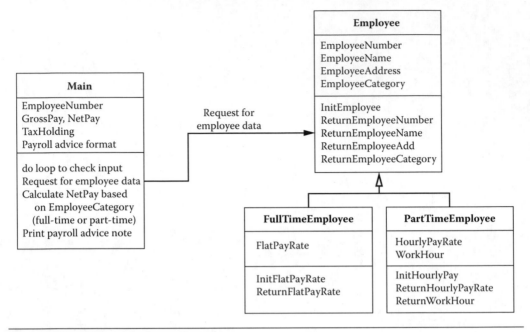

Figure 2.27   OOP design for the payroll example.

```
12   cout<<"Please type 3 digit employee ID for payroll advice note:\n";
13   cin>>EmployeeNumber;
14   } while ((strcmp(EmployeeNumber, "123")!=0)
15       && (strcmp(EmployeeNumber, "234")!=0)
16       && (strcmp(EmployeeNumber, "345")!=0)
17       && (strcmp(EmployeeNumber, "456")!=0)
18       && (strcmp(EmployeeNumber, "567")!=0));

19   //Create an employee object
20   EMPLOYEE Employee;
21   Employee.InitEmployee(EmployeeNumber);

22   //Different payroll schemes for full-time vs. part-time
23   if(strcmp(Employee.ReturnEmployeeCategory(), "F")==0 )
24   { FULLTIMEEMPLOYEE FullTimeEmployee;
25     FullTimeEmployee.InitFlatPayRate(EmployeeNumber);
26      GrossPay=FullTimeEmployee.ReturnFlatPayRate();
27   }
28   else
29   { PARTTIMEEMPLOYEE PartTimeEmployee;
30     PartTimeEmployee.InitHourlyPay(EmployeeNumber);
31     GrossPay=PartTimeEmployee.ReturnHourlyPayRate() *
32            PartTimeEmployee.ReturnWorkHour();
33    };

34   //Calculate tax holding and net pay
35   if (GrossPay>=2500) { TaxHolding=GrossPay*0.25; }
36   else {TaxHolding=GrossPay*0.15; };
37   NetPay=GrossPay-TaxHolding;

38   //Print payroll advice note
39   printf("\n======================================================");
```

```
40   printf("\n         THE    COMPANY  PAYROLL  ADVICE  NOTE          ");
41   printf("\n  -------------------------------------------- \n");
42   printf("Employee No.:   %s \n", EmployeeNumber);
43   printf("Name:           %s \n", Employee.ReturnEmployeeName());
44   printf("Address:        %s \n", Employee.ReturnEmployeeAdd());
45   printf("Gross Pay:      $%5.2f \n", GrossPay);
46   printf("Tax Holding:    $%5.2f \n", TaxHolding);
47   printf("Net Payment:                           $%5.2f \n", NetPay);
48   printf("=====================================================\n");
49 }
```

Listing 2.12(b): Example of Inheritance—employee.h

```
1  // ****  Class EMPLOYEE and its subclasses:
2  //FULLTIMEEMPLOYEE and PARTTIMEEMPLOYEE - File is "employee.h"
3  class EMPLOYEE
4  {
5  // protected attributes may be used by subclasses (derived class)
6  protected:
7    char EmployeeNumber[5];
8    char EmployeeName[30];
9    char EmployeeAddress[30];
10   char EmployeeCategory[5]; //"F" for full-time, "P" for part-time

11 public:
12    EMPLOYEE()
13    {
14 // The constructor is defined by   void InitEmployee(int);
15    };
16 // The following procedure simulates a database or data file
17    void InitEmployee(char *EmpID)  {
18      if (strcmp(EmpID, "123")==0) {
19      strcpy_s(EmployeeNumber, "123");
20      strcpy_s(EmployeeName, "Ann");
21      strcpy_s(EmployeeAddress, "A Street");
22      strcpy_s(EmployeeCategory, "F");  };
23      if (strcmp(EmpID, "234")==0) {
24      strcpy_s(EmployeeNumber, "234");
25      strcpy_s(EmployeeName, "Bill");
26      strcpy_s(EmployeeAddress, "B Street");
27      strcpy_s(EmployeeCategory, "P");  };
28      if (strcmp(EmpID, "345")==0) {
29      strcpy_s(EmployeeNumber, "345");
30      strcpy_s(EmployeeName, "Connie");
31      strcpy_s(EmployeeAddress, "C Street");
32      strcpy_s(EmployeeCategory, "F");  };
33      if (strcmp(EmpID, "456")==0) {
34      strcpy_s(EmployeeNumber, "456");
35      strcpy_s(EmployeeName, "Dany");
36      strcpy_s(EmployeeAddress, "D Street");
37      strcpy_s(EmployeeCategory, "P");  };
38      if (strcmp(EmpID, "567")==0) {
39      strcpy_s(EmployeeNumber, "567");
40      strcpy_s(EmployeeName, "Ed");
41      strcpy_s(EmployeeAddress, "E Street");
42      strcpy_s(EmployeeCategory, "F");  };
43      };
```

```
44  // Methods
45    char *ReturnEmployeeNumber()  { return EmployeeNumber; };
46    char *ReturnEmployeeName()  { return EmployeeName; };
47    char *ReturnEmployeeAdd()  { return EmployeeAddress; };
48    char *ReturnEmployeeCategory()  { return EmployeeCategory; };
49  };

50  // Subclass FULLTIMEEMPLOYEE. Its superclass is EMPLOYEE
51  class FULLTIMEEMPLOYEE : public EMPLOYEE
52  {
53   private:
54      double FlatPayRate;

55   public:
56      FULLTIMEEMPLOYEE()
57      {
58  // The constructor is defined by void InitFullPayRate(char);
59      };

60   // Initialize flat pay rate for full time employee
61   void InitFlatPayRate(char *EmployeeNumber) {

62      if (strcmp(EmployeeNumber, "123")==0) FlatPayRate=2000;
63      if (strcmp(EmployeeNumber, "345")==0) FlatPayRate=2500;
64      if (strcmp(EmployeeNumber, "567")==0) FlatPayRate=3000;
65    };

66  // Methods
67   double ReturnFlatPayRate()  { return FlatPayRate; };
68  };

69   // Subclass PARTTIMEEMPLOYEE. Its superclass is EMPLOYEE
70  class PARTTIMEEMPLOYEE : public EMPLOYEE
71  {
72   private:
73      double HourlyPayRate;
74      int WorkHour;

75   public:
76      PARTTIMEEMPLOYEE()
77      {
78  // The constructor is defined by void InitHourlyPay(char);
79      };

80    void InitHourlyPay(char *EmployeeNumber)  {
81        if (strcmp(EmployeeNumber, "234")==0)
82        { HourlyPayRate=12;
83          WorkHour=30;  };
84        if (strcmp(EmployeeNumber, "456")==0)
85        { HourlyPayRate=15;
86          WorkHour=20;  };
87     };

88    double ReturnHourlyPayRate() { return HourlyPayRate; };
89    int ReturnWorkHour() { return WorkHour;  };
90  };
```

The class in Listing 2.12(b) shows the implementation of inheritance. Line **51,** class FULLTIMEEMPLOYEE : public EMPLOYEE, defines a subclass named FULLTIMEEMPLOYEE within the EMPLOYEE class This subclass shares all common attributes and methods for the superclass EMPLOYEE, but has a unique attribute named FlatPayRate (line **54**) and unique methods including InitFlatPayRate (line **60**) and ReturnFlatPayRate (line **67**). Similarly, line **70** defines another subclass named PARTTIMEEMPLOYEE within the EMPLOYEE class. This subclass also shares the same attributes and methods of class EMPLOYEE, but has unique attributes (HourlyPayRate and WorkHour) and unique methods (InitHourlyPay, ReturnHourlyPayRate, and ReturnWorkHour).

Other minor features of C++ can also be observed in Listings 2.12(a) and 2.12(b)—for example,

- To compare strings, strcmp is used many times in the program.
- Because EMPLOYEE has subclasses, its attributes are placed in the protected section (Listing 2.12(b), line **6**).
- When the type of argument is char in a method (or function), the "*" symbol is used. Line **17** in Listing 2.12(b) is an example (void InitEmployee(char *EmpID)).

The rest of the program is straightforward. This example makes it clear that the OOP approach has the advantage of inheritance over the function-oriented programming approach. In this example, both PARTTIMEEMPLOYEE and FULLTIMEEMPLOYEE could belong to the class EMPLOYEE and share the common data attributes and operations. Figure 2.28 shows the execution result of this example.

Figure 2.28 Execution result of Payroll.cpp with employee.h.

2.8 Identify Class

In designing OOP, one must identify classes. The general rules for the identification of classes can be summarized as follows:

1. Physiomorphic class—physically existing entities (e.g., customer, book, and inventory)
2. Event class—events of routine operations (e.g., purchasing and credit approving)
3. Document class—information entities that enter the business process (e.g., order) or information entities produced by the business process (e.g., bill)
4. Microclass—in software development, widgets (e.g., button, check-box, etc.) are microclasses at the user–computer interface level.

An attribute is not a class. For example, "student name" is not a class, but can be an attribute of a class—say, STUDENT. A generic function is not a class. For example, "calculation of payment" is not a class, but could be a method of a class—say, BILL.

A beginner of programming is often confused about the difference between object oriented and function oriented. A simply or poorly designed object-oriented program can be just one method that is equivalent to a function. For example, one can use the C++ object-oriented form to rewrite the function CalculateAvg in the C program in Listing 2.4 and name it as an object—say, AvgCalculator. In principle, any function-oriented program can be converted into its object-oriented form. Although such an object-oriented program works well, the concept of object oriented is misunderstood. In fact, a good object-oriented program is "class oriented"; that is, it is designed for a class instead of a single object.

2.9 Debugging

Debugging C or C++ programs is a difficult task. After compiling (or building) a C or C++ program, the compiler will show error or warning messages if the program has a syntax error or an imperfect statement. A warning message does not prevent the program from executing but it might cause problems (e.g., loss of information when converting data types). Any error could be fatal. The programming environment (e.g., Microsoft Visual Studio) can show the error locations, and, if you click on an error item in the error message window, the cursor will move to the place in the program where the error occurs. The following tips are for debugging:

1. Start with the first error in the program to debug.
2. An error message could be vague. For beginners, do not attempt to interpret the meaning of an error message, but pay attention to the error line itself.
3. An error line identified by the compiler may seem to be correct, but is actually affected by a real error in a related line. Thus, you need to inspect all lines that can be related to the indicated error line.
4. Fix one error at a time and recompile the program after making a change.

5. Do not attempt to make the number of errors detected by the compiler smaller by making irrational changes.

Common syntax errors include:

- Typos or misspelling a word
- Omitting a symbol (e.g., missing one side of brace or parenthesis)
- Violating format
- Using an undefined user-defined variable

The compiler can detect syntax errors. The syntax error-free condition is necessary for execution, but it does not guarantee the correctives of the logic of the program. Logical errors or runtime errors often occur when the computer performs wrong operations, not as predicted. To debug logical errors, one should use data samples to test the program based on the output of the program:

1. Make the design of modules clear and logical. Do not use a "goto" or any jump statement (e.g., "return" in the middle of the module) because this tends to cause bugs and to make debugging difficult.
2. Exercise every possible option to check the computer outputs to see if the program does only as expected. Examine all if-statements to follow possible actions.
3. A program might cause a crash. Usually, this can be caused by wrong data types, wrong calculations (e.g., a number is divided by zero), wrong size of an array, or wrong data file operations.
4. If a program is "dead," you must terminate it through interruption. A "dead" program is more likely caused by an endless loop. You need to examine loop statements and if-statements thoroughly.

Warning messages often appear after the compiling. For example, if the program involves data type conversion (e.g., converting a variable from integer to floating), the compiler will give a warning that some information might be lost during the conversion.

Chapter 2 Exercises

1. Read the following C program and complete it by filling in the blanks:

```
1    #_____<iostream>
2    using namespace std;
3    _____ CommissionCalculation(_____);
4    void main()
5    _____
6    _____ i;
7    double sales;
8    double _____;
9    for (i=1_____ i<=3 _____ i++)
10     {
```

```
11      sales=10*i;
12      CommissionRate=CommissionCalculation(sales);
13      printf("The commission rate for sales of %2.2f is : __2.2f. \n",
14          sales, CommissionRate);
15      _____
16  }
17  double CommissionCalculation(double S)
18  {
19          _____ Commission;
20      if (S<=15)      {Commission=0.01; };
21      if ((S>15) && (S<=25) )_____      {Commission=0.02; };
22      if (S>25)          {Commission=0.01; };
23          _____ (Commission);
24  _____
```

2. Draw a structure diagram for the preceding C program.

3. Write the expected print result generated by the preceding C program.

4. Read the following C++ program and complete it by filling in the blanks:

```
1 #include<iostream>
2 #include<cstring>
3 #include"customer.h"
4 using namespace std;
5//The header file of the class CUSTOMER used is included
6 void main()
7 {
8 _____ Credit;
9 printf("Customer Name      Payment Due \n");
10 printf("\n");
11 Credit=100.0;
12 for (int i=1; i<=3; i++) {
13     CUSTOMER Customer;
14             _____.ConstCustomer(i);
15     printf ("%s", Customer.ReturnCustomerName());
16     printf("            %4.2f \n", Customer.CustomerDue(Credit));
17 _____
18 }
```

```
1 // **** Class CUSTOMER definition ****
2 // File is "customer.h"
3 class CUSTOMER
4 // Class declaration
5 {
6 private:
7 // Attributes
8 int CustomerNumber;
9 _____ CustomerName[20];
10 _____ CustomerBalance;
11 char CustomerPhone[15];
```

```
12 public:
13 CUSTOMER ()
14 {
15 // Constructor is actually implemented by the method
16 // void ConstCustomer(int)
17 };

18 // Operations
19 // The following procedure simulates the system to read a
20 //database/data file which records information of customer
21 void ConstCustomer(int CN) {
22    CustomerNumber=CN;
23    if (CustomerNumber==1)
24    { strcpy_s(CustomerName, "John ");
25      CustomerBalance=-200.05;
26      strcpy_s(CustomerPhone, "123 1234 ");
27    }
28    if (CustomerNumber==2)
29    { strcpy_s(CustomerName, "Anne ");
30      CustomerBalance=-200;
31      strcpy_s(CustomerPhone, "123 2345 ");
32    }
33    if (CustomerNumber==3)
34    { strcpy_s(CustomerName, "Greg ");
35      CustomerBalance-100.78;
36      strcpy_s(CustomerPhone, "123 7890 ");
37    }
38 }

39 // Next are methods of the CUSTOMER class...
40 _____  _____
41 {return CustomerName;};

42 _____ *ReturnCustomerPhone()
43 {return CustomerPhone;};

44 double ReturnCustomerBalance()
45 {return CustomerBalance;};

46 double CustomerDue(double CR) {
47    _____  _____  _____
48    if ((CustomerBalance+CR)<0)
49    { DueAmount=(CustomerBalance+CR)*-1; }
50    else
51    { DueAmount=0; };
52    _____ (DueAmount);
53 }
54 _____
```

5. Draw an object-oriented programming design diagram for the preceding C++ program.

6. Write the expected print result generated by the preceding C++ program.

7. Run the C++ programs in Listings 2.10(a) and 2.10(b). Has the `GroceryInventoryProcess` method of the `GROCERY` class ever been used in this program? Discuss the advantages of object-oriented modules. Expand the programs in Listings 2.10(a) and 2.10(b) to use the `GroceryInventoryProcess` method.

8. Develop a C project that contains one main function and two or more functions used by the main function. The document of your project includes:
   • Brief description of your project
   • A structure diagram for your program
   • Source code of your project
   • Execution results

9. Develop a C++ project that contains one main program and two or more classes. The document of your project includes:
   • Brief description of your project
   • An object-oriented programming design diagram for your programs
   • Source code of your project
   • Execution results

Appendix 2.1: Commonly Used C and C++ Keywords

C and C++ Keywords

auto	do	if	static
break	double	int	struct
case	else	long	typedef
char	enum	register	union
const	float	return	unsigned
continue	for	short	void
default	goto	signed	while

C++ Only Keywords

catch	friend	public	try
class	new	static_cast	typeid
dynamic_cast	operator	template	typename
explicit	private	this	using
false	protected	true	

3
HTML, JᴀᴠᴀSᴄʀɪᴘᴛ, ᴀɴᴅ CSS

3.1 Introduction to the Internet

The Internet has had a remarkable impact on business and organizations globally. Using the Internet, people create innovative ways of doing business. This chapter provides essential knowledge for understanding the process of creating web pages. The Internet is a network of networks. It is a linkage of smaller networks, each of which agrees to use the same communication rules (called a protocol) for exchanging information. The Internet protocol is a transmission control protocol/Internet protocol (TCP/IP). The Internet is a great place to acquire information from across the world. The user can also acquire computer software or work online. The cloud computing technology allows the user to access computing resources (hardware and software) that are delivered as services over the Internet.

To access the Internet, the computer must be linked to the Internet through an Internet provider (usually a local telephone company). Computers on the Internet play two types of roles: server and client. A server is a computer that manages its data, including text, images, video clips, and sound. A server computer is set up by an individual or organization and it allows other computers to access its data and service resources. A client is a PC that can access data and services provided by servers. On the Internet, the software supporting the client operations is called a browser. Microsoft Internet Explorer and Mozilla Firefox are the two popular web browsers of the Windows platform. A browser uses a graphical user interface (GUI), which is supported by a local operating system—for example, Microsoft Windows.

The first page encountered when one visits a website is the home page of the site. From the home page one can explore other web pages and other websites that have been linked to it. A web home page is accessed by an address. The address of a web page is referred to as its uniform resource locator (URL), because a URL is a standard means of consistently locating the web page no matter where it is physically stored on the Internet. A URL for a web page is defined by the letters `http`, which stand for hypertext transfer protocol. The documents available on the Internet make wide use of hypertext and multimedia. Using hypertext, the user can move from document to document by following hyperlinks. Hypertext and multimedia are often combined to create hypermedia. With hypermedia, a user can have an in-depth look at a web page by clicking on a graphic image and hearing an audio or seeing a video clip, or clicking on a word and seeing animation.

3.2 Creating Web Pages Using HTML

There are many software packages available for creating web pages. Like word processing software, these web page authoring tools allow the user to use menus and function buttons to create static web pages, thereby releasing the user from tedious programming work. In fact, many word processing software packages (e.g., Microsoft Word) can translate an ordinary document into a web page. However, the basic tool, the hypertext markup language (HTML), must be used when constructing a dynamic web page through the use of server-side programming. In addition, HTML allows the web page developer to better control the appearance of the web page.

HTML is the main markup language for presenting web pages that can be displayed in a web browser. To use HTML to create a web page, one needs to follow the following steps.

1. Create your own folder. Later, save your web pages and other material (such as images) in this folder.
2. Edit a text of HTML for the web page. Notepad in the Accessories group in the Windows operating system can be used for editing. Open source Notepad++ is also a good editor. As the web page developer you can write an HTML text (see an example of HTML in Listing 3.1) and save it to your folder as a file with extension .html (e.g., MyFirstPage.html). If you use Notepad, make sure you choose [All Files] for [Save as type] before you save the file.
3. Reopen the HTML text file in a web browser. In Microsoft Internet Explorer, click [File], [Open] to open the HTML file (e.g., MyFirstPage.html) you saved. The HTML file is read by the browser. The web page described by the HTML is then displayed on the screen. You can also open a web page by clicking on the icon of the web page file you saved.
4. Make changes. If modification is required, the original HTML text file should be called up in the editor (Notepad). After making modifications, you must save it before reopening it in the web browser.

HTML is written in the form of HTML elements that consist of tags that tell the browser how to display the data. HTML container tags are used in pairs to indicate the start and end of a structure. For example:

```
<TITLE>John Smith's Web Page</TITLE>
```

The tags <TITLE> and </TITLE> around the text inform the browser that these words are the title of the web page. An empty tag does not surround any components. For example, <HR> causes a horizontal line and does not hold text. HTML tags are not case sensitive.

A web page has a particular structure as follows:

```
<HTML>
 <HEAD>
 . . . . . .
 </HEAD>
 <BODY>
 . . . . . .
 </BODY>
</HTML>
```

This chapter introduces the most commonly used HTML tags.

3.3 Simple Container Tags

3.3.1 <HTML>

<HTML> indicates the document written in HTML. A web page has only one pair of <HTML> and </HTML> tags.

3.3.2 <HEAD> and <TITLE>

The <HEAD> and <TITLE> tags are used to identify the title of the document. The title of the web page will be displayed on the top of the browser window. A web page has only one pair of <HEAD> and </HEAD> tags and only one pair of <TITLE> and </TITLE> tags.

3.3.3 <BODY>

<BODY> is used to contain the main portion of an HTML document. The <BODY> tag can have its attributes. The BGCOLOR attribute controls the background color of the page. For example, <BODY BGCOLOR=LIGHTBLUE> makes a light blue background. One can also use a code to define the background color (e.g., <BODY BGCOLOR=#0FFFF>). The BACKGROUND attribute brings a background image for the web page. For example, <BODY BACKGROUND="Marble.gif"> makes the image "Marble.gif" as the background if the image file is stored with the web page in this example. A web page has only one pair of <BODY> and </BODY> tags.

3.3.4 Comments <!-- ... -->

A comment line is delimited by <!-- and -->. The comments are not displayed by the browser.

3.3.5 *Headings* `<H1>` `<H2>` ... `<H6>`

A heading tag indicates a heading. HTML allows six different levels of headings. `<H1>` has the biggest font, and `<H6>` has the smallest font.

3.3.6 `<P>`

`<P>` indicates a new paragraph. The `<P>` tag can have attributes. For example, `<P ALIGN=CENTER>` is used for centering a paragraph.

3.3.7 `<I>`

The text between `<I>` and `</I>` is displayed in italics.

3.3.8 `<TABLE>`, `<TH>`, `<TR>`, *and* `<TD>`

`<TABLE>` defines a table. Its attribute BORDER defines the type of table border. `<TH>` defines the table header. `<TR>` defines a table row. `<TD>` describes a table data cell.

3.3.9 `<A>`

The anchor tag `<A>` creates a link to another website. Its attribute HREF (hypertext reference) defines the target of the link to the URL. For example,

```
<A HREF="http://www.umassd.edu">UMD</A>
```

means that the user is allowed to access to "http://www.umassd.edu" by clicking on "UMD" on the web page.

3.3.10 `<CENTER>`

All text and images within a `<CENTER>` container will be centered on the page.

3.4 Empty Tags

Major empty tags are presented next.

3.4.1 `<HR>`

`<HR>` causes a horizontal rule.

3.4.2 `<BR>`

`<BR>` adds a line break into the text.

3.4.3 <IMG>

One of the attractions of web pages is the integration of text and images. Web browsers support a wide variety of image formats. The most popular formats are GIF (.gif files), PNG (.png files), and JPEG (.jpg files). JPEG files have a higher quality, but GIF files can be "animated" images. An animated GIF file has a series of images that are displayed in an order to form animation (e.g., rotation and motion). You can download images from the Internet by right-clicking the image you want to download and then clicking [Save As] on the displayed menu to save it. Be aware of copyright protection laws. Images can be inserted into an HTML document by using the <IMG> tag. When using this tag, its attributes must be included in the tag. The ALIGN attribute indicates the position of the image. The SRC attribute defines the source of the image. The ALT (alternate) attribute contains a text that is displayed when the browser is unable to display the actual image because of an invalid image file name. The WIDTH and HEIGHT attributes define the size, in pixels, of the image on the web page.

Listing 3.1 shows a simple web page example. The line numbers are used for explanation and are not a part of the web page. Clearly, this web page is not well designed and merely shows the basic features of some tags. Students are encouraged to learn more about the HTML through further reading the source code of well-designed web pages by clicking on [View] and [Source] in the browser to design a fancy web page for their projects.

Listing 3.1: An Example of HTML Code for a Web Page (`MyFirstPage.html`)

```
 1  <HTML>
 2   <HEAD>
 3    <TITLE>A Web Page</TITLE>
 4   </HEAD>
 5  <BODY BGCOLOR="#FFFFF">
 6     <H1>My First Web Page - The Largest Heading</H1>
 7     <H6>for practice - The Smallest Heading</H6>
 8     <HR>
 9      This page is not well designed, but just to show how HTML works.
10     <P>
11      I make a table in this paragraph:
12      <TABLE BORDER=2>
13        <TR>
14         <TD>MIS</TD>
15         <TD>Programming</TD>
-13        </TR>
16        <TR>
17         <TD>Marketing</TD>
18         <TD>Advertising</TD>
-16        </TR>
-12       </TABLE>
-10      </P>
19     <P>
20      The real power of Web pages is the ability to create links.
21     <BR>
```

```
22    To learn about <I>links</I>, I create a link to
23    <A HREF="http://www.smu.ca">Saint Mary's University</A>.
-19   </P>
24    I can also put images and email addresses on my Web page.

25    <P ALIGN=CENTER>
26    <IMG  ALIGN=MIDDLE  ALT="An Image" WIDTH=150 HEIGHT=150
27     SRC="http://smu-facweb.smu.ca/~hwang/example.gif">
28    <A HREF="mailto:MyEmail@Provider.com">demo@Provider.com</A>
-25   </P>
29    <P ALIGN=RIGHT>
30    Finally, I include icons and links to facebook and twitter...
31    <A HREF="http://facebook.com/">
32    <IMG  ALT="An Icon" WIDTH=30 HEIGHT=20
-31    SRC="http://smu-facweb.smu.ca/~hwang/facebookicon.png"> </A>
33    <A HREF="http://twitter.com/">
34    <IMG  ALT="An Icon" WIDTH=30 HEIGHT=20
-33    SRC="http://smu-facweb.smu.ca/~hwang/twittericon.png"> </A>
-29   </P>
-5  </BODY>
-1  </HTML>
```

The presentation of the preceding HTML web page in Microsoft Internet Explorer is shown in Figure 3.1. It is easy to match the presentation of the web page with the HTML code. Only a few lines need to be explained. Line **28** is included here just for demonstration of e-mail in a web page, and it may not function even when the e-mail address is valid because your e-mail system setting does not allow an insecure e-mail source. Lines **26** and **27** define an image that does not have a hyperlink. Lines **31**

Figure 3.1   Presentation of the example web page (`MyFirstPage.html`).

through **-31** define an image that has a hyperlink, and the anchor (<A>) tags must be used surrounding the <IMG> tag.

3.5 Complex Container Tags

3.5.1 <FORM>

One of the most useful features of HTML is FORM. A form allows the user to fill out data and to send the data from the filled form to the server that hosts the web page. To process the data sent from the form, the server must run a server-side program, as discussed in Chapters 6 and 7. This chapter deals with the client side only and assumes that the form data are sent back to the host server through e-mail. Again, your e-mail system may refuse to process an insecure e-mail even when the e-mail address is valid. Listing 3.2 shows an example of form in HTML (Form.html). Also, you may insert lines **5** through **-8** of Listing 3.2 into the HTML document in Listing 3.1 at the line right before </BODY> (line **-5**) to merge the two web pages.

Listing 3.2: HTML Code of Form (`Form.html`)

```
 1  <HTML>
 2   <HEAD>
 3   <TITLE> Form Web Page </TITLE>
-2   </HEAD>
 4  <BODY>
 5   <H2> SEND YOUR COMMENTS! </H2>
 6   Please fill the form and submit it :
 7   <BR>
 8   <FORM ACTION = "mailto:MyEmail@auniversity.edu" METHOD=POST>
 9    Your Name: <BR>
10    <INPUT TYPE=TEXT NAME="name" SIZE=50> <BR>
11    Your Email Address: <BR>
12    <INPUT TYPE=TEXT NAME="email" SIZE=50> <BR>
13    Your Brief Comments: <BR>
14    <TEXTAREA NAME="comm" ROWS=4 COLS=50> </TEXTAREA> <BR>
15    <INPUT TYPE=SUBMIT VALUE="Submit the Data">
16    <INPUT TYPE=RESET VALUE="Start Over Again">
-8   </FORM>
-4   </BODY>
-1  </HTML>
```

Figure 3.2 shows the presentation of Form.html. Several attributes of FORM and related tags are explained next.

3.5.1.1 Attribute ACTION   The attribute ACTION (see line **8** in Listing 3.2) points to the application that is to capture the data. The value of this attribute could be a program on the remote server specified by a URL or simply an e-mail address. You can learn more about form data processing on the server in the chapters on server-side programming (ASP.NET and PHP) of this book. In this chapter, the simple e-mail

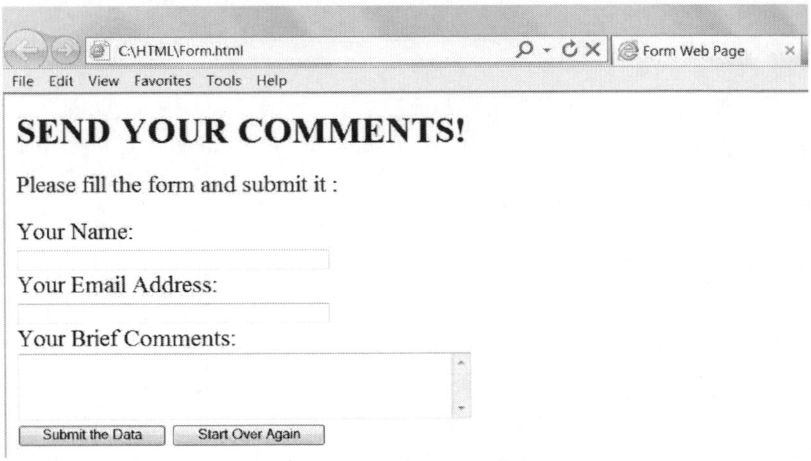

Figure 3.2   Presentation of `Form.html`.

approach is used for ACTION. If the e-mail system has been set by the e-mail system administrator to capture the form data from your exercise web page, the location of the captured data on the receiver's side is specified by the e-mail system.

3.5.1.2 Attribute METHOD   The attribute METHOD instructs the browser to send the data back to the server. The value of the attribute could be GET or POST. GET has not been recommended recently. In general cases, POST should be used.

3.5.1.3 <INPUT> *and Its Attributes* TYPE, NAME, SIZE, *and* VALUE   The INPUT tag is the tool to create input fields on a form. It has attributes such as TYPE, NAME, SIZE, and VALUE. The TYPE attribute specifies the type of the input field. TEXT is used for text entry. SUBMIT is used to create a submission command button, and RESET is used to create a reset command button. The VALUE attributes give the labels on these command buttons. Other types of input include RADIO (for radio buttons) and CHECKBOX (for checkboxes). TEXTBOX is a special input type and has its tags (see line **14** in Listing 3.2).

The NAME attribute of the INPUT tag specifies the name of the input field. The names can be passed on to the relevant JavaScript programs or the relevant server-side programs as discussed later in this book. The SIZE attribute specifies the size of the entry field.

3.5.2 FRAME *and* FRAMESET

One HTML web page can host several subpages. The space on the screen for a sub-page is called a frame. Using the <FRAMESET> and <FRAME> tags, the web page designer sets frames and defines the source of each frame, as shown in an example in Listing 3.3 (`Frame.html`).

Listing 3.3: HTML Code for Setting Frames (`Frame.html`)

```
<HTML>
<FRAMESET COLS="25%, *">
    <FRAME SRC="Frame1.html">
    <FRAME SRC="Frame2.html">
</FRAMESET>
</HTML>
```

In Listing 3.3, the frames are set in columns. The left column occupies 25% of the entire screen width. The asterisk sign means that the rest of the screen is allocated to the right column. A frame can be set in rows if attribute ROWS is used in the tag. Within the <FRAMESET> container, the two frames are defined by using the <FRAME> tags. The SRC attribute defines the two source web pages for the subpages. Clearly, you need to have the two subpages (i.e., `Frame1.html` and `Frame2.html`) to view the presentation of `Frame.html`.

Appendix 3.1 lists commonly used HTML tags.

3.6 Publish Web Page

To develop a large web page, it is a good practice to develop smaller web pages and then to merge them into a large web page. For example, you can combine Listing 3.1 and Listing 3.2 into a single HTML document by copying lines **5** through **-8** of Listing 3.2 and pasting them anywhere in Listing 3.1 after <BODY> and before </BODY>.

To publish a web page on the Internet, you need to acquire a space on a web server. You may rent a space from a Web hosting provider (e.g., a local telephone company). Some web hosting providers have their own web standards and guidelines. If the web is crucial for your business, you can create your own web server by connecting a dedicated computer to the Internet through a service provider (e.g., a telephone company).

3.7 Introduction to JavaScript

A script language is a computer programming language with limited functions, and it can be embedded in another programming language. JavaScript is a script language and is directly interspersed with HTML statements. Originally, as HTML does not possess any computational capacity, JavaScript was used to validate user inputs. Later, JavaScript was widely used to accomplish a variety of tasks, including client-side calculations, client-side lookup databases, creating image maps, and personalizing documents before they are displayed. In terms of syntax, JavaScript is very similar to C and C++. A JavaScript program is contained between the <SCRIPT> and </SCRIPT> tags in the HTML program, with the exceptions of the event handlers discussed later. JavaScript is entirely interpreted when the host web page is displayed by the web browser. JavaScript can be put in either of the two places in an HTML program: between <HEAD> and </HEAD> or between <BODY> and </BODY>. However, placing JavaScript between <HEAD> and </HEAD> could protect the presentation of the web page if the JavaScript contains errors.

JavaScript is case sensitive. Listing 3.4 is a simple example of a JavaScript program (FirstJavaScript.html) that displays a line of message in the web page created by HTML. For illustration purposes, we use bold font for the part of JavaScript in the example. Note that if your computer Internet security is set to "high," your web browser may block the JavaScript program because the JavaScript program could access your computer. Then you need to click on the [Allow blocked content] button to allow the known JavaScript program to run.

Listing 3.4: A Simple JavaScript Example (FirstJavaScript.html)

```
<HTML>
 <HEAD>
 <TITLE> Hello World Example of JavaScript </TITLE>
   <SCRIPT>
   document.write("Hello, World!  I am learning JavaScript!")
   </SCRIPT>
  </HEAD>
 <BODY>
  <BR>
  <H3>The rest part is the HTML presentation.... </H3>
 </BODY>
 </HTML>
```

The major reason for the use of JavaScript is to inject the capability of data processing for the web page on the client-side because HTML is just to present the web page. Four typical applications of JavaScript in web pages are illustrated in this section through examples: image manipulation, FORM input data verification, FORM data calculation, and cookie processing. Note that JavaScript is a client-side programming language and JavaScript programs run on the client computer for the data processing.

3.8 Image Manipulation

Listing 3.5 shows a simple example (Image.html) of image manipulation. Assume that there are two images, named photo1.jpg and photo2.jpg, in the JPEG format. In this example, these two images are placed in the folder named images, which is stored with the Image.html program in the same folder. This JavaScript program implements an image rollover task described as follows. After opening the web page, the user can see the image originally displayed on the web page (i.e., photo1.jpg). The user may click on the image to load the linked web home page. When the user moves the mouse (or cursor) out from photo1.jpg, the image rolls over to photo2.jpg. When the mouse is moved back to the image, the image rolls over back to the original. Clearly, to test this program, you must make (or copy) two images in the JPEG format and place them into the images folder. If you have incorrect image names or you have put the images in the wrong place, the program does not function. More details of the JavaScript related to this example are discussed next.

Listing 3.5: Use JavaScript to Manipulate Images (`Image.html`)

```
 1 <HTML>
 2  <HEAD>
 3   <TITLE>My Web Page of Image Rollover</TITLE>
-2  </HEAD>
 4 <BODY>
 5  <A HREF = "http://www.smu.ca"

 6  onMouseOver = "document.photo.src = 'images/photo1.jpg' "
 7  onMouseOut = "document.photo.src = 'images/photo2.jpg' ">

 8  <IMG SRC = "images/photo1.jpg" WIDTH=320 HEIGHT=400 NAME="photo">
-5  </A>
-4 </BODY>
-1 </HTML>
```

3.8.1 Object Classes and Their Methods and Attributes

JavaScript is a mixture of function-oriented and object-oriented paradigms. JavaScript has many predefined object classes that have been built in the JavaScript interpreter. These classes have built-in methods (equivalent to functions). In Listing 3.4 (`FirstJavaScript.html`), document is an object that means the current web page, and `write` is its method. Arguments (or parameters) are placed within the pair of parentheses after the method name. The JavaScript sentence in Listing 3.4 (`FirstJavaScript.html`) directs the web page (document) to write a message, "`Hello, World! …`".

In Listing 3.5 (`Image.html`), document is an object, photo is an image object within the object document, and `src` (source) is an attribute of the object photo. Note that this image name (photo) is defined in the HTML tag `<IMG...NAME...>` (see line **8** in Listing 3.5). `value` is an attribute commonly used in various objects, as can be seen in the next several examples. A basic hierarchy of predefined object classes of JavaScript is shown in Figure 3.3.

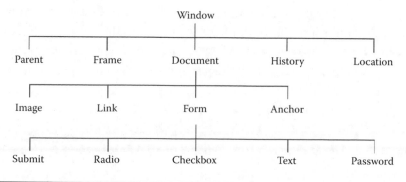

Figure 3.3 A basic hierarchy of object classes of JavaScript.

Very much like C++, the general syntax of JavaScript statements related to the built-in classes is

```
[Object Name].[Sub-object Name].[...].[Attribute Name or Method
   Name( )]
```

for example, document.write() in Listing 3.4 (FirstJavaScript.html) and document.photo.src in Listing 3.5 (Image.html).

3.8.2 Event Handler

An event is an action the user performs while visiting the web page. Moving the mouse and submitting a form are examples of an event. JavaScript deals with events with commands called event handlers. An event handler is usually applied within an HTML tag. Commonly used event handlers are

EVENT HANDLER	EVENT
onMouseOver	The mouse is moved over an object.
onMouseOut	The mouse is moved off an object.
onSubmit	The user submits a form.
onBlur	The user closes the object.
onClick	The user clicks the object.
onFocus	The object becomes active.
onSelect	The content of the object is selected.

onMouseOver and onMouseOut are used in the JavaScript program in Listing 3.5 (Image.html). They instruct the computer to swap the images on the screen in accordance with the user's cursor movement. Note that some event handlers may not work if the web browser is not set properly.

3.9 FORM Input Data Verification

A major utility of JavaScript is to verify the input of the user. Listing 3.6 (VarifyData. html) exhibits a JavaScript program that verifies the e-mail address typed by the user when he or she submits a FORM back to the web server. The program assumes that if the textbox for the e-mail address on the FORM has not been filled or the typed e-mail address string contains any illegal characters, such as slash (/), comma (,), space, colon (:), and semicolon (;), then the computer displays an error message and asks the user to retype the e-mail address.

Listing 3.6: Use JavaScript to Verify Typed E-mail Address (VerifyData.html)

```
1 <HTML>
2 <HEAD>
3 <TITLE> Verify FORM data </TITLE>
```

```
 4 <SCRIPT>
 5 // Define a function for the action after verify the email address
 6 function VerifyForm(form) {
 7 // If VerifyEmailAdd function returns false (wrong address),
 8 // then signals alert. Move the cursor back and highlight for retyping.
 9  if (!VerifyEmailAdd(form.email.value)) {
10      alert("OOPS! Invalid email address. Please input again!")
11      form.email.focus()
12      form.email.select()
13    return false
-9    }
14    return true    // Otherwise, it is OK.
-6 }

15 // Define a function to verify the email address types on the form
16 function VerifyEmailAdd(EmailString)  {
17 // If the email address is empty, then gives false
18  if (EmailString == "") {
19      return false
-18  }

20 // Define five bad characters (incl. space) in illegal email address
21  BadChars = "/, :;"
22 // For each of the 5 bad characters (including a space), check the typed
23 // email address.  If a bad character has been found, then gives false
24  for (i=0; i<=4; i++) {
25      aBadChar=BadChars.charAt(i)
26      if (EmailString.indexOf(aBadChar,0) >= 0) {
27       return false    }
-24      }
28 // Otherwise (i.e., the above two errors are not found), gives true
29  return true
-16 }
-4 </SCRIPT>
-2 </HEAD>

30 <BODY>
31 <H2> SEND YOUR COMMENTS! </H2>
32 Please fill the form and submit it :
33 <BR>
34  <FORM onSubmit="return VerifyForm(this)"
35      ACTION = "mailto:MyEmail@auniversity.edu" METHOD=POST>
36   Your Name: <BR>
37   <INPUT TYPE=TEXT NAME="name" SIZE=50> <BR>
38   Your Email Address: <BR>
39   <INPUT TYPE=TEXT NAME="email" SIZE=50> <BR>
40   Your Brief Comments: <BR>
41   <TEXTAREA NAME="comm" ROWS=4 COLS=50> </TEXTAREA> <BR>
42   <INPUT TYPE=SUBMIT VALUE="Submit the Data">
43   <INPUT TYPE=RESET VALUE="Start Over Again">
-34  </FORM>
-30 </BODY>
-1 </HTML>
```

We examine how VerifyData.html works. The JavaScript program is highlighted in bold in Listing 3.6. Line **6** defines a function named VerifyForm. This function has one argument named form. This means that this function works on the form assigned by the calling function in line **34**. Lines **9** through **-9** are an if-statement. This statement calls another function named `VerifyEmailAdd`. Line **9** means that if `VerifyEmailAdd` returns "false," then the computer signals an alert (line **10**), moves the cursor back to the e-mail textbox, and allows the user to retype an e-mail address (lines **11** and **12**). If the `VerifyEmailAdd` returns "true," then this function returns "true" back to the calling function (line **14**). In this example, "true" represents "no error has been detected" and "false" represents "an error has been detected."

Lines **16** through **-16** implement the function `VerifyEmailAdd` that verifies the e-mail address typed in the e-mail textbox on the FORM. The argument of this function is `EmailString`, which is supposed to be replaced by the value of the textbox named "`email`" (see the argument in line **9** and its source in line **39**). Lines **18** and **19** let the function return "false" if the string is empty. Line **21** defines all illegal characters for any e-mail address. As an example, five bad characters (including space) are defined. Lines **24** through **-24** are a search procedure to find whether there is any bad character in the e-mail address string. Since we have defined five bad characters, the for-loop repeats five times. For each time, one character is selected for checking (line **25**). Lines **26** and **27** instruct the computer that if the selected bad character is found in `EmailString`, then return "false." We will explain line **26** in detail shortly. If the e-mail string is not empty and contains no bad characters, then the computer executes line **29** and returns "true" to the calling function.

Now we examine line **34**. This line means that when FORM is submitted, the computer passes "`this`" (which means the current form) to the `VerifyForm` function and executes the function. In line **34**, "**`return`**" means the computer keeps calling the function until the called function returns "true." In other words, the "**`return`**" keyword in line **34** has a meaning different from that of the "return" keyword in functions (e.g., line **29**).

Figure 3.4 shows the execution result when an error in the e-mail address has been detected and the alert signal generated by the JavaScript program appears on the screen. You may see other alert signals sent by the Windows operating system or the e-mail system warning that the insecure e-mail sent by this web page does not go through, but those alert signals are not part of JavaScript and should be ignored in learning this example.

3.9.1 Comparison of JavaScript with C and C++

The syntax of JavaScript is very similar to C and C++. In terms of function declaration and calling, JavaScript is of the style of C language. On the other hand, JavaScript has many built-in object classes, and the use of the built-in object classes is of the style of C++ language. JavaScript is case sensitive. A comment line in a JavaScript program is placed after // or is delimited by /* and */.

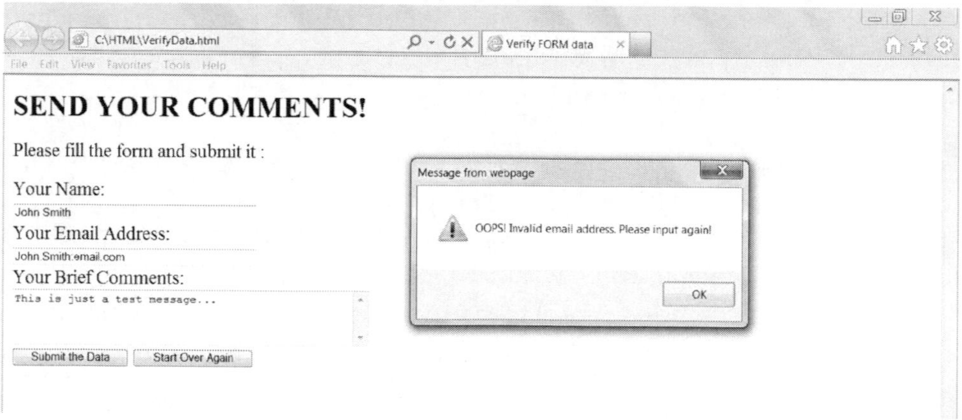

Figure 3.4 JavaScript (`VerifyData.html`) verifies input data.

A few features of JavaScript programs are different from those of C/C++. In JavaScript, data types of variables do not need to be declared. The type of a variable is automatically determined based on the assigned value. For instance, in Listing 3.6, `BadChars = "/, :;"` means that a string is assigned to the variable `BadChars`, and the type of this variable automatically becomes string.

In JavaScript, a semicolon (;) is not needed after a sentence. JavaScript has its keywords or reserved words—that is, words that are not recommended for user-defined words (see Appendix 3.2).

In JavaScript, you can use "function" to define a user-defined object class. Compared with C++, JavaScript is weak in the object-oriented feature.

3.9.2 Function and Calling a Function

Similar to C, a function of JavaScript is a set of JavaScript statements that perform a specific task. A function can be called by an external JavaScript statement. The format of a JavaScript function is

```
function [user-defined function name](arguments) {
[statements of the function]
}
```

In Listing 3.6, `VerifyEmailAdd` is a function name, and `EmailString` is its argument. Similarly to C, a JavaScript function can return a value back to the calling function. The value returned can be numerical or Boolean (i.e., "true" or "false"). There are usually two ways to call a function. One is to call a function within another function, using

```
[called function name](passing arguments)
```

In Listing 3.6, function `VerifyForm` calls `VerifyEmailAdd` by passing the value of `form.email.value` to substitute `EmailString`. The other way of calling a function is the use of an event handler:

```
[event handler]="[called function name](passing arguments)"
```

In Listing 3.6, `onSubmit` (line **34**) calls function `VerifyForm` by passing the argument `this`. `this` represents the current active object. In this example, the current active object is the `FORM`. Since the `VerifyForm` function has argument `form` (line **6**), `this` (i.e., the current `FORM`) substitutes `form` in `VerifyForm` in line **6**.

3.9.3 String Processing

JavaScript has string (character) object class that has many built-in methods of string processing. In Listing 3.6, `BadChars` (line **21**) is a string object, and `charAt()` (line **25**) is the method that identifies the character at the position specified in parentheses. In JavaScript, the index of the position of a character in the string starts with 0. `EmailString` is also a string object, and `indexOf()` (line **26**) is another built-in method that finds the location of a substring in the string. `EmailString.indexOf(aBadChar,0)` means "to search `EmailString` from position 0 to find the location of the substring specified in `aBadChar` and to return the value of the location." If the search fails to find the substring, the entire string processing returns value –1.

Strings can be added together. There will be an example of a cookie later in Listing 3.8, where it is to be observed that

```
document.cookie = "UserName=" + UserName + ";expires="
                + expireDate.toGMTString()
```

This means that the string operation (+) adds the four strings together and hands over the long string to `document.cookie`. Note the difference between string and string name. A specific string is placed in a pair of quotation marks (" "), while a string name is a variable name and must not have quotation marks.

3.9.4 if-Statement

The format of if-statement of JavaScript is very similar to that of C. In Listing 3.6, `if(!VerifyEmailAdd(form.email.value))` (line **9**) means that if the function `VerifyEmailAdd` based on `form.email.value` is not "true" (i.e., it returns "false"), then the actions specified in the action statements will be executed. Here, the "!" symbol is used to specify the negative condition.

3.9.5 `alert`-*Statement*

`alert` is used to alert the user with a warning message. It results in an alert window. The user can click on the [OK] button to close the alert window.

3.10 `FORM` Data Calculation

In this section, we examine the third typical JavaScript application: client-side calculation. JavaScript allows the user on the client side to find more information from the web page based on the input data on the FORM. In this example, the user is allowed to input the weight of a package for delivery, the days needed for transportation, and the destination, and then to find the delivery service charge.

Listing 3.7: Use JavaScript to Make Calculation on Client Side (`Delivery.html`)

```
 1  <HTML>
 2  <HEAD>
 3  <TITLE>Delivery fee </TITLE>
 4  <SCRIPT>
 5  function CalPayment(form)
 6  { form.Payment.value = "";
 7    DeliveryWeight=eval(form.Delivery.value);
 8    DeliveryDays=eval(form.Days.value);
 9    if(form.State[0].checked)  {
10      form.Payment.value = DeliveryWeight * DeliveryDays * 1;
-9    }
11    if(form.State[1].checked)  {
12      form.Payment.value = DeliveryWeight * DeliveryDays * 2;
-11   }
-6  }
-4  </SCRIPT>
-2  </HEAD>
13  <BODY>
14   <H2>Estimate the delivery charge by yourself.</H2>
15   <FORM NAME="PAY">
16    <P> Input the weight of package for the delivery:
17    <INPUT TYPE=TEXT SIZE=10 NAME="Delivery"> lb<BR>
-16   </P>
18    <P>Input the days needed for transportation:
19    <INPUT TYPE=TEXT SIZE=10  NAME="Days"><BR>
-18   </P>
20    <P>Choose the destination State:</P>
21    <INPUT TYPE=RADIO NAME="State">In State<BR>
22    <INPUT TYPE=RADIO NAME="State">Out State
-20   <BR></P>
23    <INPUT TYPE=BUTTON VALUE="Estimate Payment",
24          onClick="CalPayment(PAY)">
25    <INPUT TYPE=RESET  VALUE="Reset">
26    <P>The delivery charge would be:  $
27    <INPUT TYPE=TEXT SIZE=10  NAME="Payment"><BR>
-26   </P>
```

```
-15   </FORM>
-13   </BODY>
 -1   </HTML>
```

In Listing 3.7, lines **15** through **-15** implement the FORM. There are three text-boxes. In the first textbox (line **17**), the user inputs the weight of the package. The second one (line **19**) is used for the user to input the days for the delivery. The third (line **27**) is used to display the calculation result of the delivery charge. There are two radio buttons (lines **21** and **22**). The user is expected to select the delivery destination. The name of the radio buttons is "State" and only one of them can be activated. Thus, the JavaScript automatically assigns State[0] to the first radio button and State[1] to the second radio button. Lines **23** and **24** implement a command button. On clicking this button, the CalPayment() function is called. Note that, as the FORM has its specific name (PAY) (line **15**), the name of the argument of the calling function is PAY.

Now we examine function CalPayment(), programmed in lines **5** through **-6**. Line **5** declares the function name. Line **6** cleans up the textbox for the new answer. Line **7** captures the weight of the package for the delivery. Note the argument name, Delivery, in line **7**, which is the name of the textbox in line **17**. The eval internal function converts the string in the textbox into a numerical number. Line **8** captures the days permitted for the delivery. Lines **9** through **-9** calculate the delivery charge if the user selects "In State" using the radio button. Lines **11** through **-11** calculate the delivery charge if the user selects "Out State."

Figure 3.5 shows an execution result of Delivery.html. It also shows the source code, which the client can view through clicking [View] and [Source] in the browser. If the web page owner does not want to reveal the formulas of calculation to the user, she or he must create a JavaScript program in a protected folder on the server that contains the formulas and can be called by the web page for execution. For complex web application tasks such as manipulating data on the server and producing

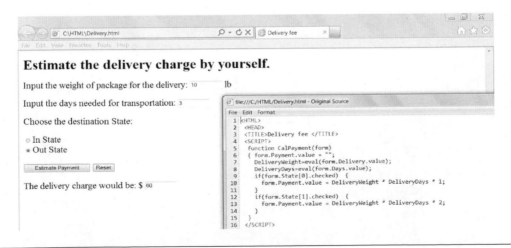

Figure 3.5 JavaScript (Delivery.html) calculate data on client side.

dynamic web pages, one must use server-side programs as discussed in the chapters on ASP.NET and PHP.

3.11 Cookies

In web applications, a cookie is a piece of information that a web page gives to the user's browser when the two first meet. It is a small file containing information about the web server and the web pages visited, and it is stored on the client-side computer hard disk as a plain text file. On the server side, the remote server saves its part of the cookie and information about the user. The issue of cookies is controversial, since people prefer anonymous access of websites. To control the computer's behavior with respect to cookies, the web browser can be set to allow or disallow a computer to send a cookie to the server. Nevertheless, cookies exist, and a JavaScript programmer can perform many useful tasks with cookies. For instance, a web server can remember the visitor's name. A cookie is a text string with the following format:

```
[Cookie Name]=[Value of the cookie];
expires=expirationDateGMT;
path=[URL path];
domain=[site domain]
```

Only the first two lines are mandatory. The first line defines the cookie's name and its value. The second line defines the expiration date (the standard Internet time based upon Greenwich Mean Time [GMT]) after which the browser will automatically delete the cookie. The next two lines allow the programmer to store a URL and a domain value in the cookie.

The following JavaScript example of cookie manipulations involves two web pages with HTML and JavaScript programs. The first web page (WriteCookie.html in Listing 3.8) allows the user to input his or her name. The input user's name is then written to a cookie that is in turn stored on the web page's server. The second web page (ReadCookie.html in Listing 3.9) uses the cookie created by WriteCookie.html. In this example, when the user downloads ReadCookie.html (note that it must be stored with WriteCookie.html on the same server), it will retrieve the user's name from the cookie and display it for the user.

Listing 3.8: Use JavaScript to Write Cookie to the Server (WriteCookie.html)

```
1  <HTML>
2  <HEAD>
3  <TITLE> Write a cookie </TITLE>
4  <SCRIPT>
5    expireDate = new Date
6    expireDate.setTime(expireDate.getTime() + (24*60*60*1000*365))
7    // Write a cookie function
8    function WriteCookie() {
```

```
 9   UserName = ""
10   // If the cookie is not empty, then retrieve the cookie
11     if (document.cookie != "") {
12      UserName = document.cookie.split("=")[1]
-11    }
13   // If the NameBox is not empty then obtain the user name from the box
14     if (document.CustomerForm.NameBox != "") {
15      UserName = document.CustomerForm.NameBox.value
-14    }
16   // Write cookie
17     document.cookie = "UserName=" + UserName + ";expires="
18          + expireDate.toGMTString()
-8   }
-4  </SCRIPT>
-2  </HEAD>
19  <BODY>
20   <H3>Customer relationships: </H3>
21   <FORM NAME=CustomerForm>
22    Please enter your name for cookie:
23    <INPUT TYPE=TEXT  NAME=NameBox onBlur="WriteCookie()">
-21  </FORM>
24   <P>After you close the Web page, please visit
25    (ReadCookie.html) to view warmest greetings!
-24  </P>
-19 </BODY>
 -1 </HTML>
```

We examine how `WriteCookie.html` in Listing 3.8 works. Line **5** defines variable `expireDate`, which is an object of `Date` class. The `Date` class is a built-in class in the JavaScript library. There are many standard methods of the `Date` class. Line **6** uses two of these methods: `setTime` (to set a new time) and `getTime` (to get the current time). In JavaScript, time is measured in milliseconds. Line **6** sets the expire time 1 year ahead (i.e., 365 days per year, 24 hours per day, 60 minutes per hour, 60 seconds per minute, and 1,000 milliseconds per second). Line **8** starts the `WriteCookie` function. Line **9** defines variable `UserName`. Lines **11** through -**11** retrieve the user name if the cookie for the user is not empty. This ensures that the user's name previously stored in the cookie is not lost if the user does not input his or her name this time. Lines **14** through -**14** obtain the user's name from the textbox (note the `FORM` name `CustomerForm` in line **21** and the textbox name `NameBox` in line **23**). Lines **17** and **18** generate a string and write the string to the cookie. In line **23,** the `onBlur` command instructs the computer to write a cookie when the user leaves the web page.

Listing 3.9 shows the JavaScript program (`ReadCookie.html`) that retrieves the cookie.

Listing 3.9: Use JavaScript to Read Cookie from the Server (`ReadCookie.html`)

```
<HTML>
 <HEAD>
 <TITLE> Read a cookie </TITLE>
 <SCRIPT>
```

```
      if (document.cookie != "") {
      document.write("Hello, " + document.cookie.split("=")[1] + "!")
     }
   </SCRIPT>
   </HEAD>
   <BODY>
   <H4> Welcome back!</H4>
   </BODY>
   </HTML>
```

The lines in bold in Listing 3.9 (ReadCookie.html) are the JavaScript program that retrieves the user's name stored in the cookie and displays it on the web page. If you understand WriteCookie.html in Listing 3.8, this program is straightforward.

The execution results of Listings 3.8 and 3.9 are shown in Figures 3.6 and 3.7. Again, you need to click on the [Allow blocked content] button in the browser every time to allow the JavaScript program to run. In addition, a setting of your computer (and the browser) might block the JavaScript programs completely unless the web page with the JavaScript is reloaded after [Allow blocked content] is activated. This is because cookies are stored on your computer and the browser does not allow an unsafe program to access your computer. If you run the program in Listing 3.8 on your local computer, you can view the cookie in a folder on the C: drive,

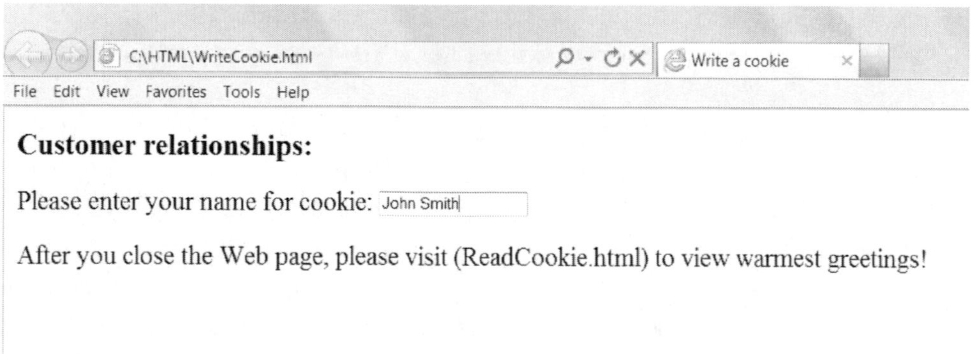

Figure 3.6 JavaScript (WriteCookie.html) writes cookie.

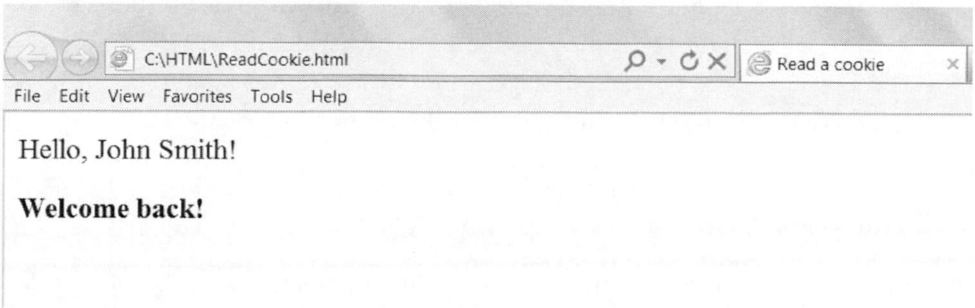

Figure 3.7 JavaScript (ReadCookie.html) reads cookie.

depending on the setting of the browser. Various JavaScript statements used in the previous examples are further explained next.

3.12 Miscellaneous JavaScript Statements

3.12.1 new *Statement*

JavaScript is a multiparadigm language, supporting object-oriented and function-oriented programming styles. It uses function as modules and uses objects of the built-in classes. new statement creates a new object of the specified class. In Listing 3.8, line **5,** Date is a JavaScript predefined object class, and expireDate is a user-defined new object of Date. Its data type is time string.

3.12.2 *Miscellaneous Functions and Methods*

JavaScript provides a variety of methods of built-in classes. In Listing 3.6 (VerifyData.html), line **11,** focus() is a method of the textbox class that moves the cursor to the textbox. In line **12,** select() is also a method of the textbox class that highlights the textbox.

In lines **7** and **8** of Listing 3.7 (Delivery.html), the eval() function evaluates the string in the input textbox and converts it to a numerical value. For instance, if you input "200+300" in the Delivery textbox, DeliveryWeight ends up with 500. This feature is powerful.

In line **6** of Listing 3.8 (WriteCookie.html), getTime() is to get the current time from the time string. setTime() is to set a time string. In line **18,** toGMTString() is a method of Date that converts the expireDate into the standard Internet time string.

In line **12** of Listing 3.8 (WriteCookie.html), split("=") is a method of cookie. It splits a cookie record into fields based on the "=" symbol in the cookie (see the cookie format discussed right before Listing 3.8). After splitting the cookie, [0] represents the first field of the cookie or the cookie's name (i.e., "UserName" in WriteCookie.html), and [1] represents the second field of the cookie or the value of the cookie (i.e., the string typed in the textbox in WriteCookie.html). The operation of line **12,** document.cookie.split("=") [1], finds the value of the cookie. The operation of line **17,** document.cookie = ..., actually writes the cookie to the client's disk and to the server.

3.13 Cascading Style Sheet

Cascading style sheet (CSS) is a language for expressing the presentation of structured documents in HTML and other markup languages. CSS is often used with HTML to describe the presentation semantics (i.e., the appearance and formatting) of web pages. The use of CSS offers several advantages:

1. CSS enables the separation of web page contents expressed in HTML from document presentation.
2. CSS is able to change the default settings of the web browser for displaying HTML documents.
3. CSS supports rich instructions of typographical styles that are not supported by HTML.

The main criticism of CSS is a lack of uniform support by different web browsers.

There are three methods to embed CSS codes in HTML: inline CSS, internal CSS, and external CSS. For inline CSS, the CSS code is specified for and applied to a single HTML tag. For internal CSS, the CSS code is specified in the head section of an HTML document and allows the same formatting style to be applied to multiple HTML tags within the web page. For external CSS, the CSS code is stored in a separate text file that can be linked by an HTML document. Like internal CSS, external CSS also allows the same formatting style to be applied to multiple HTML tags in the web page.

3.13.1 Inline CSS

To specify inline CSS, the `style` attribute must be added to the HTML tag as follows:

```
<tag-name style="property1:value1; property2:value2;
                 . . . . . . .
                    propertyN:valueN;">
```

where the value of the `style` attribute contains the CSS properties that specified the formatting style associated with the HTML tag. Listing 3.10 shows an example of the CSS code of `style`.

Listing 3.10: Example of CSS Code of `style`

```
<p style="background-color:#FF0000; color:#FFFF00;
font-family:'Times New Roman', Arial, Courier;
font-size:xx-large;">

<p style="background-color:#FF0000; color:#FFFF00;
font-family:'Times New Roman'; font-size:20pt;">
```

In the example of Listing 3.10, the CSS property "`color`" specifies the text color, and the CSS property "`background-color`" specifies the background color. The color code #FF0000 represents the red color, and #FFFF00 represents the yellow color.

You can find the color code from the Internet. The CSS property "font-family" specifies the list of fonts. A font is a collection of similar characters with a specific design. For the list of fonts specified as the value of the CSS "font-family" property, the browser uses the first font in the list if it supports it. If the browser does not support any of the specified fonts, the browser will use its default font. If the font name has more than one word, it should be delimited by single quotes. The CSS property "font-size" specifies the size of the text in terms of either an absolute value or a relative value. Absolute values of the font size are measured in points (pt) or pixels (px), such as 20pt and 20px. A point is 1/72 of an inch, and a pixel is a tiny dot on the monitor screen that displays a single color. Relative values of the font size include "xx-small," "x-small," "small," "medium," "large," "x-large," "xx-large," etc.

To apply inline CSS to a group of HTML tags, the HTML tags should be nested inside <div> and </div> or inside <span> and </span>. Both <div> and <span> are HTML tags for grouping multiple HTML tags together without signifying specific meaning. The inline CSS specified in <div> or <span> will be applied to all HTML tags inside <div> and </div> or inside <span> and </span>. Listing 3.11 shows simple examples of <div> and <span>.

Listing 3.11: Example of CSS Code with <div> and <span>

```
<html>
<div style="background-color:#FF8000; color:#FFFFFF;
font-family:'Microsoft Sans Serif'; font-size:24pt;">
 <h1> div: </h1>
 <p> Style for an entire section of the page.  </p>
 <p> The same format style is applied to the entire block. </p>
 <p> (The block is ended here...) </p>
</div>

<span style="background-color:#FF8000; color:#FFFFFF;
font-family:'Microsoft Sans Serif'; font-size:20pt;">
 <h2> span: </h2>
 <p> Style for surrounding text.  </p>
 <p> The same formatting style is applied to lines.</p>
 <p> (These lines are highlighted...) </p>
</span>
</html>
```

The only difference between <div> and <span> is that <div> divides the web page into sections with the same formatting styles, while <span> highlights text lines. Figure 3.8 is the presentation of Listing 3.11 and shows the difference between <div> and <span>.

3.13.2 Internal CSS

Internal CSS is specified in the head section of an HTML document with the syntax

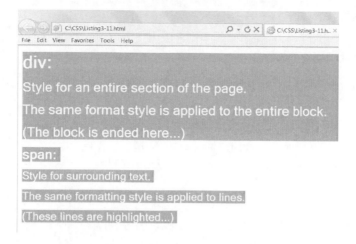

Figure 3.8   Presentation of CSS with `<div>` and `<span>`.

```
<head>
  <style type="text/css">
      selector1 {property1:value1; property2:value2; ...
                   propertyN:valueN;}
    selector2 {...}
        ...
  </style>
</head>
```

where a selector refers to the HTML tags to which the style will be applied. If the value of a property has more than one word, it should be delimited by double quotes, such as `"Times New Roman"`.

There are five different types of selectors defined in CSS:

1. *Simple selector*—corresponding to a single HTML tag, such as

```
<head>
<style type=="text/css">
          h1 {font-size: 30pt;}
          h2 {font-size: 20pt;}
    </style>
</head>
```

   This CSS code means that all `<h1>` tags in the HTML document will use the font size of 30 points and all `<h2>` tags in the HTML document will use the font size of 20 points, regardless of the default settings of the web browser.

2. *Contextual selector*—corresponding to a sequence of HTML tags, such as

```
<head>
<style type=="text/css">
h1 b {color:#FF0000; font-size: 20pt;}
</style>
</head>
```

This CSS code means that all texts within <h1><b> and </b></h1> throughout the HTML document will use the font size of 20 points and appear in the red color.

3. *Class selector*—specifying different classes for a single HTML tag, such as

```
<head>
<style type=="text/css">
          p.normal {font-size:20pt;}
          p.warning {font-size: 24pt; color: #FF0000;}
     </style>
</head>
```

This CSS code implies that there are two different classes of the <p> tag in the HTML document: "normal" and "warning". To refer to a particular class in the HTML document, the <p> tag should include a "class" attribute. For example,

```
<p class="normal"> texts with the 20pt font size </p>
<p class="warning"> texts with the 24pt font size and the red
color </p>
```

4. *Generic class selector*—specifying classes for multiple HTML tags, such as

```
<head>
<style type=="text/css">
          .warning {color:#FF0000;}
</style>
</head>
```

This CSS code implies that any HTML tag in the web page can refer to the class "warning" in order to change the associated texts to the red color. For example,

```
<p class="warning"> a paragraph in the red color</p>
<h1 class="warning">a heading in the red color </h1>
```

5. *Pseudo class selector*—specifying special mouse effects to other types of selectors; the syntax is

```
selector:pseudo-class {property1:value1; property2:value2; ...
                            propertyN:valueN;}
```

Currently, most pseudo classes defined in CSS, except for the "hover" pseudo class, are not uniformly supported by different browsers. The hover pseudo class specifies the formatting style to be applied when the mouse pointer hovers over a particular selector. For example,

```
<head>
<style type=="text/css">
    a:hover {background-color:#FF0000;}
```

```
    input:hover {background-color:#FFFF00;}
    h1 b:hover{background-color:#FF0000;}
    p.important:hover{background-color:#FFFF00;}
    .warning:hover {background-color:#FF0000;}
</style>
</head>
```

implies that the background will change when the mouse pointer hovers over any link defined by the `<a>` tag, any textbox defined by the `<input>` tag, the texts within `<h1><b>` and `</b></h1>`, any paragraph defined by the `<p class="important">` tag, and any HTML tags of the class "warning" such as `<p class="warning">` and `<h1 class="warning">`.

Listing 3.12 is an example of the `hover` pseudo class. Note that `<!DOCTYPE>` must be declared for the `hover` pseudo class to work in Microsoft Internet Explorer.

Listing 3.12: Example of CSS Code with `hover` Pseudo Class

```
<!DOCTYPE html>
<html>
<head><title>CSS-hover Example</title>
<style type="text/css">
    a:hover {background-color:#FFFF00;}
    a.important:hover {background-color:#FF0000;color:#0000FF;}
    input:hover {background-color:#FFFF00;}
    h1 b:hover{background-color:#FF0000;}
</style>
</head>
<body>
  <h1><b>Pseudo class selector</b></h1>
  <form action="mailto:demo@Provider.com" method="post">
   <a href="http://www.umassd.edu">University of Massachusetts
      Dartmouth</a><br><br>
   <a class="important" href="http://www.smu.ca">Saint Mary's
      University</a><br><br>
   <input type="text">
</form></body></html>
```

3.13.3 External CSS

The syntax for external CSS is the same as that for internal CSS. External CSS allows multiple HTML documents to share the same CSS codes. For external CSS, the actual CSS codes between the `<style>` and `</style>` tags for internal CSS are stored in a separate text file, which normally has a file name with extension `.css`. For example, the following CSS code can be stored in a text file named "FileName.css":

```
p.normal {font-size:20pt;}
p.warning {font-size: 24pt; color: #FF0000;}
```

For any HTML document to use the CSS code, it should link to this text file in the head section as follows:

```
<head>
  <link rel="stylesheet" href="FileName.css">
</head>
```

3.14 Debugging Source Code of Web Pages

Web page browsers are more tolerant of errors in the HTML and JavaScript programs than other language compilers or interpreters. Usually, the browser can continue to interpret and execute the HTML and JavaScript programs when an error is encountered. In many cases of error, the browser dumps compromised results on the web page (e.g., a broken icon for an image) without fatal interruptions.

When designing a large web page, it is a good practice to develop a small HTML document for each of the components of the web page. Test all the small components and then assemble them into a large web page.

A browser can provide built-in debugger functions. Common errors in HTML and JavaScript programming include:

- Misspelling words
- Missing a tag
- Omitting symbols
- Violation of formats
- Incorrect URL
- Incorrect folders for images
- Incorrect image format (JPG or GIF)

After debugging a web page written in HTML, JavaScript, and CSS, one should reopen the web page file in the browser, instead of clicking on the web page icon or clicking on the "refresh" button, to discharge the old programs completely.

Chapter 3 Exercises

1. Access an interesting web page on the Internet, and view the HTML source code.
2. Create a web page by using the HTML language. Include tags that are not mentioned in the book examples.
3. Create an electronic document by using a software package (e.g., Microsoft Word) and then convert it into an HTML document. View the HTML code and give comments.
4. Fill blanks in the following HTML and JavaScript program. Sketch the web page and discuss how this page works:

```
1   <HTML>
2   _____
3   <TITLE> Web Page with JavaScript </TITLE>
```

```
 4   <SCRIPT>
 5   // Define a function to verify the name types on the form
 6   function VerifyName(NameString)  {
 7   // If the name is empty, then give false
 8       if (_____ == "") {
 9       return false
10       }
11   // Define 7 bad characters which are illegal in names
12       IllegalChar = "/, :;[]"
13   // For each of the 7 bad characters, check the typed name
14   // If a bad character has been found, then give false
15    for (i=0; i<=_____; i++) {
16          aBadChar=_____.charAt(i)
17        if (_____.indexOf(aBadChar,0) >= 0) {
18        return false
19          }
20    }
21   // Otherwise (the above two errors are not found), give true
22   return _____
23   }

24   // Define a function for the action after verify the name
25   function SubmitForm(_____) {
26   // If the verification returns false based on typed address
27   // then signals alert
28   // and move the cursor back to the name box and highlight it
29   // and return true (move on to the next task)
30    if (!VerifyName(form._____.value)) {
31      alert("Ha-ha! Invalid name. Please input again!")
32      form._____.focus()
33      _____.name._____()
34      _____ false
35    }
36    return true
37   _____
38   _____
39   </HEAD>
40   _____
41   <H3> SEND YOUR INFORMATION! </H3>
42   Please fill the form and submit it :
43   <BR>
44    <FORM onSubmit="return _____(this)"
45      ACTION="mailto:MyEmail@U.edu" METHOD=POST>
46   Your Name: <BR>
47   <INPUT TYPE=TEXT NAME="name" SIZE=50> <BR>
48   Your Address: <BR>
49   <INPUT TYPE=TEXT _____="address" SIZE=50> <BR>
50   Your Request: <BR>
51   <INPUT _____=TEXT NAME="request" _____=100> <BR>
```

```
52  <INPUT TYPE=SUBMIT _____="Submit Information">
53  <INPUT TYPE=RESET VALUE="Reset the Form">
54  _____
55  </BODY>
56  </HTML>
```

5. Fill blanks in the following HTML and JavaScript program. Sketch the web page and discuss how this page works:

```
1   <HTML>
2   <HEAD>
3   <TITLE> Housing Expenses </TITLE>
4   _____
5    function _____(form)
6     { form.HousingExpense._____ = "";
7       Months=eval(form._____.value);
8       Meals=eval(form.MealsPerDay.value);
9       if(form._____[0].checked)  {
10      form.HousingExpense._____ = Months * (1000 + Meals * 300);
11      _____
12      if(form._____[1].checked)  {
13      form.HousingExpense._____ = Months * (800 + Meals * 300);
14      }
15     }
16  </SCRIPT>
17  _____
18  <BODY>
19   <H2>Estimate the Housing Expenses.</H2>
20   <_____ NAME="Housing">
21    <P>How many months do you want to rent?
22    <INPUT TYPE=TEXT SIZE=10 NAME="Duration"> Months<BR>
23    </P>
24    <P>How many meals per day would you order?
25    <INPUT TYPE=TEXT SIZE=10  NAME="MealsPerDay"><BR>
26    </P>
27    <P>Choose the type of dorm:</P>
28    <INPUT TYPE=RADIO NAME="Type">Single<BR>
29    <INPUT TYPE=RADIO NAME="Type">Shared<BR></P>
30    <INPUT TYPE=BUTTON VALUE="Estimate Housing Expenses",
31      onClick="HousingEstimation(_____)">
32    <INPUT TYPE=RESET  VALUE="Reset">
33    <P>The total expenses would be:  $
34    <INPUT TYPE=TEXT SIZE=10  NAME="HousingExpense"><BR>
35    </P>
36   </FORM>
37  </BODY>
38  </HTML>
```

6. Use a web browser to open the completed web page in question 5. The user types two numbers in the first two textboxes (12 and 3, respectively), clicks on the first radio button, and clicks on the first command button. What is the calculation result and where will it show up?

7. Fill blanks in the following HTML and JavaScript program. Discuss how to use this program.

```
1   <HTML>
2   <HEAD>
3   <TITLE> Set a cookie based on a form _____
4   _____
5   expireDate = new Date
6   expireDate.setTime(expireDate.getTime()+(24*60*60*1000*365))
7   StudentAddress = ""
8   if (document.cookie != "") {
9    StudentAddress = document.cookie.split("=")[1]
10  }
11  function SetCookie() {
12  StudentAddress = document._____.AddressBox.value
13   document.cookie = "StudentAddress=" + _____
14       + ";expires=" + _____
15  }
16  </SCRIPT>
17  _____
18  <BODY>
19  <H4>We will keep your address updated!
20  </H4>
21  <FORM _____=StudentForm>
22  Please Enter Your Address:
23  <INPUT TYPE=TEXT  NAME=AddressBox onBlur="SetCookie()">
24  </FORM>
25  _____
26  </HTML>
```

8. Use JavaScript to verify a form.
9. Use JavaScript to manipulate an image.
10. Use JavaScript to read a cookie.
11. Fill blanks in the following demonstration document of CSS. Sketch the appearance of each line of the web page:

```
1 <html>
2 <head>
3  <title>CSS Assignment</title>
4  <style type="_____/css">
5     h1 {font-size:medium;}
```

```
 6     h3 b {color:#FF0000;}
 7     p.important {background-_____:#FFFF00;}
 8     p.large {font-_____:large;}
 9     .myColor {color:#FF0000;}
10   <_____>
11 </head>
12 <body>

13 <h1>Welcome to CSS!</h1>
14 <h3>CSS: <_____>Cascading Style Sheet</b> describes the
15         document presentation semantics.</h3>

16 <p class="important">One can highlight parts of the Web page
17         based on a criterion across the entire Web page.</p>
18 <p _____="large">Or, one can set a particular font for a type
19         of paragraph across the entire Web page.</p>

20 <p _____="myColor">The color of this line is "myColor."</p>

21 <div _____="_____-color:#00FFFF;font-family:Arial;font-size:large;">
22 <p>One can also<u>divide</u> the Web page into blocks.</p>
23 <p>(Note: #FF0000 is Red.  #FFFF00 is Yellow. #00FF00 is Green.)_____
24 <_____>

25 </body>
26 </html>
```

12. Use HTML and CSS to implement the following table as a menu of links to the websites: blue color font, 16 pt, light color background.

```
Google
eBay
Amazon.com
SMU
```

13. Develop a web page with business contents to meet the following minimum requirements:
    • Well-designed contents and hyperlinks
    • Well-designed images and colors
    • At least one well-designed form
    • JavaScript for verifying the form
    • JavaScript for client-side calculation
    • CSS components

Appendix 3.1: List of HTML Commonly Used Tags

Tag	Description
`<!-- . . . -->`	Comments
`<A> . . . </A>`	Anchor; creates a hyperlink (att: `HREF`)
`<APPLET> . . . </APPLET>`	Define and trigger a Java applet
`<B> . . . </B>`	Bold font
`<BASE>`	Defines the base URL for all relative URLs in the current document
`<BIG> . . . </BIG>`	Big font
`<BLINK> . . . </BLINK>`	Cause annoying blink text
`<BODY> . . . </BODY>`	Defines the body of an HTML document (att: `BGCOLOR`, `BACKGROUND`)
` `	Break line
`<CAPTION> . . . </CAPTION>`	Creates a caption for a table
`<CENTER> . . . </CENTER>`	Centers the text
`<DD> . . . </DD>`	The text is the definition part of a definition-list
`<DT> . . . </DT>`	The text is the term part of a definition-list
`<FONT> . . . </FONT>`	Set font (att: `COLOR`, `SIZE`)
`<FORM> . . . </FORM>`	Delimits a form
`<FRAME> . . . </FRAME>`	Delimits a frame
`<FRAMESET>.</FRAMESET>`	Set multiple frames
`<Hx> . . . </Hx>`	Headers, where x is a number 1–6 for the level
`<HEAD> . . . </HEAD>`	Delimits the document's head
`<HR>`	Horizontal rule
`<HTML> . . . </HTML>`	Contains the HTML document
`<I> . . . </I>`	Italic font
`<IMG>`	Inserts image (att: `ALIGN`, `ALT`, `SRC`, `HEIGHT`, `WIDTH`)
`<INPUT TYPE=CHECKBOX>`	Creates a checkbox-input within a form
`<INPUT TYPE=RADIO>`	Creates a radio button within a form
`<INPUT TYPE=IMAGE>`	Creates an image input element within a form
`<INPUT TYPE=SUBMIT>`	Creates a submit button within a form (att: `NAME`, `VALUE`)
`<ISINDEX>`	Creates a searchable HTML document (att: `ACTION` and `PROMPT`)
`<LI> . . . </LI>`	List
`<LINK>`	Establishes a link
`<P> . . . </P>`	Delimits a paragraph (att: `ALIGN`)
`<PARAM>`	Set parameters for Java applets
`<S> . . . </S>`	Causes struck
`<SELECT> . . . </SELECT>`	Creates a multiple-choice menu

`<TABLE>` . . . `</TABLE>`	Delimits a table (att: `ALIGN`, `BORDER`, `VALIGN`, `WIDTH`)
`<TD>` . . . `</TD>`	Describes a table data cell
`<TH>` . . . `</TH>`	Table header
`<TR>` . . . `</TR>`	A table row
`<TITLE>` . . . `</TITLE>`	Creates the title
`<U>` . . . `</U>`	Underlines

Appendix 3.2: JavaScript Reserved Words and Other Keywords

JavaScript Reserved Words

break	false	if	null	true	while
continue	for	in	return	var	with
else	function	new	this	void	

The following words are not reserved, but are not recommended to use as user-defined words:

alert	Date	getClass	name	onSubmit	status
Anchor	defaultStatus	history	navigator	open	String
Area	document	Image	netscape	Option	Submit
Array	Element	JavaClass	Number	parent	sun
assign	focus	length	Object	Password prompt	Text
blur	Form	Link	onClick	Radio	top
Button	Frame	location	onError	Reset	valueOf
Checkbox	frames	Location	onFocus	scroll	window
close	function	Math	onLoad	Select	WINDOW

4

VB.NET

4.1 Graphical User Interface

In business computer applications such as order processing, payroll program, and billing, the users of computer programs require customized applications to accommodate the needs of the business processes in the organization as well as the individuals' preferences. One of the important aspects in business computer applications is the design of the graphical user interface (GUI).

A GUI allows the user to click on boxes for entering text, to click on buttons to initiate a process, and so forth. By using a GUI, the user can better control the execution of the computer application program. Figure 4.1 shows an example of an online price quote GUI. The GUI allows the user to interact with the system to receive needed information.

Visual Basic is Microsoft's product. It provides tools that make it easier for the programmer to create good GUI. As most business applications require frequent modification, the programmer can change the user interface and the code behind the user interface promptly. Visual Basic has several versions. In this chapter, we introduce the recent version VB.NET, which is not totally compatible with the old versions of Visual Basic. VB.NET is one part of the .NET framework that is a complete set of development tools for building comprehensive business applications including web applications.

4.2 Microsoft Visual Studio and VB.NET Environment

VB.NET is a part of the Microsoft .NET framework and is supported by the Microsoft Visual Studio programming environment—the software tool specifically designed to facilitate the development of applications in the .NET platform. One can use it to construct and test applications easily. Figure 4.2 shows the instruction to use the Microsoft Visual Studio environment to create a VB.NET project. Note that you should create a folder for your project to avoid misplacing the project. The folder holds many files that are used for the project. You can copy or move the entire folder, but are not supposed to make a change to the folder unless you know exactly what will happen. To open a project that has been already created, you access the folder and find the project solution file (with extension .sln) to open.

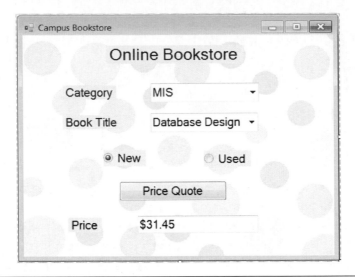

Figure 4.1   An example of GUI.

Once a VB.NET project is created in the Microsoft Visual Studio environment, the VB.NET programming environment starts to operate. VB.NET provides two major facilities to the programmer:

1. A set of development tools that enable the programmer to create the GUI by including control elements such as command button, radio button, etc.
2. The VB.NET programming language, which enables the programmer to specify how the computer performs the tasks required by the control elements of the GUI

Figure 4.3 shows the major components in the VB.NET environment.

1. *Menu bar:* This gives many functions needed to develop projects. The menu bar is similar to those in other Microsoft software.
2. *Tool bar:* This contains icons for most frequently used functions specified in the menu bar.
3. *Form window:* A VB.NET project has two modes. In the design mode, the form window is a working space for the design of form, a GUI unit. In the run mode (when you click on [Debug] and [Start] in the menu bar), the entire GUI is executed.
4. *Toolbox:* This is a collection of tools for the design of a GUI at design time. It allows the programmer to place control elements on the form.
5. *Properties window:* This is used at the design time to examine and change the settings for the properties of each element on the GUI.
6. *Coding window:* This allows the programmer to view and write VB.NET code for any element on the form. If it is not visible, one can double click on an element on the form.

Create your own folder for your project.

Start Microsoft Visual Studio.

Click on [File].

Choose [New Project].

In the Templates Window:

choose [Visual Basic] in left pane;

choose [Windows Forms Application]

in right pane;

click on [OK] button.

You will see the project created.

Click on [File].
Choose [Save All].

In the Save Project window:

find your own folder using

[Browse...] button;

confirm project name;

click on [OK] button.

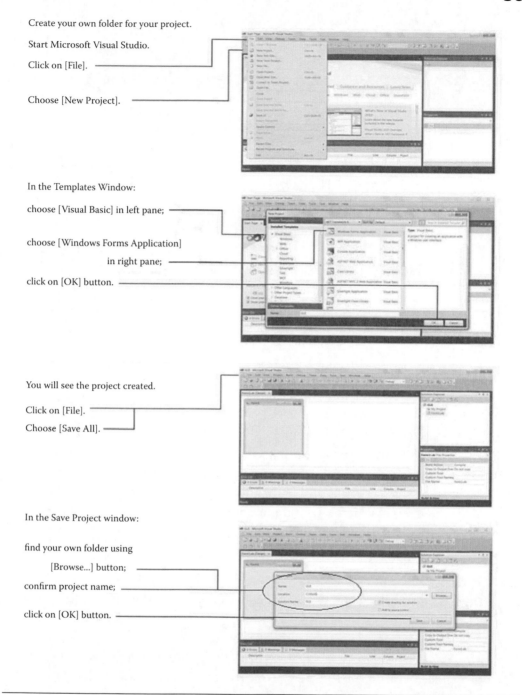

Figure 4.2 Create VB.NET project in Microsoft Visual Studio environment.

7. **Solution explorer window:** This lists all the forms, classes, code modules, and resource files of the VB.NET project.

8. **Error message window:** This shows messages of error and warning for the program.

If a window discussed here is not visible, you may click [View] on the menu bar to bring it up.

Toolbox   Menu (Debug for execution)   Form window   Project window

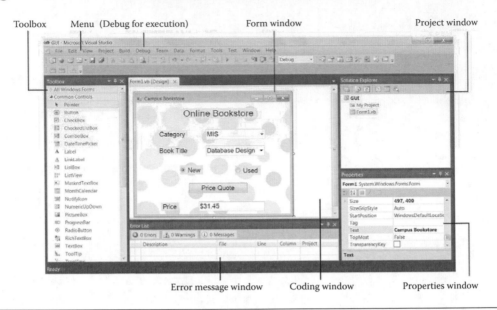

Error message window   Coding window   Properties window

Figure 4.3   VB.NET environment.

4.3 Event Driven

In VB.NET, a GUI unit is a form. A form is a class, which can have attributes, methods, and subclasses. One of the major tasks of developing a GUI application using VB.NET is to write event-driven programs for these classes. In this section, we will learn how VB.NET works implementing GUI. We use a toy example to show the essential steps to designing a GUI by using VB.NET. Suppose we are designing a GUI so that when the user clicks on a button, the window displays a message "Hello, World!" on the screen. We implement this example by performing the following steps:

1. Create a VB.NET project, named HelloWorld, by following the procedure shown in Figure 4.2.
2. In the VB.NET environment (see Figure 4.3), work on [Form1.vb [Design]]. Click on the "Label" control element on the toolbox (the control element marked "A Label") and drag a space on the form to indicate where the message is supposed to be displayed.
3. Bring the Properties Window up by clicking the icon on the toolbar if it is not visible. Work on the Properties Window and change the label Text to nothing by deleting "Label1." This label has its default name "Label1" but does not have any text now (see Figure 4.4). Note that you may change the label name (e.g., to "MsgLabel"), using the Property Window. For programming, the programmer needs to cite the name correctly. For simplicity, we always use the default names of the control elements in our examples. Continue to work on Properties Window and set the Font of the label to a larger font (e.g., 16 point) if the default font is small.

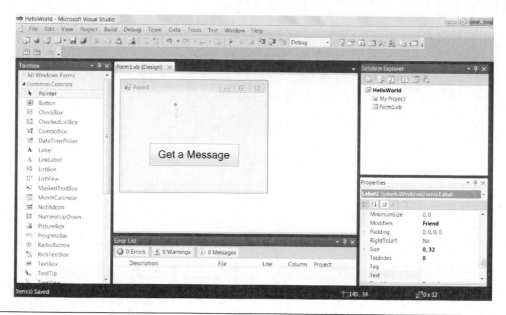

Figure 4.4 Create label and button.

4. Click on the [Button] control element on the toolbox (shown as Button). Draw a button on the form below the label. You can resize the button. The command button has its default name "Button1." In its Properties Window, change the Text to "Get a Message"; its caption is now "Get a Message" (see Figure 4.4). Change the font of the text in the Property Window as you like. Again, you may change the name of the button (e.g., to "MsgButton") in the Property Window, but we do not do this in our examples to avoid confusion.

5. Double click on the "Get a Message" button (Button1) on the form to bring the code window up. Now you can write an event-driven program in the code window for the "Get a Message" button (Button1) to specify what will happen if the user clicks on this button. You may find that the VB.NET environment has formatted the program and has templates similar to the following:

```
Public Class Form1
    Private Sub Form1_Load(ByVal sender As System.Object, _
            ByVal e As System.EventArgs) Handles MyBase.Load

    End Sub

    Private Sub Button1_Click(ByVal sender As System.Object, _
            ByVal e As System.EventArgs) Handles Button1.Click

    End Sub
End Class
```

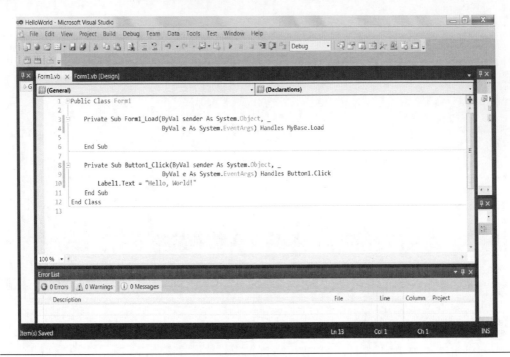

Figure 4.5   Write event-driven program in the coding window.

Since we want the GUI to display a message "`Hello, World!`" in the label, we simply add a statement in the template of `Button1 _ Click`, as shown in Listing 4.1 by the bold line. We will return to explain the template later in this chapter.

Listing 4.1: Code for `Button1 _ Click`

```
Private Sub Button1_Click(ByVal sender As System.Object, _
                ByVal e As System.EventArgs) Handles Button1.Click
    Label1.Text = "Hello, World!"
End Sub
```

The coding window is shown in Figure 4.5. Note that, in the added statement, `Label1` is an object, `Text` is the property (or attribute) of "`Label1`," and the command statement assigns "`Hello, World!`" to the `Text` of `Label1`.

6. Run the program by clicking on `[Debug]` on the menu bar and then `[Start Debugging]`. Now the form starts to execute in the run mode. If you click on the "`Get a Message`" button, then the GUI displays "`Hello, World!`" in the label, as shown in Figure 4.6. Notice the differences between the design mode and the run mode. If you want to make changes to the GUI (e.g., the font for the message), you have to return to the design mode by closing the execution window.

7. Quit the run mode by closing the execution window. Save the project by clicking on `[File]` and then `[Save All]`. The next time you can retrieve the project after logging into the VB.NET environment. To do so, access the folder, find the project solution file (with extension `.sln`), and open it.

Figure 4.6 Execution of VB.NET project.

In fact, once you successfully run the project, the project has been compiled into executable code that can run without the support of the VB.NET programming environment. You go to the folder where you saved the project and go to the [bin] folder and then the [Debug] folder; you will see the executable code HelloWorld.exe in this example.

4.4 Example of a Single Form

In this section, we learn more features of VB.NET. Suppose the project, named LoanPayment, is to calculate the monthly payment based on the amount and the term of the loan. The GUI accepts these data from the user, allows the user to select a current interest rate from a combo menu, and then calculates the monthly payment for the user. The design of Form1 is shown in Figure 4.7. On this form, five labels are created to display headings including "STUDENT TRUST CO.," "Loan Amount $," "Term(year)," "Annual Interest Rate," and "Monthly Payment." Two textboxes are created to catch the data, and the third textbox is used to display the calculated monthly payment result. The difference between textbox and label is that a textbox can catch data as well as display data, but a label can only display text. Close to the "Annual Interest Rate" label, a combobox is created to show the alternative interest rates applied. Finally, a command button is created for the user to find the answer. To write a VB.NET program, you must remember the names of these control element objects (e.g., Label1, TextBox2, ComboBox1, and so on).

Double click on the body of Form1 (other than any objects on the form) to bring the coding window up. Type in the code in bold in Listing 4.2 in the Form1_Load subroutine that will add items to ComboBox1 when the form is loaded.

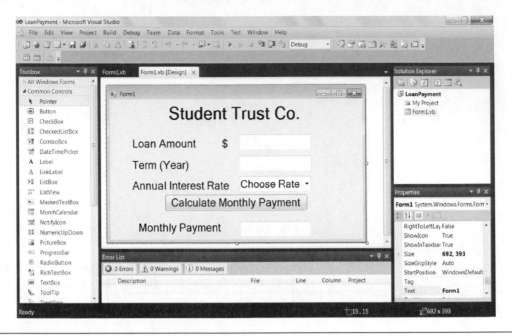

Figure 4.7   Design of form for `LoanPayment` project.

Listing 4.2: Visual Basic Codes for the Combo Menu

```
1 Private Sub Form1_Load(ByVal sender As System.Object, _
2     ByVal e As System.EventArgs) Handles MyBase.Load
3     Dim InterestRate As Decimal
4     For InterestRate = 0.05 To 0.12 Step 0.005
5         ComboBox1.Items.Add(InterestRate)
6     Next InterestRate
7 End Sub
```

The program in Listing 4.2 shows us how to load a combobox and how to write a for-loop in VB.NET. Lines **1** and **2** are the declaration of method `Form1_Load` and are actually a part of the template displayed by the programming environment to allow you to define anything you want the computer to execute during loading the form. In VB.NET, if a method does not return a value, it is called subroutine, and if a method returns a value, it is called a function. A subroutine or function can have parameters (or arguments) to communicate with the request. We do not explain the parameters in this example because beginners do not use them. In VB.NET, if a line of code is too long to print on paper, you may use a space followed by the underscore sign "_" to divide the line. Practically, you do not really need to divide a line in the programming environment. Line **3** declares a variable used by this program. We will explain data types later in this chapter. Lines **4–6** are a for-loop. `InterestRate` is the loop controller. It is set initially to 0.05 and increases 0.005 each step. The for-loop is ended when the value of `InterestRate` reaches 0.12. Line **5** instructs the computer to add an item to the combobox with the value of InterestRate for each step. Line **6** defines the boundary of the for-loop.

Go back to Form1, double click on the designed command button in Form1, and bring the coding window up for the button. Type the program in bold in Listing 4.3 in the Button1_Click subroutine. This program is to catch the data from the textboxes and the combobox and to calculate the payment by using a built-in function named Pmt.

Listing 4.3: VB.NET Code for the Button

```
 1 Private Sub Button1_Click(ByVal sender As System.Object, _
 2    ByVal e As System.EventArgs) Handles Button1.Click
 3    Dim LoanAmount, LoanTerm, InterestRate, MonthlyPayment As Double
 4    LoanAmount = Val(TextBox1.Text)
 5    LoanTerm = Val(TextBox2.Text)
 6    InterestRate = Val(ComboBox1.Text)
 7    MonthlyPayment = -Pmt(InterestRate / 12, _
 8                        LoanTerm * 12, LoanAmount, 0, 0)
 9    TextBox3.Text = Format(MonthlyPayment, "Currency")
10 End Sub
```

We examine how the program in Listing 4.3 works. Lines **1** and **2** are a part of the template displayed by the programming environment. It allows you to define the subroutine when the user clicks the command button. Line **3** declares four variables used in this program. Line **4** catches a value from TextBox1 for LoanAmount. Line **5** catches a value from TextBox2 for LoanTerm. Line **6** catches a value from ComboBox1 for InterestRate. Lines **7** and **8** are one statement that calculates the monthly payment using function Pmt. Pmt is a built-in function in VB.NET that returns the monthly payment based on the monthly interest rate, terms in months, loan amount, etc. If one wants to show the payment without a sign, a negative sign must be applied because a payment is always negative in terms of balance. Finally, line **9** displays the monthly payment in TextBox3 in the currency format (e.g., $30.08). Note that Format() is a function that specifies the format of the data item.

VB.NET provides many built-in calculation functions such as Pmt. To make it easier for the user to learn a variety of topics and functions, the .NET environment provides online help. Using online help, the user is allowed to use keywords to search relevant topics. (Click on [Help] in Visual Studio, select [View Help], and then search Pmt in the Visual Studio online help site.) Figure 4.8 shows a screenshot of online help for the explanation of the Pmt function.

Now you are ready to test the program. Press the [F5] key. If there is no typo in the program, an execution result similar to the one shown in Figure 4.9 is expected. The user of the GUI is allowed to input data of loan amount and term in the respective textboxes, and to select the annual interest rate by clicking on the combo menu. Upon clicking on the [Calculate Monthly Payment] button, the program will give the number of monthly payments in the textbox for "MonthlyPayment."

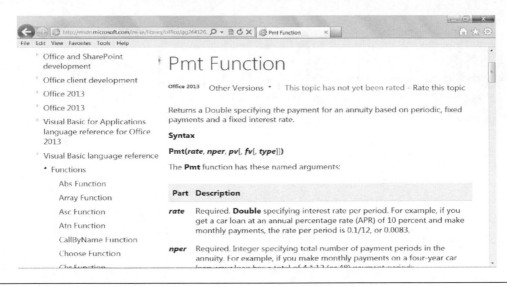

Figure 4.8 Online help for Pmt function.

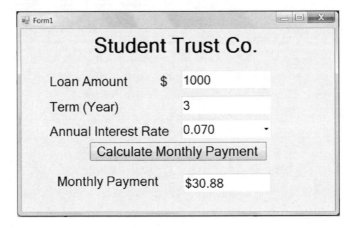

Figure 4.9 Execution result of LoanPayment project.

4.5 Multiple Forms

This section gives an example of a VB.NET project, named FastLunch, with multiple forms. The GUI of this example allows the user to choose the food items and input the purchase for lunch, to view the purchase summary, and to print the receipt on the default printer.

4.5.1 Design Forms

The programmer designs Form1 for the primary GUI as shown in Figure 4.10. To make the GUI attractive, the form is decorated with a color background. Note that when you download images from the Internet, you must be aware of the copyright laws. Form1 has three comboboxes and three textboxes created to accept inputs from the user. It also has a pair of radio buttons to allow the user to indicate the club membership. In their

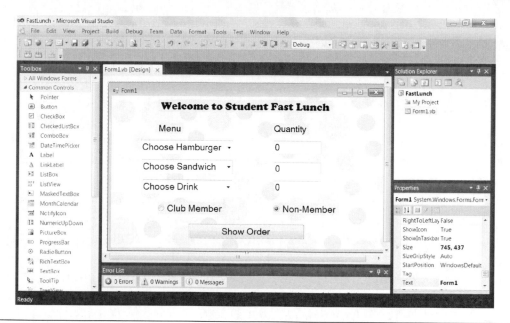

Figure 4.10 Design Form1.vb.

default setting, these two radio buttons belong to the same group and have exclusive choices. If the user wants to have a number of groups of radio buttons, group setting must be applied. The form has a button to allow the user to view the order.

To display order information on the screen, you need another form. Click on [PROJECT] on the menu and then [Add Windows Form...]; the templates pane shows up. Choose [Windows Form] in the templates pane, click on the [Add] button, and Form2 will be added to the project. Figure 4.11 shows the design of Form2 for this

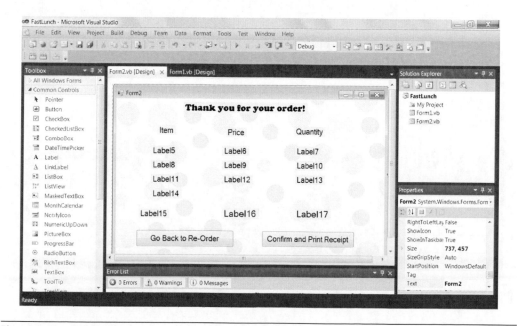

Figure 4.11 Design Form2.vb.

project. Several labels are employed to display information on the screen. To allow the user to go back to Form1 and hide Form2, one command button named [Go Back to Order] is created. The second command button is to print a receipt for the user.

4.5.2 Module

Module is a special class in VB.NET to define global constants, variables, or subroutines that can be shared by all classes of the project. In the current example, prices of food items, membership fee, and sales tax rate are all global constants that can be used by all control elements of the project. Placing global constants in a module not only makes the programming easier, but also is useful for system maintenance because one fact is stored in the project in just one place. Click on [PROJECT] on the menu and then [Add Module...]; the templates pane shows up. Choose [Module] in the templates pane, click on the [Add] button, and Module1 will be added to the project. Figure 4.12 shows the coding window of Module1 for this project. Listing 4.4 is the code of Module1. Note that you must use the keyword Public to define any shared constant and variable. As shown in Listing 4.4, you can use the apostrophe sign "'" for a comment line for self-documentation.

Listing 4.4: Code of Module1.vb

```
1 Module Module1
2  ' At the Module level one can define constants or
```

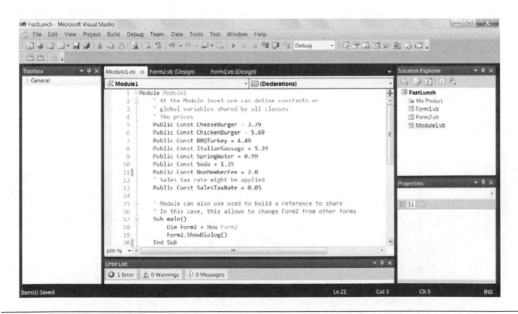

Figure 4.12   Write code for module.

```
 3  ' global variables shared by all classes
 4  ' The prices
 5  Public Const CheeseBurger = 3.79
 6  Public Const ChickenBurger = 5.69
 7  Public Const BBQTurkey = 4.49
 8  Public Const ItalianSausage = 5.39
 9  Public Const SpringWater = 0.99
10  Public Const Soda = 1.35
11  Public Const NonMemberFee = 2.0
12  ' Sales tax rate might be applied
13  Public Const SalesTaxRate = 0.05

14  ' Module can also be used to build a reference to share
15  ' In this case, this allows to change Form2 from other forms
16  Sub main()
17      Dim Form2 = New Form2
18      Form2.ShowDialog()
19  End Sub
20 End Module
```

In Listing 4.4, lines **1** and **20** are the pregenerated template. Lines **2–4** are notations. A notation line starts with the apostrophe "'" sign. Lines **5–13** define the prices of food items, membership fee, and tax rate for all classes to share.

Note Sub main() in line **16.** In VB.NET, the control elements (labels, textboxes, etc.) on a form are unable to be accessed from an external entity unless a dialog reference is built. Lines **16–19** serve this purpose so that the components of Form2 can be addressed from Form1 for making changes. Thus, modules are also often used to store subroutines and functions that can be requested by any class within the project.

4.5.3 Class

A form is a class. However, in VB.NET, two forms do not share information unless a superclass is created to make sure that the two forms are shared throughout the application project. To create a class, click on [PROJECT] on the menu and then [Add Class...]; the templates pane shows up. Choose [Class] in the templates pane, click on the [Add] button, and Class1 will be added to the project. Figure 4.13 shows the coding window of Class1 for this project. The code in Listing 4.5 for Class1 is to make sure the two forms share each other so that one form can access the other form.

Listing 4.5: Code for Class1.vb

```
1 Public Class Class1
2 ' To create a class and make objects shared within the class
3 ' In this case, share Form1 and Form2 throughout the application
4     Public Shared Form1 As Form
5     Public Shared Form2 As Form
6  End Class
```

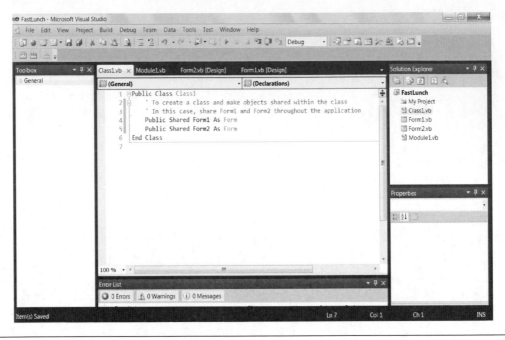

Figure 4.13 Write code for class.

4.5.4 Coding

Now we return to Form1 to write code for the class. Double click on the body of the form or Button1 in the design mode, enter the coding window for the form, and write code as shown in Figure 4.14. Note that it is unnecessary to type the templates; simply double click on the concerned control element to obtain its template. The entire program for Form1 is shown in Listing 4.6.

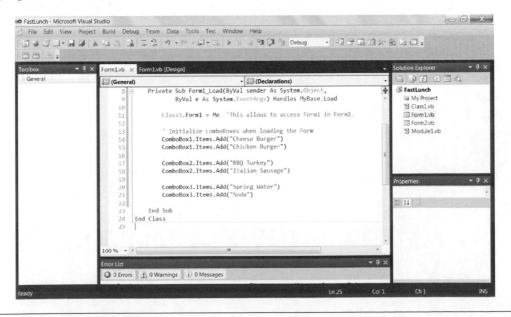

Figure 4.14 Write code for form.

Listing 4.6: Code for Form1.vb

```vb
1 Public Class Form1

2 Private Sub Form1_Load(ByVal sender As System.Object, _
3          ByVal e As System.EventArgs) Handles MyBase.Load

4 Class1.Form1 = Me  'This allows to access Form1 in Form2.

5 ' Initialize comboBoxes when loading the Form
6 ComboBox1.Items.Add("Cheese Burger")
7 ComboBox1.Items.Add("Chicken Burger")

8 ComboBox2.Items.Add("BBQ Turkey")
9 ComboBox2.Items.Add("Italian Sausage")

10 ComboBox3.Items.Add("Spring Water")
11 ComboBox3.Items.Add("Soda")

12 End Sub
```
```vb
13 Private Sub Button1_Click(ByVal sender As System.Object, _
14          ByVal e As System.EventArgs) Handles Button1.Click
15   ' Build references to use Form2
16   Dim Form2 As New Form2

17   ' Declare variables
18   Dim Hamburger As Double
19   Dim Sandwich As Double
20   Dim Drink As Double
21   Dim MemberFee As Double
22   Dim Total As Double

23   ' Find prices
24   If ComboBox1.Text = "Choose Hamburger" Then
25       Hamburger = 0.0
26   Else
27      If ComboBox1.Text = "Cheese Burger" Then
28          Hamburger = CheeseBurger
29      End If
30      If ComboBox1.Text = "Chicken Burger" Then
31           Hamburger = ChickenBurger
32      End If
33   End If

34   If ComboBox2.Text = "Choose Sandwich" Then
35       Sandwich = 0.0
36   Else
37      If ComboBox2.Text = "BBQ Turkey" Then
38          Sandwich = BBQTurkey
39      End If
40      If ComboBox2.Text = "Italian Sausage" Then
41          Sandwich = ItalianSausage
42      End If
43   End If

44   If ComboBox3.Text = "Choose Drink" Then
45       Drink = 0.0
46   Else
47      If ComboBox3.Text = "Spring Water" Then
```

```
48          Drink = SpringWater
49       End If
50       If ComboBox3.Text = "Soda" Then
51          Drink = Soda
52       End If
53    End If

54    If RadioButton1.Checked = True Then
55       MemberFee = 0
56    Else
57       MemberFee = NonMemberFee
58    End If

59  ' Calculate Total
60    Total = (Hamburger * Val(TextBox1.Text) + _
61             Sandwich * Val(TextBox2.Text) + _
62             Drink * Val(TextBox3.Text)) * (1 + SalesTaxRate) + _
63             MemberFee

64  ' Fill Form2
65    If ComboBox1.Text = "Choose Hamburger" Then
66       Form2.Label5.Text = "No Hamburger"
67       Form2.Label6.Text = ""
68       Form2.Label7.Text = "0"
69    Else
70       Form2.Label5.Text = ComboBox1.Text
71       Form2.Label6.Text = Format(Hamburger, "Currency")
72       Form2.Label7.Text = TextBox1.Text
73    End If
74    If ComboBox2.Text = "Choose Sandwich" Then
75       Form2.Label8.Text = "No Sandwich"
76       Form2.Label9.Text = ""
77       Form2.Label10.Text = "0"
78    Else
79       Form2.Label8.Text = ComboBox2.Text
80       Form2.Label9.Text = Format(Sandwich, "Currency")
81       Form2.Label10.Text = TextBox2.Text
82    End If
83    If ComboBox3.Text = "Choose Drink" Then
84       Form2.Label11.Text = "No Drink"
85       Form2.Label12.Text = ""
86       Form2.Label13.Text = "0"
87    Else
88       Form2.Label11.Text = ComboBox3.Text
89       Form2.Label12.Text = Format(Drink, "Currency")
90       Form2.Label13.Text = TextBox3.Text
91    End If

92    Form2.Label14.Text = _
93    "------------------------------------------------------------"
94    If RadioButton1.Checked = True Then
95       Form2.Label15.Text = "Club member: No fee."
96    Else
97       Form2.Label15.Text = "Non-Member: $2 fee."
98    End If
99    Form2.Label16.Text = "TOTAL"
100   Form2.Label17.Text = Format(Total, "Currency")

101 ' Use message box
102   If ComboBox1.Text = "Choose Hamburger" And _
```

```
103      ComboBox2.Text = "Choose Sandwich" And _
104      ComboBox3.Text = "Choose Drink" Then
105      MsgBox("You haven't chosen anything!", , "Choose Items")
106   End If

107   'Show Form2
108   Form2.Show()
109 End Sub

110 End Class
```

We examine how the program for Form1 in Listing 4.6 works. Line **1** declares class Form1 and is paired with the last line, **110,** as the class template generated by the environment. Lines **2** and **3** declare the method Form1_Load and are paired with line **12** as the method template. Line **4** allows Form1 to be accessible from other forms. Here, the Me keyword means the current object. In this example, it makes Form1 a shared form for other forms. Lines **6–11** load the three comboboxes.

Lines **13** and **14** declare the Button1 _ Click method for Button1 and are paired with line **109** as the method template. Line **16** declares Form2 as a shared form for this button. As will be shown later, Form2 is a summary of the order and allows the user to print a receipt. Lines **18–22** declare variables for this method.

Lines **24–33** are one if-then-else statement that in turn has nested if-then-else statements to obtain the prices for food items of hamburger. Lines **34–43** and **44–53** do similar work for other types of food. Lines **60–63** calculate the total price of the chosen food items after sales tax plus fees. A space and the underscore sign "_" must be used if one sentence is divided into more than one line.

Lines **65–73** are one if-then-else sentence that fills information of the hamburger order to the corresponding labels (Label5 through Label7) in Form2. Lines **74–82** and **83–91** do similar work for other labels of Form2.

Lines **92** and **93** fill a line to the label of Form2. Lines **94–98** fill Label15 for the membership fee. Line **100** fills the total field on Form2. Lines **102–106** show a message box for warning the user if no food item has been chosen for the order. Finally, line **108** brings Form2 up to the screen.

The next program is made for Form2, as listed in Listing 4.7. There are two buttons on Form2. One is to hide Form2 and allow the user to go back to Form1 to make changes to the order, and the other is to print the receipt. There are two ways to print. From the Windows operating system, the user can press the [PrintScrn] key on the computer keyboard and then paste it in Word to print a form window. However, this method is inefficient. First, a form image is used for screen display, but is dark on paper and consumes much ink. Second, a form image is small and is unable to contain many lines for a large report. To print a good report for users, one needs to use a print method as shown in this example. As shown in Listing 4.7, printing a document in VB.NET is rather tedious.

Listing 4.7: Code for `Form2.vb`

```vb
1 Imports System.Drawing.Printing

2 Public Class Form2
3 ' Declare an array of labels to make printing code shorter
4 Dim LabelArray(3, 3) As Label

5 Private Sub Form2_Load(ByVal sender As System.Object, _
6          ByVal e As System.EventArgs) Handles MyBase.Load
7 ' To make Form2 a shared by other forms to show/hide it
8 Class1.Form2 = Me
9 End Sub

10 Private Sub Button1_Click(ByVal sender As System.Object, _
11         ByVal e As System.EventArgs) Handles Button1.Click
12 Class1.Form2.Hide()
13 End Sub

14 ' Declare a print document as an object
15 Private WithEvents myDocument As PrintDocument

16 Private Sub Button2_Click(ByVal sender As System.Object, _
17          ByVal e As System.EventArgs) Handles Button2.Click
18 ' This button is to print document
19 ' Retrieve data in all labels into LabelArray
20 LabelArray(1, 1) = Label5
21 LabelArray(1, 2) = Label6
22 LabelArray(1, 3) = Label7
23 LabelArray(2, 1) = Label8
24 LabelArray(2, 2) = Label9
25 LabelArray(2, 3) = Label10
26 LabelArray(3, 1) = Label11
27 LabelArray(3, 2) = Label12
28 LabelArray(3, 3) = Label13

29 ' Initialize the print document
30   myDocument = New PrintDocument

31 ' Use the Print method (_PrintPage) to print the document
32   myDocument.Print()
33 End Sub

34 ' Specific methods for printing the document
35 Private Sub myDocument_PrintPage(ByVal sender As Object, _
36          ByVal e As System.Drawing.Printing.PrintPageEventArgs) _
37          Handles myDocument.PrintPage
38 ' Declare a string line
39 Dim myText As String
40 ' Declare number of lines
41 Dim N As Integer = 1
42 ' Declare counters
43 Dim I, J As Integer
44 ' Declare font for the print document
45 Dim myFont As New Font("Courier New", 12, FontStyle.Regular, _
46                            GraphicsUnit.Point)

47 ' Print the heading with margin starting at (50, 50) point
48    e.Graphics.DrawString(Label1.Text, myFont, _
49                            Brushes.Black, (50 + 50), 50)
```

```
50 ' Print today date starting at (150, 74) point
51    e.Graphics.DrawString(Date.Today(), myFont, _
52                          Brushes.Black, (50 + 100), (50 + 24))

53 ' Use for-loops to print all items
54    For I = 1 To 3
55    ' Screen out non-selected items (0 Quantity)
56    If Val(LabelArray(I, 3).Text) <> 0 Then
57       N = N + 1          'Next line
58       ' Print three fields at the corresponding location
59       For J = 1 To 3
60          e.Graphics.DrawString(LabelArray(I, J).Text, myFont, _
61             Brushes.Black, (50 + (J - 1) * 480 / J), (50 + N * 24))
62       Next
63    End If
64    Next
65 ' Print member fee
66    myText = Label15.Text
67    N = N + 1
68    e.Graphics.DrawString(myText, myFont, _
69                          Brushes.Black, 50, (50 + N * 24))
70 ' Print a line
71    myText = "---------------------------------"
72    N = N + 1
73    e.Graphics.DrawString(myText, myFont, _
74                          Brushes.Black, 50, (50 + N * 24))

75 ' Print the Total.  Note the space
76    myText = Label16.Text + "                    " + Label17.Text
77    N = N + 1
78    e.Graphics.DrawString(myText, myFont, _
79                          Brushes.Black, 50, (50 + N * 24))
80 End Sub
```

```
81 ' You can make page setting
82 Private Sub PrintDocument1_QueryPageSettings(ByVal sender _
83          As Object, ByVal e As   _
84    System.Drawing.Printing.QueryPageSettingsEventArgs) _
85          Handles myDocument.QueryPageSettings
86    e.PageSettings.Landscape = False
87 End Sub

88 End Class
```

We examine how the program in Listing 4.7 for Form2 works. Line **1** imports the library for printing. Generally, a programming manual is needed to determine what library is needed for a particular task. Line **2** declares class Form2 and is paired with the last line, **88,** as the class template generated by the environment. Line **4** declares an array, named LabelArray(3, 3), to hold information in the labels for food items in Form2. This would make the code for printing concise.

Lines **5–9** define the task for loading Form2. In this example, line **8** makes Form2 accessible to other forms.

Lines **10–13** define the task for Button1. In line **12,** Class1 is used as a super-class in order to hide Form2.

The program after line **14** is to print a receipt. Line **15** declares `myDocument` as a `PrintDocument` object for printing

Lines **16–33** define the task for `Button2`. Lines **20–28** retrieve information from the labels to the array in order to use one for-loop to print all food items. Line **30** initializes the `PrintDocument` object (`myDocument`) and makes it ready to use. Line **32** applies the `Print` method to print the document. This method is implemented in a separate subroutine named `myDocument_PrintPage` because the object is named `myDocument`.

Lines **35–80** specify the task of subroutine `myDocument_PrintPage`. Note that, in lines **35–37,** the subroutine name must be the document object name followed by `_PrintPage`, and the handled event is the document object name followed by `.PrintPage`.

Lines **38–46** declare variables for printing. Line **45** declares the font used for printing. `Courier New` is a fixed-width font and makes words easy to line up.

Lines **48** and **49** draw a line for the heading, which is stored in `Label1`. Note that the margin is defined by the start position of the line (x-y coordinates in numbers of pixels). In VB.NET, anything for printing is treated as graphics. Lines **51** and **52** draw a line for the current date. Lines **54–64** are nested for-loops that print out all data from the two-dimensional array `LabelArray(I, J)`. Line **56** screens out all food items with no order quantity. In line **61,** the locations of fields are defined by the x-y coordinates, which may not be straightforward. Lines **66–69** print the member fee. Lines **71–79** print a line and the total for the receipt.

Lines **82–87** show how to set the page orientation to landscape or portrait.

An example of execution of the `FastLunch` project is shown in Figure 4.15, which includes examples of `Form1` and `Form2` in the run mode and printed document.

4.6 Programming with VB.NET

This section provides detailed explanations of essential VB.NET programming techniques and instructions.

4.6.1 General Format of Code, Comments, and Keywords

The VB.NET coding environment automatically provides formats and pull-down lists of available attributes and methods for coding. In the editor window, if a line is too long to be displayed, the window rolls automatically. For printing the source code, one can use a space followed by the line divider sign "_" to divide a code line. Programmers insert comments to document programs and make the programs readable. A comment line begins with the apostrophe "'" sign. VB.NET has its keywords, such as `Public`, `Private`, `Sub`, `End`, `Button1_Click`, `Me`, `ByVal`, `Dim`, `As`, etc.

Figure 4.15 Execution result of `FastLunch` project.

Each keyword represents its specific meaning and cannot be used as a user-defined word. A practical approach is to use application-specific words for user-defined words (e.g., `NonMemberFee`). The `Me` keyword is difficult for beginners to understand. Generally, the `Me` keyword refers to the current instance of an object. We will explain most commonly used keywords in the following subsections.

4.6.2 Class and Object

VB.NET is a blended language of object oriented and function oriented. A form is a class, a module is a class, a data type is a class, etc. Many classes (e.g., data types) have been built into VB.NET. The programmer can use the following syntax to define a user-defined object of a built-in class:

```
[access-modifier] Class [class identifier]
[Inherits class-name]
    [class body]
End Class
```

See Listing 4.5 for an example of class. The access modifier is typically the keyword `Public`, which means the class can be accessed globally. The inheritance part is optional. In VB.NET, there are many built-in classes. To make an actual class instance, or object, the programmer must declare the object. Two steps are needed to instantiate an object:

Step 1. Declare the object by writing an access modifier and an instance of the class—for example,

```
Private WithEvents myDocument As PrintDocument
```

where `PrintDocument` is a class and `myDocument` is the declared object of this class

```
Dim myText As String
```

where `String` is a class; the `myText` is the declared object of this class.

Step 2. Allocate memory for the object using the `New` keyword for example,

```
myDocument = New PrintDocument
```

The two steps can be combined into a single line—for example,

```
Dim T As New Date
```

4.6.3 Methods

VB.NET code for a method is written between the procedure definition header and the end of the method (subroutine or function). The environment generates a predisplayed template with the header and end for each event handler such as `Button_Click` and `Form_Load`. The procedure definition header

```
Private Sub [sub_name](ByVal sender As System.Object, _
        ByVal e As System.EventArgs) Handles [event_name]
```

defines the parameters for the method.

An event handler has two parameters. The first parameter is of the object type and controls the event. It is called sender. The second parameter is of the EventArgs class type, and it passes information about the event. The method is appended with the Handles keyword followed by the event name. VB.NET differentiates between passing parameters by value (ByVal) and passing parameters by reference (ByRef). ByVal is commonly considered by beginners.

4.6.4 Constant Variables

Programmers can create variables whose values do not change during the program execution. These variables, called constant variables, are defined by the const keyword. The use of constant variables makes the program easy to maintain.

4.6.5 Data Types

VB.NET provides many data types, including:

Boolean	True or false
Char	unicode character
DateTime	for example, 12/31/2099
Decimal	Decimal number
Double	Double-precision floating point
Integer	Integer
String	A sequences of characters

The Dim (stands for dimension) and As keywords are used to define the data type for a user-defined class, variable, or array. One can also assign the initial value to a variable. In VB.NET, the default value of a numerical variable is zero.

Textboxes can be used to receive numerical data from the user. In principle, the data type of text string is different from that of numeric data. The Val() function converts a string in the textbox to a number (e.g., Listing 4.3, line **4**).

4.6.6 Arithmetic Operations

The arithmetic operations of VB.NET are similar to those of C. For instance:

```
AssignValue = 50
TotalAmount = Amount1 + Amount2
DifferenceAmount = Amount1 - Amount2
MultiplyAmount = Amount1 * Amount2
DivideAmount = Amount1 / Amount2
```

4.6.7 If-Then-Else *Statement*

The if-then-else statement has the following syntax and format:

```
If [condition] Then
      [action block 1]
Else
      [action block 2]
End If
```

The condition is a logical expression. Note that the format is rigidly defined; that is, the three subsentences (If ... Else ... End If) must not be written in the same line. There are variations of the if-then-else statement in VB.NET, such as the if-then-elseif-then and IIF (if and only if) statements, which might not be easy to use by beginners.

4.6.8 For-*loop*

For-loop is used when the times of iteration are predetermined. The syntax of the for-loop statement is

```
For [counter] = [start] To [end] [step]
     [action block]
Next [counter]
```

See an example in Listing 4.2. In the Next phrase, [counter] can be omitted. If [step] is omitted, the counter increases by 1 on each iteration.

4.6.9 String Processing and Format Statement

In VB.NET, there are many methods for string manipulation, such as concatenating, testing, finding substrings, etc. In our examples (see line **76**, Listing 4.7), we use the plus sign "+" for concatenating strings. One may use the "&" sign to join strings and numbers to avoid a plus operation. The programmer can use the format function Format() to control the appearance of string that is displayed or printed (see an example in Listing 4.3). The format function specifies exactly how the string should appear.

4.6.10 Print Document

Printing a document in VB.NET seems to be tedious. The syntax used for the statements for printing a document is not straightforward. As shown in Listing 4.7, three basic steps are involved in printing a document:

Step 1. Declare a `PrintDocument` object. The syntax is

```
Private WithEvents [document_name] As PrintDocument
```

Step 2. In the subroutine of the button that is to print the document, initialize the `PrintDocument` object, and trigger the `Print()` method. The syntax is

```
Private Sub [button]_Click(ByVal sender As System.Object, _
     ByVal e As System.EventArgs) Handles [button].Click
        . . . .
     [document_name] = New PrintDocument
     [document_name].Print()
        . . . .
End Sub
```

Step 3. Write a subroutine to print the document. The general structure is

```
Private Sub [document_name]_PrintPage(ByVal sender As Object, _

   ByVal e As System.Drawing.Printing.PrintPageEventArgs) _
   Handles myDocument.PrintPage
      . . . .
Dim [string_name] As String
      . . . .
Dim [font_name] As New Font("[font_type]", [font_size], _
            FontStyle.Regular, GraphicsUnit.Point)
      . . . .
e.Graphics.DrawString([string_name], [font_name], _
            Brushes.[color], [x-coordinate], [y-coordinate])
      . . . .
End Sub
```

Note that in these methods we use e as the print event argument to pass the parameters.

4.6.11 Message Box

The MsgBox statement displays a message window to the user when it is executed. Its syntax is

```
MsgBox [message body], [message box type], [message title]
```

4.7 Debugging

Traditional Visual Basic programs are easy to debug. However, since Visual Basic migrated to VB.NET, debugging VB.NET programs becomes difficult. First, unlike other object-oriented languages such as C++, the structure of the entire VB.NET project is rather disjointed. Although the VB.NET environment can help one to avoid syntax errors by showing available properties and methods for a class and automatically placing the cursor at the location of a syntax error, it does not provide much help for debugging logical errors (or semantic errors). Common syntax errors include a misuse of user-defined variables, mismatching between the class name defined in the program and the actual control element on the GUI, and references among the classes. The coordination of the control elements of the entire VB.NET project is crucial for avoiding logical errors.

Chapter 4 Exercises

1. Given the VB.NET window in the "run mode," describe how you would design this GUI (Form1) by filling the table:

NAME OF THE GUI OBJECT	PROPERTIES: (INDICATE "TEXT" ONLY)
Label1	

2. Read the flowing VB.NET program for the preceding GUI and fill the blanks. Note that your answers must be consistent with your table in question 1.

```
1 Public Class Form1
2   Inherits System.Windows._____.Form
```

```
3   Private Sub Form1_Load(ByVal sender As System.Object, _
4                ByVal e As System.EventArgs) Handles MyBase.Load
5
6       ComboBox1._____("Computer")
7       ComboBox1._____("Cell Phone")
8       ComboBox1._____("Web Camera")
9       ComboBox1._____("Laser Printer")
10  End Sub
```

```
11  Private Sub Button1_Click(ByVal sender As System.Object, _
12             _____ e As System.EventArgs) Handles Button1.Click
13      If (Val(TextBox1.Text) = 0) _
14         Or (ComboBox1.Text = "Choose Item") _____
15        MsgBox("Please Input your bid!", , "Missing input data")
16      Else
17        MsgBox("Offer is accepted.  Please find the result!")
18      _____
19  End Sub
```

```
20  Private Sub Button2_Click(ByVal sender As System.Object, _
21         ByVal e As System.EventArgs) Handles _____
22    Dim CurrentHighestBid As _____
23    If ComboBox1.Text = "Computer" Then
24        CurrentHighestBid = 1000
25      _____
26    If ComboBox1.Text = "Cell Phone" Then
27        CurrentHighestBid = 200
28    End If
29    If ComboBox1.Text = "Web Camera" Then
30        CurrentHighestBid = 100
31    End If
32    If ComboBox1.Text = "Laser Printer" Then
33        CurrentHighestBid = 400
34    End If
35    If _____(TextBox1.Text) > CurrentHighestBid Then
36        MsgBox("You win!", , "You win!")
37    Else
38        MsgBox("Sorry, your bid is not high enough.  Bid again!")
39    End If
40  End Sub
41  _____
```

3. In the "run mode" of the preceding VB.NET program, if the user selects "Computer" using the combos, inputs 900 in the textbox, and then clicks on the "Bid" and "Find Bidding Result" buttons, what is the expected result and where does it appear?

4. In the "run mode" of the preceding VB.NET program, if the user selects "Computer" using the combos, inputs nothing in the textbox, and then clicks on the "Bid" button, what is the expected result and where does it appear?

5. In the "run mode" of the preceding VB.NET program, if the user selects "Web Camera" using the combos, inputs 200 in the textbox, and then clicks on the "Bid" and "Find Bidding Result" buttons, what is the expected result and where does it appear?

6. Learn more features of VB.NET from online help. Create a VB.NET project that uses features of VB.NET that are not fully explained in the book.

7. Develop a VB.NET project that has one form, one combo box, three to five labels or textboxes, and two to four buttons.

8. Develop a VB.NET project that has two forms with good design and interactions, at least three buttons, several labels or textboxes, at least two comboboxes, one module, one class, and message boxes. One of the buttons is to print a report on the default printer.

5
C#.NET

C#.NET, or simply C#, is a modern, general-purpose, object-oriented programming language developed by Microsoft within the .NET initiative. Like C++, C# is also derived from C. The name C# is inspired by the musical notation #, which indicates the written note should be made a semitone higher in pitch. C# has been standardized by the international standardization organizations ECMA (European Computer Manufacturers Association) and ISO (International Organization for Standardization). To make the book concise, we assume that the reader has basic knowledge of C and C++ (presented in Chapter 2) as a prerequisite of this chapter.

5.1 Microsoft Visual Studio and C# Programming Environment

Like VB.NET and other .NET programming languages, C# is supported by the Microsoft Visual Studio programming environment. C# supports console application and Windows forms application. A console application is a computer program designed to be used via a text-only computer interface. The user typically interacts with a console application using only a keyboard and display screen. A Windows forms application is a graphical user interface (GUI), which normally requires the use of a mouse or other pointing device.

Figure 5.1 shows the instruction to use the Microsoft Visual Studio environment to create a C# console application program. Once the C# console application project is created, you will see the initial automatically generated source code as shown in Listing 5.1, which you can continue to work on.

Listing 5.1: Initial Automatically Generated C# Source Code

```
1   using System;
2   using System.Collections.Generic;
3   using System.Linq;
4   using System.Text;

5   namespace ConsoleApplication1
6   {
7     class Program
8     {
9       static void Main(string[] args)
10      {
11      }
12    }
13  }
```

Start Microsoft Visual Studio

Click on [File]

Choose [New Project]

In New Project Window:

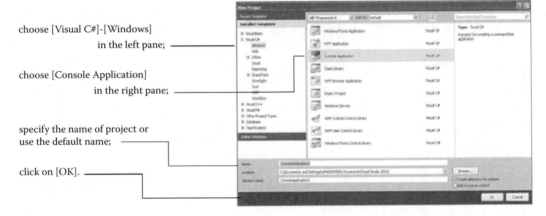

choose [Visual C#]-[Windows]
in the left pane;

choose [Console Application]
in the right pane;

specify the name of project or
use the default name;

click on [OK].

Source Code Editor Window
will be launched.

Figure 5.1 Create C# project in Microsoft Visual Studio environment.

5.2 C# Program Structure

In C#, a large program can consist of many pieces of small programs (or modules), which can be written by different programmers. Hence, the same name may be used in different small programs but actually correspond to different identifiers. Namespace in C# is used to avoid confusion. A namespace is an abstract container created to hold a logical grouping of names. A C# program contains one or more namespaces. In Listing 5.1, the C# program defines one default namespace called "ConsoleApplication1" as shown in line **5**.

To access the identifiers from other namespaces, the C# program must declare these namespaces through the "using" statements as shown in lines **1** through **4** of Listing 5.1. The identifiers following the "using" keyword are the namespaces to be used.

A C# namespace can contain one or more classes. Line **7** in Listing 5.1 indicates that the namespace contains only one class named "Program." In a C# console application project, only one namespace and only one class with this namespace can have a special method called Main. This Main method is the entry point of the C# program. As shown in line **9** of Listing 5.1, the Main method must be static, its return data type must be void, and its parameter must be "string[] args."

In C#, a static method or attribute is not associated with any instance of the class. A static method is always callable even when no instance of the class has been created. Static methods and static attributes are often used to represent data or calculations that do not change in response to object state. For instance, a math class may include static methods for calculating absolute value and logarithm.

The parameter string[] args of the Main method enables command line arguments once the program has been compiled and is executed directly under the operating system environment. Section 5.4.2 will explain command line arguments in detail.

5.3 Run a C# Console Application Program

As an example, edit the following simplest C# program by inserting a line (line **11** in Listing 5.2) into the automatically generated code:

Listing 5.2: Example of a Simple C# Program

```
1   using System;
2   using System.Collections.Generic;
3   using System.Linq;
4   using System.Text;

5   namespace ConsoleApplication1
6   {
7      class Program
8      {
9         static void Main(string[] args)
```

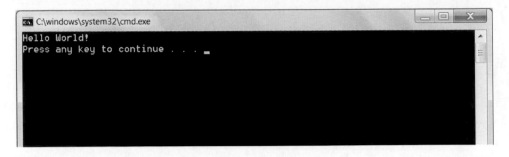

Figure 5.2   Execution result of C# program in Listing 5.2.

```
10          {
11              Console.WriteLine("Hello World!");
12          }
13      }
14 }
```

In line **11** of Listing 5.2, "Console" is a predefined class in the System name-space, and "WriteLine" is one of its static methods that prints "Hello World!" on the screen. The "Console.WriteLine" method can print out a value of any data type as a text string on the screen.

After editing the program, click on the [Save] icon on the top menu to save the program. The default class name "Program" is the name of the program file (i.e., "Program.cs" under the default project folder). You may change the program name in the Solution Explorer window, and the class name in the program will be changed to the program name automatically. To compile the program, click on [Build] on the top menu and then click on [Build Project]. If your program is correct, you should have [0 Errors] on the error list. Now the program is ready to execute. Press the [Ctrl] and [F5] keys simultaneously, and you will see the execution window as shown in Figure 5.2. Alternatively, you click on [Debug] on the top menu and then click on [Start Without Debugging] to see the execution window. Visual Studio allows the execution result to stay on the screen until you press any key to close it.

5.4 C# Syntax

Much of C# syntax is very similar, if not identical, to that of C and C++. The syntax of comments, data types, operators, statements, decisions, loops, classes and objects, attributes and methods, and public and private are the same as in C and C++, as discussed in Chapter 2.

There are a few differences between C# and C and C++ programs. They are described in the following subsections.

5.4.1 Arrays and `foreach` *loop*

Array is a data structure that contains a collection of elements of the same data type. The size of the array is the number of elements in the array. Each element in the array can be used as a variable to store a value for computation. To declare an array in C#, the square brackets [] must be included after the data type. For example,

```
int[] numbers;    // declare an integer array named numbers
string[] names;   // declare a string array named names
```

Once the array is declared, you must initialize it before using it in your program, such as

```
numbers = new int[3]{10,9,8}; // numbers is a 3 element array with
                              // initial values 10, 9, and 8

names = new string[3]{"John","Jane", "James"};
                    // names is a 3 element array with initial values
                    // "John", "Jane", and "James".
```

Array declaration and initialization may be combined into a single statement. For example,

```
int[] numbers = new int[3]{10, 9, 8};
string[] names = new string[3]{"John","Jane", "James"};
```

Once the array is initialized, array index is used to access the elements in the array. The array index is specified inside the square brackets [] after the array name to refer to a particular array element. The index of the first element in an array is zero. Each element is equivalent to a variable. For example,

```
numbers[0]  = 100;
numbers[1] = numbers[0] + 1;
numbers[2] = numbers[2] + 1;

for (int i = 0; i <= 2; i++) {
    Console.WriteLine(numbers[i]); // print out the array element
}
```

When you declare an array, you may only reserve the space without initial values, but you have to initialize each element before using the element. For example,

```
numbers = new int[5];                // numbers is a 5 element array
numbers[0] = 1;
numbers[1] = numbers[0] + 1;
```

```
numbers[2] = numbers[1] + 1;
numbers[3] = numbers[2] + 1;
numbers[4] = numbers[3] + 1;
```

Arrays are actually objects belonging to the "Array" class in the "System" namespace. You can access all attributes and methods defined in the "System.Array" class once you declare an array. An example is to get the length of an array through the "Length" attribute as follows:

```
int[] numbers = new int[5] {10, 9, 8, 7, 6};
for (int i = 0; i < numbers.Length; i++) { // numbers.Length is 5
    Console.WriteLine(numbers[i]);
}
```

Note that the "Length" attribute is read-only and it is automatically set by C# once you declare an array. The "System.Array" class also provides many useful methods, such as methods for sorting, searching, and copying arrays.

In addition to using a for-loop statement to iterate through an array, you may use a foreach loop statement. For example,

```
int[] numbers = new int[5] {10, 9, 8, 7, 6};
foreach (var x in numbers) {
    Console.WriteLine(x); // x corresponds to an element
```

In this example, the variable x is a temporary variable that corresponds to an array element. The data type of x is automatically determined by that of the array named "numbers." In the first iteration of the foreach loop, x corresponds to the first array element. In the second iteration, it corresponds to the second array element, and so on.

5.4.2 Command Line Arguments

The parameter string[] args of the Main method is an array of the string data type. It enables command line arguments once the program has been compiled and is executed directly under the Microsoft Windows operating system environment. The command line arguments are the optional text strings after the executable program name. The advantage of command line arguments is that any .NET program to meet a particular need by defining specific arguments can call the compiled C# program. This feature would make C# programs more flexible for reuse. Calling a compiled C# program with different command line arguments has the same effect as calling a function with different parameters. The program in Listing 5.3 shows how the command line arguments are processed.

Listing 5.3: Example of Processing Command Line Arguments

```
1   using System;
2   using System.Collections.Generic;
3   using System.Linq;
4   using System.Text;

5   namespace ConsoleApplication1
6   {
7      class Program
8      {
9         static void Main(string[] args)
10        {
11           Console.WriteLine("Number of command line arguments: "+
12                 args.Length);
13           Console.WriteLine("Command line arguments are:");
14           foreach (var x in args)
15           {
16              Console.WriteLine(x);
17           }
18        }
19     }
20 }
```

In line **12** of Listing 5.3, "args.Length" corresponds to the length of the string array "args" automatically set by C#. It is the number of command line arguments after the program name. If there is no command line argument, then it is zero. The foreach loop between lines **14** and **17** prints all command line arguments.

Once the project has been built, the command line arguments can be added in Microsoft Visual Studio for testing the program with different command line arguments. To do so, go to the "Solution Explorer" window, right-click on the project name (e.g., "ConsoleApplication1"), click on [Properties], and the "Project Properties" window will appear. Click on [Debug] in the "Project Properties" window, in the "Command line arguments" text area; enter the command line arguments (e.g., a b c). Save the changes and run the program. The output will be displayed in the console window, as shown in Figure 5.3. You may repeat this test procedure for other command line arguments.

Alternatively, you can use the Windows Command Prompt to execute the program with different command line arguments. However, you need to find the .exe program by tracing the path of the program.

5.4.3 Functions

A function is a module that performs a calculation task. However, unlike C language, functions in C# do not exist by themselves. They are part of a class because C# is an object-oriented programming language. In C#, a function is a member of the class and is actually a method of the class.

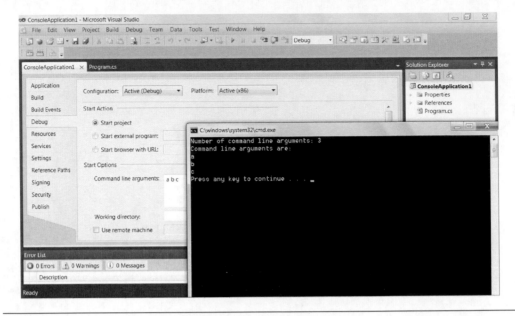

Figure 5.3   Example outputs of program in Listing 5.3.

There are two types of functions: instance function and static function. Further discussion on the two types of functions is beyond the scope of this book, and we study static functions in this chapter. C# has two approaches to parameter passing, and parameters can be passed either by value or by reference. The default parameter passing in C# is passing by value. The actual value of the parameter is passed into the function. Any changes made to the parameter passed into the function will be discarded when the function terminates. The value of the parameter before and after the function call will be the same. Listing 5.4 shows an example.

Listing 5.4: Value Parameter Passing

```
using System;
using System.Collections.Generic;
using System.Linq;
using System.Text;

namespace ConsoleApplication1
{
    class Program
    {
        static void fun(int a, int b)
        {
            a = a + 1;
            b = b + 1;
        }

        static void Main(string[] args)
        {
            int x, y;
            x = 1;
            y = 2;
            fun(x, y);
```

```
                  Console.WriteLine("x=" + x + " y=" + y);
              }
          }
      }
```

The output of this example will be "x=1 y=2". C# also supports passing parameter by reference. In reference parameter passing, the reference (memory address) of the parameter is passed into the function. Any changes made to the parameter in the function will be permanent. Listing 5.5 shows an example.

Listing 5.5: Reference Parameter Passing

```
1 using System;
2 using System.Collections.Generic;
3 using System.Linq;
4 using System.Text;

5 namespace ConsoleApplication1
6 {
7     class Program
8     {
9         static void swap(ref int a, ref int b)
10        {
11            int c = a;
12            a = b;
13            b = c;
14        }
15        static void Main(string[] args)
16        {
17            int x, y;
18            x = 1;
19            y = 2;
20            swap(ref x, ref y);
21            Console.WriteLine("x=" + x + " y=" + y);
22        }
23    }
24 }
```

For passing by reference, the parameter must be preceded by "ref." When calling the function, the corresponding function argument must be a variable and must also be preceded by "ref." In addition, the function argument must be initialized before calling the function. For this example, the output is "x=2 y=1," which means the values of "x" and "y" have been exchanged.

5.5 Examples of Console Application

This section presents examples of C# console application. In the first example, the program (named `ArrayFun.cs`) in Listing 5.6 allows the user to input three numbers for grade points and prints out the GPA. The `Main` function accepts the user's input numbers and places them into an array named `Numbers`. It then calls a function, named `Avg`, which has an array argument, named `AR`, and returns the average of the numbers in the array. Finally, the `Main` function prints the GPA based on the input grade points. The logic of the program is rather straightforward if the reader possesses prerequisite knowledge of C and C++ and has learned the previous sections of this chapter. The emphasis of this example to learn includes:

- Array and `foreach`
- Function and parameter passing
- Similarity and dissimilarity of syntax between C# and C++
- Other miscellaneous commands (e.g., C# equivalent of "`cin`" and "`cout`")

Listing 5.6: An Example of Console Application (`ArrayFun.cs`)

```
 1 using System;
 2 using System.Collections.Generic;
 3 using System.Linq;
 4 using System.Text;

 5 namespace ArrayFunction
 6 {
 7  class ArrayFun
 8  {
 9   static double Avg(ref double[] AR)
10     {
11       double Total=0;
12       for (int i = 0; i < AR.Length; i++)
13       {
14          Total=Total + AR[i];
15       }
16       Total=Total/AR.Length;
17       return(Total);
18     }

19    static void Main(string[] args)
20     {
21      double[] Numbers;
22      Numbers = new double[3];
23      Console.WriteLine("Enter first grade point:");
24      string line = Console.ReadLine();
25      Numbers[0] = Convert.ToDouble(line);
26      Console.WriteLine("Enter second grade point:");
27      line = Console.ReadLine();
28      Numbers[1] = Convert.ToDouble(line);
29      Console.WriteLine("Enter third grade point:");
30      line = Console.ReadLine();
31      Numbers[2] = Convert.ToDouble(line);

32      foreach (var ANumber in Numbers)
33        {   // numbers.Length is 3
34          Console.WriteLine("Entered grade point is:" + ANumber);
35        }
36      double GPA=Avg(ref Numbers);
37      Console.WriteLine("GPA is:" + GPA);
38     }
39  }
40 }
```

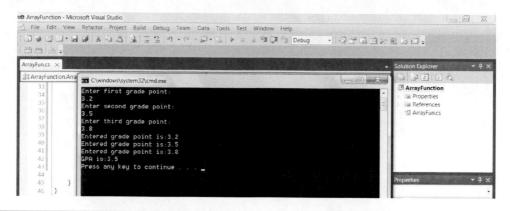

Figure 5.4 Execution result of `ArrayFun.cs`.

Figure 5.4 shows the execution result of `ArrayFun.cs` in Listing 5.6.

The second example of C# console applications is batch file processing, where the program processes multiple disk files without interaction with the user. The C# program (`FileProcessing.cs`) in Listing 5.7 merges two data files into one file. In this example, the two input files are named `file1.txt` and `file2.txt`, and the generated (output) file is named `file3.txt`. Suppose `file1.txt` contains the following computer log entries in a text editor (e.g., Notepad):

```
John, 7:37
Jack, 7:58
James, 8:23
```

and that `file2.txt` contains the following computer log entries in a text editor (e.g., Notepad):

```
Smith, 9:34
Smile, 10:50
```

After merging, `file3.txt` will contain the following text once the program is executed successfully:

```
John, 7:37
Jack, 7:58
James, 8:23
Smith, 9:34
Smile, 10:50
```

To test `FileProcessing.cs`, you need to create `file1.txt` and `file2.txt` using Notepad and then save the two files in the [\bin\debug] folder in the project folder of the C# console applications project created for this program. After execution of this program, you can see `file3.txt` in the same [\bin\debug] folder.

Listing 5.7: Example of Console Application for File Processing (`FileProcessing.cs`)

```
1 using System;
2 using System.Collections.Generic;
3 using System.Linq;
4 using System.Text;

5 using System.IO;

6 namespace FileProcessing
7 {
8  class FileProcessing
9  {
10    static void Main(string[] args)
11    {
12     string FileName1 = "file1.txt";
13     string FileName2 = "file2.txt";
14     string FileName3 = "file3.txt";
15     int FailureFlag = 0;    // Flag used for process status

16     // Open all three files
17     StreamWriter OutputFile;
18     FileInfo File3Info = new FileInfo(FileName3);
19     if (File3Info.Exists == false)
20        { OutputFile = File.CreateText(FileName3); }
21     else
22        {
23        Console.WriteLine("The original merged file is overwritten!");
24         OutputFile = File.CreateText(FileName3); // Overwrite file
25        }

26     StreamReader InputFile1, InputFile2;
27     FileInfo InputFile1Info = new FileInfo(FileName1);
28     FileInfo InputFile2Info = new FileInfo(FileName2);
29     if (InputFile1Info.Exists == true)
30        {
31         InputFile1 = File.OpenText(FileName1);
32        // Write the contents of the input file to the output file
33         while (InputFile1.Peek() > 0)
34        { OutputFile.WriteLine(InputFile1.ReadLine()); }
35          InputFile1.Close();  // Close the input file
36        }
37     else
38        {
39         Console.WriteLine("The input file #1 does not exist!");
40         FailureFlag = 1;
41        }
42     if (InputFile2Info.Exists == true)
43        {
44         InputFile2 = File.OpenText(FileName2);
45        // Write the contents of the input file to the output file
46         while (InputFile2.Peek() > 0)
47        { OutputFile.WriteLine(InputFile2.ReadLine()); }
48          InputFile2.Close();   // Close the input file
49        }
50     else
```

```
51        {
52         Console.WriteLine("The input file #2 does not exist!");
53         FailureFlag = 1;
54        }

55     OutputFile.Close();  // Close the output file

56     if (FailureFlag == 0)
57       Console.WriteLine("Two files have been merged into output file!");
58     else
59       Console.WriteLine("The operation failed due to incorrect files!");
60    }
61  }
62 }
```

For file processing, the program needs to import the System.IO namespace, as shown in line **5** of Listing 5.7. Four classes are required for file processing in C#, as shown in Listing 5.7 and discussed next:

1. The StreamWriter (line **17**) and StreamReader (line **26**) classes represent the files for writing and reading, respectively. The WriteLine() method of StreamWriter (lines **34** and **47**) writes a line to the file. The ReadLine() method of StreamReader (lines **34** and **47**) reads a line from the file. Before calling the ReadLine() method, the Peek() method (lines **33** and **46**) must be called to make sure that the end of the file has not already been reached.

2. The File class (lines **20, 24, 31,** and **44**) defines the operations for opening the data file. The File.CreateText() method (lines **20** and **24**) creates the file for writing. The File.OpenText() method (lines **31** and **44**) opens the file for reading.

3. The FileInfo class (line **18** and lines **27** and **28**) holds information about the files, such as whether they exist, to avoid errors.

5.6 Windows Forms Application

In addition to console application, C# also supports Windows forms application, which enables GUI design and programming user interface. To create a C# Windows forms application, you follow the steps in Figure 5.1 except for choosing [Windows Forms Application] instead of [Console Application] in the New Project window. Once a Windows forms application is created, a GUI design environment similar to the one in VB.NET will be launched and you can create GUI for your program. The interested reader is referred to Chapter 4 to learn more about the GUI design environment. Figure 5.5 shows a GUI design example.

Double-clicking the "Submit" button in "Form1" will launch the Source Code Editor window shown in Figure 5.6.

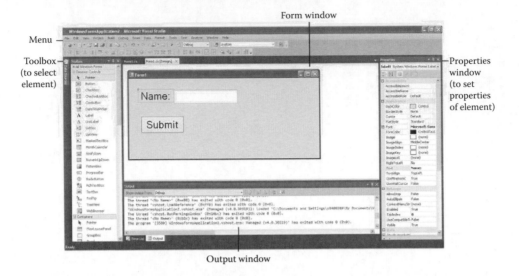

Figure 5.5   GUI design of C# Windows forms application.

Figure 5.6   Source code editor window for Windows forms application.

The `Source Code Editor` window contains the initial automatically generated source code shown in Listing 5.8.

Listing 5.8: Initial Automatically Generated Source Code

```
using System;
using System.Collections.Generic;
using System.ComponentModel;
using System.Data;
using System.Drawing;
using System.Linq;
```

```
using System.Text;
using System.Windows.Forms;

namespace WindowsFormsApplication1
{
    public partial class Form1 : Form
    {
        public Form1()
        {
            InitializeComponent();
        }

        private void button1_Click(object sender, EventArgs e)
        {

        }
    }
}
```

In the initial automatically generated code template, the function "button1 _ Click" corresponds to the event that the user clicks on the "Submit" button on "Form1." The programmer can add the code inside this function. For example, one can add the code shown in Listing 5.9 to display a greeting message, which includes the user's input in textBox1, in label2 below the Submit button. One can change the properties (such as font, color, etc.) of these control elements in the Properties window.

Listing 5.9: Example of Windows Forms Application

```
private void button1_Click(object sender, EventArgs e)
{
    label2.Text = "Welcome! " + textBox1.Text;
}
```

Click on [Build] on the top menu of the environment and choose [Build Project] to compile the program. If there is no error, click on [Debug] and then choose [Start ...], or simply press the [F5] key, to run the application. Figure 5.7 shows the result of the program in Listing 5.9, given certain settings of the properties of the elements of the GUI (e.g., the color of the text of Label2 is set to red).

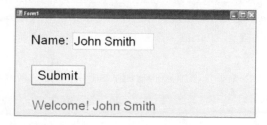

Figure 5.7   Example output of C# Windows forms application.

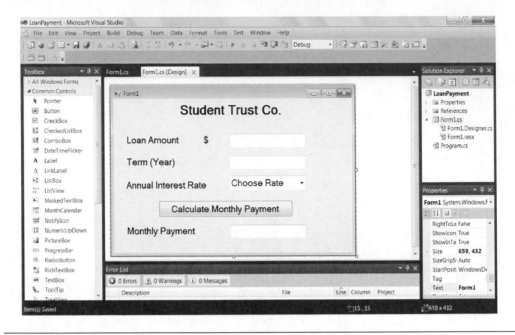

Figure 5.8   Design of form for C# `LoanPayment` project.

5.7 Examples of Windows Forms Application

In this section, we learn more features of C# of Windows forms application by using examples. The first example, named `LoanPayment`, is to calculate the monthly payment based on the amount and the term of the loan. The GUI accepts these data from the user, allows the user to select a current interest rate from a combo menu, and then calculates the monthly payment for the user. The design of `Form1` is shown in Figure 5.8. On this form, five labels are created to display headings: "STUDENT TRUST CO.," "Loan Amount $," "Term(year)," "Annual Interest Rate," and "Monthly Payment." Two `textBoxes` are created to catch the data, and the third `textBox` is used to display the calculated monthly payment result. Close to the "Annual Interest Rate" label, a `comboBox` is created to show the alternative interest rates applied. Finally, a command button is created for the user to find the answer. To write a C# program for Windows forms application, you must remember the names of these control element objects (e.g., textBox1, comboBox1, button1, etc.).

You double-click on the form, enter the coding window, and write the C# code as shown in the lines in bold in Listing 5.10.

Listing 5.10: C# Code for `LoanPayment` Project

```
1 using System;
2 using System.Collections.Generic;
3 using System.ComponentModel;
4 using System.Data;
5 using System.Drawing;
```

```
 6 using System.Linq;
 7 using System.Text;
 8 using System.Windows.Forms;

 9 namespace LoanPayment
10 {
11    public partial class Form1 : Form
12    {
13        public Form1()
14        {
15            InitializeComponent();
16        }

17        private void button1_Click(object sender, EventArgs e)
18        {
19         double LoanAmount, LoanTerm, InterestRate, MonthlyPayment;
20         LoanAmount = Convert.ToDouble(textBox1.Text);
21         LoanTerm = Convert.ToDouble(textBox2.Text);
22         InterestRate = Convert.ToDouble(comboBox1.Text);
23         MonthlyPayment = (LoanAmount * Math.Pow((1 +
24                          InterestRate/12),(LoanTerm*12))
25                          * InterestRate/12) / (Math.Pow((1 +
26                          InterestRate/12),(LoanTerm*12)) - 1);
27         textBox3.Text = MonthlyPayment.ToString("c2");
28        }

29        private void Form1_Load(object sender, EventArgs e)
30        {
31         for (int i = 0; i < 7; i++)
32         {
33            comboBox1.Items.Add(0.040 + 5*i*0.001);
34         }
35        }
36    }
37 }
```

As shown in Listing 5.10, the structure of C# code for Windows forms application is very similar to the structure of VB.NET code presented in Listings 4.2 and 4.3. As the syntax of C# is similar to C++, there are differences of features between C# and VB.NET that can be learned through a comparison of Listing 5.10 and Listings 4.2 and 4.3, including:

- Data type conversion (e.g., line **20**)

```
LoanAmount = Convert.ToDouble(textBox1.Text);
```

This converts a string to a double type number.
- Data format for output (e.g., line **27**)

```
textBox3.Text = MonthlyPayment.ToString("c2");
```

This passes the format of currency (with two digits after the decimal point) to the ToString method. Similarly, ToString("0.00"); or ToString("n2"); can be used to display ordinary numbers.

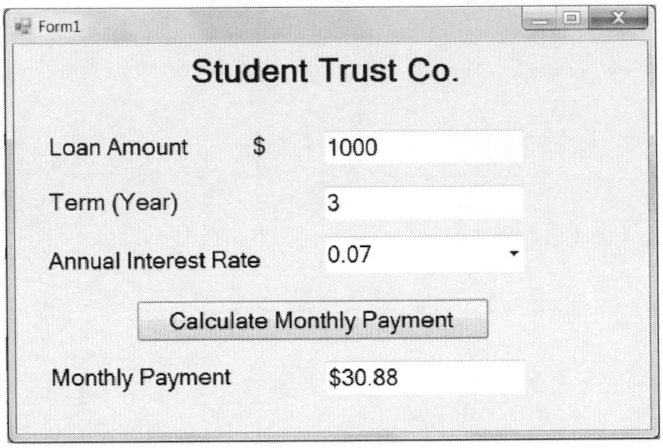

Figure 5.9   Execution result of C# `LoanPayment` project.

- Format of the for-loop statement (e.g., line **31**)
- Many built-in business calculation functions in VB.NET, such as `Pmt`, are not available in C# (e.g., lines **23–26**); apply arithmetic operators (include `Math.Pow`) to calculate the payment.

Figure 5.9 shows an example of the execution result, which is almost identical with the VB.NET example in Section 4.4. As demonstrated in this example, C# Windows forms application is very similar to VB.NET.

The second example, named `SignatureDesign`, is to demonstrate the use of multiple forms. The project is to allow the user to input a name and to choose options for designing a personal signature. This example employs two forms: One is to collect the user's input and the other is to display the designed personal signature based on the user's input. The GUI design and example execution results are shown in Figure 5.10.

The first form, named `Form1`, contains two `TextBox` controls to collect the user's first name and last name, respectively. A `GroupBox` control is used to contain two radio buttons for the signature options, which include the full name signature and initial-only signature. The `GroupBox` control ensures that only one radio button in the group can be selected by the user at a time, and the previously selected radio button will be automatically unselected if the user selects another radio button. A `ListBox` control is used to allow the user to select a design option for the personal signature. The design options are various types of font design. Once the user clicks on the [`Generate Signature`] button on `Form1`, validation will be performed to ensure the presence and correctness of the user's input. For example, as shown in Figure 5.11, the first and last names must contain only alphabetical letters. Once all validation tests have been successfully passed, the second form, named `Form2`, will be displayed (Figure 5.10). It shows the designed personal signature using a `Label`

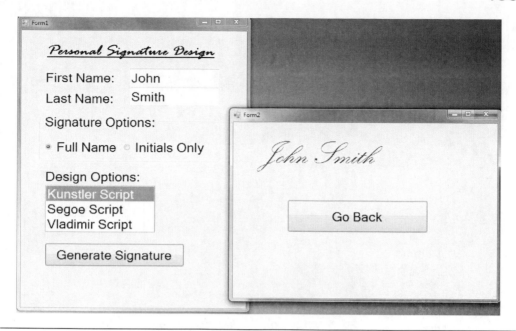

Figure 5.10 The GUI design and execution result of C# `SignatureDesign` project.

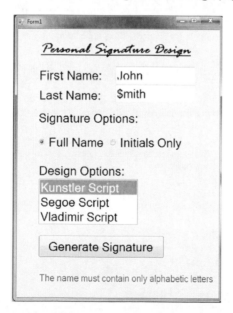

Figure 5.11 Example validation result of C# `SignatureDesign` project.

control and a [Go Back] button, which closes the Form2 window and returns the execution to the Form1 window.

To add a form (e.g., Form2) in the C# project development environment, right-click on the project name in the Solution Explorer window, point to [Add] in the menu, and then click on [Windows Form], as shown in Figure 5.12.

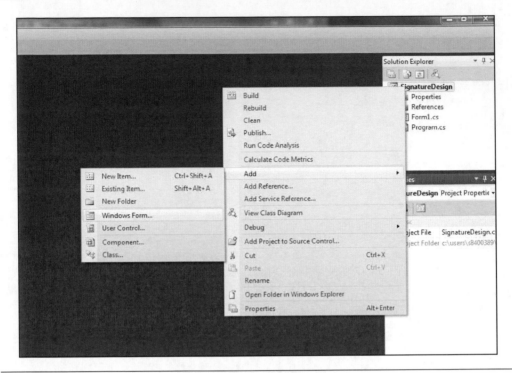

Figure 5.12 Steps to adding a new form in C# Windows forms application.

The source code associated with Form1 is shown in Listing 5.11.

Listing 5.11: C# Code for Form1 of the SignatureDesign Project

```
1    using System;
2    using System.Collections.Generic;
3    using System.ComponentModel;
4    using System.Data;
5    using System.Drawing;
6    using System.Linq;
7    using System.Text;
8    using System.Windows.Forms;

9    namespace SignatureDesign
10   {
11     public partial class Form1 : Form
12     {
13         public Form1()
14         {
15             InitializeComponent();
16         }

17         private void button1_Click(object sender, EventArgs e)
18         {
19             label5.Text = "";

20             // check if the user has entered the first name
21             if (string.IsNullOrEmpty(textBox1.Text))
```

```
22              {
23                  label5.Text = "Warning: Please input your first name";
24              }

25          // check if the user has entered the last name
26          else if (string.IsNullOrEmpty(textBox2.Text))
27          {
28              label5.Text = "Warning: Please input your last name";
29          }

30          // check if the user has selected a signature option
31          else if ((radioButton1.Checked == false) &&
32                      (radioButton2.Checked == false))
33          {
34              label5.Text = "Warning: Please select a signature option";
35          }

36          // check if the user has selected a design option
37          else if (listBox1.SelectedIndex == -1)
38          {
39              label5.Text = "Warning: Please select a design option";
40          }

41          else
42          {
43              bool flag = true;

44              // check if the first name contains only alphabetic letters
45              for (int i = 0; i < textBox1.Text.Length; i++)
46              {
47                if (!char.IsLetter(textBox1.Text[i]))
48                {
49                  label5.Text = "The name must be alphabetic letters";
50                  flag = false;
51                }
52              }

53              // check if the first name contains only alphabetic letters
54              for (int i = 0; i < textBox2.Text.Length; i++)
55              {
56                if (!char.IsLetter(textBox2.Text[i]))
57                {
58                  label5.Text = "The name must be alphabetic letters";
59                  flag = false;
60                }
61              }

62              if (flag == true)   // validation tests have been passed
63              {

64                  // make sure the first chars of the first and last
65                  // names are always capital letters
66                  textBox1.Text = char.ToUpper(textBox1.Text[0]) +
67                                      textBox1.Text.Substring(1);
68                  textBox2.Text = char.ToUpper(textBox2.Text[0]) +
69                                      textBox2.Text.Substring(1);

70                  string signatureText, designOption;
```

```
71                  if (radioButton1.Checked == true)
72                  {    signatureText = textBox1.Text + " " +
73                                              textBox2.Text;
74                  }
75                  else          // if (radioButton2.Checked == true)
76                  {
77                       signatureText = textBox1.Text[0].ToString() +
78                                              textBox2.Text[0].ToString();
79                  }

80                  if (listBox1.SelectedIndex == 0)
81                  {
82                       designOption = "Kunstler Script";
83                  }
84                  else if (listBox1.SelectedIndex == 1)
85                  {
86                       designOption = "Segoe Script";
87                  }
88                  else          // if (listBox1.SelectedIndex == 2)
89                  {
90                       designOption = "Vladimir Script";
91                  }

92                  // create and show the second form
93                  // pass signatureText and designOption to the second form
94                  Form2 showForm = new Form2(signatureText, designOption);
95                  showForm.ShowDialog();
-63              }
-42          }
-18      }
-12  }
-10 }
```

The user's input in a textbox is always a text string. This program contains several validation methods. In lines **21** and **26** of Listing 5.11, the `string.IsNullOrEmpty()` function tests whether the user has entered a text string in a textbox. Line **37** shows that the value of the `SelectedIndex` property of the listbox is `-1` if no item in the listbox has been selected. If the user selects an item in the listbox, the value of the `SelectedIndex` property of the listbox is the index of the selected item (e.g., line **80** deals with the case when the user selects the first item). In lines **47** and **56,** the `char.IsLetter()` function tests whether a character in the user's input is an alphabetic letter. To assist the validation, line **43** declares a Boolean variable named `flag` to record the validation status. Lines **31–35** and **71–79** examine the user's selection for the group of radio buttons, while lines **37–40** and **80–91** examine the user's selection for the `listBox`.

As shown in lines **26, 31, 37,** and **84** of Listing 5.11, `else  if` statements are applied. The syntax of the `else  if` statement is

```
if (condition 1)
{ action block 1 }
else if (condition 2)
```

```
{ action block 2 }
else
{ action block 3 }
```

This is the same as the following standard nested if-then statement:

```
if (condition 1)
{ action block 1 }
else
{  if (condition 2)
   { action block 2 }
   else
   { action block 3 }
}
```

As shown in lines **66–79** of Listing 5.11, the first character of a string is indexed at the position 0, and it is of the char data type, not of the string data type. C# treats the char data type and the string data type differently. The ToString() method of any character will convert the character into the string data type so that it can concatenate with other strings. The SubString(x) method of any string will extract a substring from the original string, starting at the position x. For example, SubString(1) will result in a new string, without the first character of the original string.

As shown in line **94** of Listing 5.11, Form2 is dynamically created in the source code of Form1, and the data to be passed from Form1 to Form2 are the parameters of the constructor of Form2. In line **95** of Listing 5.11, the ShowDialog() method will display this newly created Form2 and transfer the execution of the program to Form2.

The source code of Form2 is shown in Listing 5.12, where line **13** indicates that the data passed from Form1 are the parameters of the constructor of Form2. Line **18** shows that the font and font size of label1 can be dynamically changed in the program so that the text associated with the label will be displayed differently. Line **22** shows that once the user clicks on the [Go back] button on Form2, the Form2 window will be closed and the execution of the program will be returned to Form1.

Listing 5.12: C# Code for Form2 of the SignatureDesign Project

```
1   using System;
2   using System.Collections.Generic;
3   using System.ComponentModel;
4   using System.Data;
5   using System.Drawing;
6   using System.Linq;
7   using System.Text;
8   using System.Windows.Forms;
```

```
 9  namespace SignatureDesign
10  {
11     public partial class Form2 : Form
12     {
13          public Form2(string signatureText, string fontName)
14          {
15              InitializeComponent();

16              // signatureText and fontName are passed from Form1
17              label1.Text = signatureText;
18              label1.Font = new Font(fontName, label1.Font.Size);
19          }

20          private void button1_Click(object sender, EventArgs e)
21          {
22              this.Close();
23          }
24     }
25  }
```

The interested reader is referred to Chapter 4, "VB.NET," for examples of GUI with advanced features such as printing documents and others.

5.8 Debugging

Debugging C# programs could be time consuming. After compiling (or building) a C# program, the compiler will show error or warning messages if the program has a syntax error or an imperfect statement. A warning message does not prevent the program from executing, but it might cause problems (e.g., loss of information when converting data types). Any error could be fatal. The programming environment (e.g., Microsoft Visual Studio) can show the error locations, and, if you click on an error item in the error message window, the cursor will move to the place in the program where the error occurs. The following tips are for debugging:

1. Start with the first error in the program to debug.
2. An error message could be vague. For beginners, do not attempt to interpret the meaning of an error message, but pay attention to the error line itself.
3. An error line identified by the compiler may seem to be correct, but is actually affected by a real error in a related line. Thus, you need to inspect all lines that can be related to the indicated error line.
4. Fix one error a time and recompile the program after making a change.
5. Do not attempt to make the number of errors detected by the compiler smaller by making irrational changes.

The compiler can detect syntax errors. The syntax error-free condition is necessary for execution, but it does not guarantee the correctives of the logic of the program.

Logical errors or runtime errors often occur when the computer performs wrong operations, not as predicted. To debug logical errors, one should use data samples to test the program based on the output of the program.

1. Make the design of modules clear and logical. Avoid using a "goto" or any jump statement (e.g., "return" in the middle of the module) because it tends to cause bugs and to make debugging difficult.
2. Exercise every possible option to check the computer outputs to see if the program does only as expected. Examine all if-statements to follow possible actions.
3. A program might cause a crash. Usually, it could be caused by wrong data types, wrong calculations (e.g., a number is divided by zero), wrong size of an array, or wrong data file operations.
4. If a program is "dead," you must terminate it through interruption. A dead program is more likely caused by an endless loop. You need to examine loop statements and if-statements thoroughly.

Chapter 5 Exercises

1. Create a C# console application that defines a function and calls this function from the main function. The function takes three parameters, all of the integer data type, and returns the value of the smallest among the three parameters. Test the program with the following combinations of the function arguments:
0, 2, 1
1, 2, 3
5, 4, 3
and display the results in the console window.

2. Create a C# console application that defines a user-defined void function and calls this function from the main function. The user-defined void function takes two parameters, x and y, both of which are of the integer data type and of passing by reference parameter passing. In this function, the following computation will be executed:
x = x + y
y = x − y
x = x − y
Test the program and display the values of two variables before and after calling this function in the console window. Explain the effect of this user-defined function.

3. Fill blanks in the following C# console application program. Sketch the execution result of the program if the user inputs two numbers: 5 and 6.

```
 1 using System;
 2 using System.Collections.Generic;
 3 using System.Linq;
 4 using System.Text;

 5 namespace AreaFunction
 6 {
 7   class AreaFun
 8   {

 9     static double _____(ref double[] Dimensions)
10       {
11         double _____ = 1;
12         for (int i = 0; i < Dimensions._____; i++)
13         {
14             Product = Product * Dimensions[_____];
15         }
16         return (Product);
17       }

18     static void Main(string[] args)
19       {
20         double[] Measurements;
21         Measurements = new double[____];
22         Console.WriteLine("Enter length:");
23         string Side = Console.ReadLine();
24         Measurements[0] = Convert._____(_____);
25         Console.WriteLine("Enter width:");
26         Side = Console.ReadLine();
27         Measurements[1] = Convert._____(_____);

28         double Area = CalArea(_____ Measurements);
29         Console.WriteLine("Area is:" + Area);
30       }
31   }
32 }
```

4. (a) Given the following execution window, describe how you would design this GUI (Form1) by filling the table:

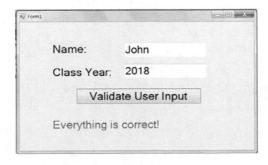

NAME OF THE GUI OBJECT	PROPERTIES: (INDICATE "TEXT" ONLY)
Label1	

(b) Read the flowing C# program for the preceding GUI and fill the blanks. Note that your answers must be consistent with your table in question 4(a).

```
1 using System;
2 using System.Collections.Generic;
3 using System.ComponentModel;
4 using System.Data;
5 using System.Drawing;
6 using System.Linq;
7 using System.Text;
8 using System.Windows.Forms;

9 namespace WindowsFormsApplication1
10 {
11     public partial class Form1 : Form
12     {
13         public Form1()
14         {
15             InitializeComponent();
16         }

17         private void button1_Click(object sender, EventArgs e)
18         {
19             label3.Text = "";
20             int OKFlag = 0;
21         // Check whether the user has entered the name and GPA
22             if (string.IsNullOrEmpty(_____.Text))
23             {   MessageBox.Show("Please input your name!");
24                 OKFlag = 1;

25             _____
26             if (string.IsNullOrEmpty(textBox2.Text))
27             {   MessageBox.Show("Please input your Class Year!");
28                 OKFlag = 1;
29             }
30         // Check whether the name contains only alphabetic letters
31             for (int i = 0; i < textBox1.Text.Length; i++)
32             {
```

```
33              if (!char.IsLetter(textBox1.Text[i]))
34              { MessageBox._____("The name must be alph. letters!");
35                OKFlag = 1;
36              }
37            }
38          // Check class year is an integer between 1900-2020
39            for (_____ i = 0; i < textBox2.Text.Length; i++)
40            {  if (!char.IsDigit(textBox2.Text[i]))
41            { MessageBox.Show("Year must be integer 1900-2020!");
42                 OKFlag = 2; }
43            }
44          if (OKFlag==0)
45          { int year = Convert.ToInt32(textBox2.Text);
46              if ((year < 1900) || (year > 2020)_____
47            { MessageBox.Show("Year must be integer 1900-2020!");
48                OKFlag=1;  }
49            }
50          // Validation had been passed
51            if (OKFlag==0)
52            _____.Text = "Everything is correct!";
53          }

54          private void Form1_Load(object sender, EventArgs e)
55          {
56          }
57      }
58 }
```

(c) During the test of the preceding C# program, if the user does not input anything but clicks on the "Validate User Input" button, what is the expected result and where does it appear?

(d) During the test of the preceding C# program, if the user inputs $100 in the first textbox, 2010 in the second textbox, and then clicks on the "Validate User Input" button, what is the expected result and where does it appear?

(e) During the test of the preceding C# program, if the user inputs Smith in the first textbox, 2030 in the second textbox, and then clicks on the "Validate User Input" button, what is the expected result and where does it appear?

(f) Discuss validation of user inputs in C#.

5. Create a C# Windows forms application that contains the following form: Once the user clicks on the submit button, the user's input should be displayed below the submit button for confirmation. For example,

Credit card: Visa

Name on Credit Card: John Smith

Credit Card Number: 1234567890123456

Expiration Date: 01/2020

If the user has missed any data item before clicking on the submit button, a warning message will be displayed.

6. Learn more features of C# from the online help. Create a C# project that uses features that are not fully explained in the book.

7. Develop a C# project that has one form, one combobox, three to five labels or textboxes, and two to four buttons.

8. Develop a C# project that has two forms with good design and interactions, at least three buttons, several labels or textboxes, at least two comboboxes, one group of radio box, one class, and message boxes. One of the buttons is to print a report on the default printer.

6

ASP.NET

6.1 Introduction to ASP.NET

ASP.NET is a framework for building web applications. It is a server-side programming technology. Its predecessor is ASP. ASP.NET supports all .NET programming languages for web application development, including VB.NET and C#.NET. To publish an ASP.NET web application on the web, an IIS (Internet information services) server and the Microsoft .NET framework are required. In terms of the roles of web applications, ASP.NET is not much different from other server-side programming languages such as PHP. A general process of a web application supported by ASP.NET is illustrated in Figure 6.1. The user on the client side sends a request, which might include data, over the Internet to the web server. The request and data received by the web server are used as the input for an ASP.NET program. The ASP. NET program processes the request and generates a dynamic HTML web page. A dynamic web page is different from a static web page in that a dynamic web page does not reside at a URL and its contents can vary depending on the request of a user or a computer program. The dynamic web page generated by the ASP.NET program is sent back to the client side. The web browser on the client-side computer presents the dynamic web page to the user.

The Microsoft Visual Studio development environment allows the programmer to develop ASP.NET programs on a personal computer without having a remote web server. It creates a local server on a personal computer to emulate the remote server for testing ASP.NET programs. The local server can also be a database server if the database is connected to the server through ODBC (open database connectivity). One can set the database connectivity in the Windows operating system using `Administrative Tools` in `Control Panel`. If a Microsoft Access database is used for ASP.NET as demonstrated in the examples in this chapter, it is more likely that the connectivity has been set by the system already.

This chapter includes two parts: ASP.NET with VB.NET and ASP.NET with C#.NET. Clearly, the two parts share many common characteristics. Each part needs its prerequisite of VB.NET or C#.NET. APS.NET with VB.NET and APS.NET with C#.NET are very similar. The concept and knowledge learned from one part can be straightforwardly applied to the other part. This chapter highlights the important features of ASP.NET without unnecessary replications of material. For example, the use of ADO.NET for a database process is mainly presented in the part of ASP.NET with VB.NET, and the use of the `<asp:SqlDataSource>` control is presented in

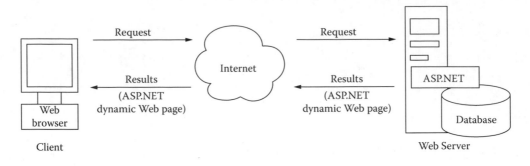

Figure 6.1 Execution cycle of an ASP.NET program.

the part of ASP.NET with C#.NET. However, either of the two features is applicable to any APS.NET application.

6.2 ASP.NET with VB.NET

One may use Microsoft Visual Studio to create an ASP.NET web application project in the Visual Basic template. The project created by the environment contains many predeveloped modules, resources, and structured query language (SQL—pronounced "sequel") server connections. However, an application of ASP.NET with VB.NET can be created in a simple way without using a website project. To avoid the distraction of those automatically generated modules and code lines, we use program files of ASP.NET with VB.NET in this section to learn and understand how ASP.NET with VB.NET programs works. In other words, we edit ASP.NET with VB.NET programs in Microsoft Visual Studio or Notepad and use the Microsoft Visual Studio environment to compile and execute the programs. The following steps are the general procedure of editing a program of ASP.NET with VB.NET and viewing the execution result:

1. Create a folder on your computer to store all ASP.NET programs. The folder name must not contain the # sign.
2. Start Microsoft Visual Studio. Click on [File] and choose [New File]. In the New File pane on the left [Installed Template], choose [Web]– [Visual Basic]; in the right pane, choose [Web Form]. Click on the [OK] button. When the editing window comes up, click on the [Source] button at the bottom of the editing window. You may delete the template code altogether and start editing your own ASP.NET program here (see Listing 6.1 for an example). After editing, save the program to your folder as *FileName*.aspx (e.g., HollowWorld.aspx). Alternatively, you may use Notepad to edit your ASP.NET program and save it to the folder. Make sure that you choose [All Files] for [Save as type] before you save the file as *FileName*.aspx.

Menu - [Open File...] [View in Browser]...

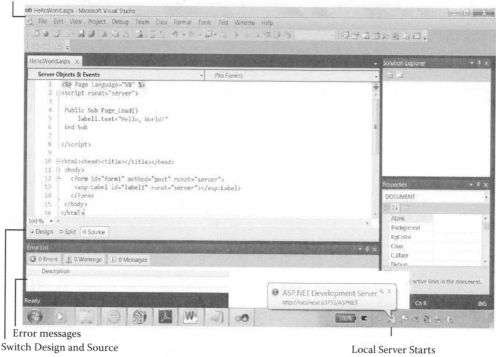

Error messages
Switch Design and Source   Local Server Starts

Figure 6.2 Microsoft visual studio environment for ASP.NET.

3. In the menu of Microsoft Visual Studio, click on [File] and then on [Open File …] to open your ASP.NET program file.

4. After opening the APS.NET program file, you can see error messages if there is an error.

5. If the program is error free, click on [View in Browser] in [File]. You will see the local server start and then the execution result presented by the browser on the client side will show up.

In case [View in Browser] is not in the [File] menu, it can be added to the menu by clicking on [Tools] on the Menu Bar, choosing [Customize], clicking on the [Commands] tab, and then adding [View in Browser] to the [File] menu.

Figure 6.2 shows the important features of the Microsoft Visual Studio environment for using ASP.NET files.

6.2.1 Structure of ASP.NET Program

Generally speaking, an ASP.NET program includes two parts: the user interface logic and the web form. In this part, we use VB.NET for user interface logic. We present a simple ASP.NET program, named HelloWorld.aspx, in Listing 6.1. As usual, the line numbers are added for explanation and should not be included in the program.

Bold font is used for highlighting some important words that connect the user interface logic and the web form.

Listing 6.1: Example of ASP.NET with VB.NET (`HelloWorld.aspx`)

```
 1 <%@ Page Language="VB" %>
 2 <script runat="server">
 3 Public Sub Page_Load()
 4   label1.text="Hello, World!"
-3 End Sub
-2 </script>

 5 <html><head><title></title></head>
 6 <body>
 7 <form id="form1" method="post" runat="server">
 8   <asp:Label id="label1" runat="server"></asp:Label>
-7 </form>
-6 </body>
-5 </html>
```

As shown in Listing 6.1, the ASP.NET program has one heading line (line **1**) and two parts. The heading line informs the web browser that this is an ASP.NET program and uses VB.NET language. The first part (lines **2** through **-2**) is a script block containing the VB.NET code that is used for the second part of the ASP.NET program. The second part (lines **5** through **-5**) is an HTML web form that holds all ASP.NET instructions for the server to execute. These instructions are called server controls. Lines **2** and **-2** are the pair of tags of the VB.NET script block. We always use the attribute `runat="server"` for the script tag. Lines **3** through **-3** are the VB.NET code that instructs the web browser to load the page and display the `"Hello, World!"` string in the label named `label1`. The `Page _ Load()` subroutine runs every time when the page, which is defined by the HTML block, is loaded. We will return to the VB.NET code after explaining the HTML part. Lines **5** and **-5** contain the pair of tags for the HTML block. Lines **7** through **-7** define the form. Line **7** uses several attributes. The `id` attribute specifies the name of the form. The other two attributes are quite standardized; that is, when creating a web form, we always specify `runat="server"` and `method="post"` for the attributes. Note that there are no `NAME` and `ACTION` attributes, which are normally used in the HTML `FORM` tag, here. Line **8** defines an ASP.NET control that outputs plain text (as label). You can use / in the open tag (i.e., `<asp:Label ... />`) to replace the closing tag (e.g., `</asp:Label>`) if there is nothing in the container. The entire line outputs plain text (label). When creating an ASP.NET control, we always need the `id` attribute, which assigns a unique name to the control. Again, we use the `runat="server"` attribute for ASP.NET control. This specifies that your control is based on the server and allows your code to interact with the server directly.

Now we return to the first part and examine the VB.NET code in detail. In line **3**, `Page _ Load()` is a special subroutine defined by ASP.NET that will be executed when the ASP.NET program is requested (i.e., when the dynamic web page is loaded

Figure 6.3 Dynamic web page generated by `HelloWorld.aspx`.

into the web browser). In line **4**, `label1` is bounded to the `<asp:Label>` control by the identical identification name `label1`.

The entire execution process can be described as follows. When a user requests `HelloWorld.aspx` through the browser, the server passes this request to ASP.NET. ASP.NET will compile the `HelloWorld.aspx` file and run the `Page _ Load()` subroutine. Upon the execution, ASP.NET transforms the control to the HTML tags and generates an HTML document (a dynamic web page) as specified in the web form block. The HTML document is sent back to the client side and is displayed by the web browser. Figure 6.3 shows the result and the source of the dynamic web page generated by `HelloWorld.aspx` in the browser on the client side.

6.2.2 HTML Controls Versus ASP.NET Web Controls

An ASP.NET program instructs the server to execute a certain sequence of actions. The instructions are called server controls. A server control is a tag that can be executed by the server. Server controls specified by the HTML form object tags are called HTML controls, and server controls specified in the ASP.NET `<asp>` tag are called web controls. Some web controls can do the jobs that HTML controls are unable to do, and others do jobs similar to those that HTML controls do but support more built-in features. For example, in Listing 6.1, line **8** is an example of the label web control, which is more flexible to use than the label HTML control. Next, we learn the two types of server controls through typical examples.

6.2.3 HTML Controls

In this section, we learn several typical HTML server control tools.

6.2.3.1 Submit Button   Listing 6.2 shows an ASP.NET program that generates a submit button through the HTML block. Running this ASP.NET program, the user can receive a message "Hello, World!" by clicking the submit button on the screen.

Listing 6.2: ASP.NET Program (SubmitButton.aspx)
with HTML Submit Button Control

```
 1 <%@ Page Language="VB" %>
 2 <script runat="server">
 3  Public Sub Page_Load()
-3  End Sub

 4  Public Sub HelloWorld(sender As Object, e As EventArgs)
 5    label1.text="Hello, World!"
-4  End Sub
-2 </script>
 6 <html><head><title></title></head>
 7 <body>
 8  <form id="form1" method="post" runat="server">
 9  <input id="submit1" type="submit" value="Greeting"
10       runat="server" onserverclick="HelloWorld" />
11  <asp:Label id="label1" font-names ="Forte"
12            font-size ="48" runat="server"></asp:Label>
-8  </form>
-7 </body>
-6 </html>
```

We examine the HTML part first. Line **8** defines a form, and lines **9** and **10** define the submit button on the form. Note line **9**, where an HTML submit button control is implemented. It specifies the subroutine to be run through the use of the onserverclick attribute of the server control. The button click will trigger a so-called postback process that runs the VB.NET program on the server, and it will post the execution result back to the same page on the client side. Lines **11** and **12** define an ASP.NET web control that outputs plain text as labels with specific font name and font size.

Now we examine the VB.NET block. The Page_Load() subroutine (lines **3** and **-3**) is always included even though it has no specific action except for loading the page defined by the HTML block. In this example, the VB.NET block has a subroutine with the same name as the HTML control instructs to run; that is, HelloWorld() (see lines **4** and **10**). The subroutine must be declared as Public. The argument of the subroutine must be (sender As Object, e As EventArgs).

6.2.3.2 Textbox   The ASP.NET web page in Listing 6.3 implements a postback process so that the user is allowed to type the user's name in the textbox; the server then posts a greeting in the label back to the client side.

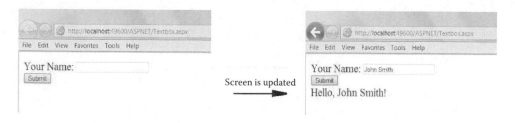

Figure 6.4 Screen updating (`Textbox.aspx`).

**Listing 6.3: ASP.NET Program (`Textbox.aspx`)
with HTML Textbox Control**

```
 1 <%@ Page Language="VB" %>
 2 <script runat="server">
 3 Public Sub Page_Load()
-3 End Sub

 4 Public Sub Greeting(sender As Object, e As EventArgs)
 5   label1.text="Hello, " + textbox1.value + "!"
-4 End Sub
-2 </script>

 6 <html><head><title></title></head>
 7 <body>
 8  <form id="form1" method="post" runat="server">
 9   Your Name:
10  <input type="text" id="textbox1" runat="server" />
11  <br />
12  <input type="submit" id="submit1" value="Submit"
13          runat="server" onserverclick="Greeting" /><br />
14   <asp:Label id="label1" runat="server"></asp:Label>
-8  </form>
-7 </body>
-6 </html>
```

In Listing 6.3, line **4** corresponds to lines **12** and **13** for the submit button control. Lines **5** and **10** correspond to the HTML textbox control. Here, `Value` is the property of the HTML textbox control. The label control is specified in line **14**. On the client side, the label appears after the submit button, which is specified in line **12**. Note in line **5** that the "+" symbol is used to join the strings. When you run the ASP. NET program, you can see that the screen is updated after clicking the submit button without losing the original form on the screen, as shown in Figure 6.4.

6.2.3.3 Checkbox Listing 6.4 lists an example (`Checkbox.aspx`) of checkbox control. By activating this ASP.NET program, the user is allowed to choose merchandise by checking on a checkbox and then clicking on the submit button to find the total price. The server then calculates the total price and posts it back to the client side. The connection elements between the VB.NET part and the HTML form part are highlighted in Listing 6.4. Note that an empty HTML tag (e.g., <br>) needs to include "/" to avoid warning messages in ASP.NET. In line **13**, the "&" sign is used to join a string and a double type number.

Listing 6.4: ASP.NET Program (`Checkbox.aspx`) with HTML Checkbox Control

```
 1 <%@ Page Language="VB" %>
 2 <script runat="server">
 3 Public Sub Page_Load()
-3 End Sub

 4 Public Sub CheckOut(sender As Object, e As EventArgs)
 5 Dim TotalPrice As Integer
 6 label1.text = ""
 7 if (chk1.checked) then
 8    TotalPrice = TotalPrice + 10
-7 end if
 9 if (chk2.checked) then
10    TotalPrice = TotalPrice + 20
-9 end if
11 if (chk3.checked) then
12    TotalPrice = TotalPrice + 30
-11 end if
13 label1.text="Total Price is:  $" & TotalPrice
-4 End Sub
-2 </script>

14 <html><head><title></title></head>
15 <body>
16 <form id="form1" method="post" runat="server">
17   Check :
18   <input id="chk1" type="checkbox" name="checkbox1" runat="server" />
19   CD
20   <input id="chk2" type="checkbox" name="checkbox1" runat="server" />
21   DVD
22   <input id="chk3" type="checkbox" name="checkbox1" runat="server" />
23   TV
24   <br />
25   <input id="submit1" type="submit"
26    value="View total price" runat="server" onserverclick="CheckOut" />
27   <br />
28   <asp:Label id="label1" runat="server"></asp:Label>
-16 </form>
-15 </body>
-14 </html>
```

6.2.3.4 Radio Button   A group of radio buttons allows the user to make just one choice. An example of HTML radio button control is shown in Listing 6.5 (`Radiobutton. aspx`). The connection elements between the VB.NET part and the HTML form part are highlighted in Listing 6.5.

**Listing 6.5: ASP.NET Program (`Radiobutton.aspx`)
with HTML Radio Button Control**

```
 1 <%@ Page Language="VB" %>
 2 <script runat="server">
 3  Public Sub Page_Load()
-3  End Sub
 4 Public Sub FindOut(sender As Object, e As EventArgs)
 5  Dim Price As Double
 6  label1.text = ""
 7  if (rad1.checked) then
 8     Price = 20.50
-7  end if
 9  if (rad2.checked) then
10     Price = 30.50
-9  end if
11  if (rad3.checked) then
12     Price = 100.50
-11 end if
13  label1.text = "The Price is:  $" & Price
-4 End Sub
-2 </script>

14 <html><head><title></title></head>
15 <body>
16 <form id="form1" method="post" runat="server">
17   Choose:
18 <input id="rad1" type="radio" name="radio1" runat="server"  />
19 CD
20 <input id="rad2" type="radio" name="radio1" runat="server"  />
21 DVD
22 <input id="rad3" type="radio" name="radio1" runat="server"  />
23 TV
24 <br />
25 <input id="submit1" type="submit" value="Submit"
26        runat="server" onserverclick="FindOut" />
27 <br />
28 <asp:Label id="label1" runat="server"></asp:Label>
-16 </form>
-15 </body>
-1 </html>
```

6.2.3.5 Select   The HTML select control allows the user to view a dropdown (combobox) menu and select a menu item for an action. An example of HTML select control is shown in Listing 6.6 (`Select.aspx`). The connection elements between the VB.NET part and the HTML form part are highlighted.

Listing 6.6: ASP.NET Program (`Select.aspx`) with HTML Select Control

```
<%@ Page Language="VB" %>
<script runat="server">
  Public Sub Page_Load()
  End Sub
```

```
    Public Sub Choice(ByVal sender As Object, ByVal e As EventArgs)
       label1.text = "Thank you for purchasing " & list1.value
    End Sub
</script>

<html><head><title></title></head>
<body>
<form id="form1" method="post" runat="server">
 Select:
 <select id="list1" runat="server">
   <option>CD</option>
   <option>DVD</option>
   <option>TV</option>
 </select>
 <br />
 <input id="submit1" type="submit" value="Submit"
        runat="server" onserverclick="Choice" />
 <br />
 <asp:Label id="label1" runat="server"></asp:Label>
</form>
</body>
</html>
```

6.2.4 Web Controls

A web control is specified in the <asp> tag. A web control is a programmed object. As you can see in this section, some web controls can do the jobs HTML controls are unable to do, and others do jobs similar to those that HTML controls do but support more features (attributes or properties) that HTML controls do not have. Listing 6.7 lists major web controls of ASP.NET.

Listing 6.7: List of Web Controls

Label	`<asp:Label>`
Button	`<asp:Button>`
TextBox	`<asp:TextBox>`
CheckBox	`<asp:CheckBox>`
RadioButton	`<asp:RadioButton>`
ListBox	`<asp:ListBox>`
DropDownList	`<asp:DropDownList>`
CheckBoxList	`<asp:CheckBoxList>`
RadioButtonList	`<asp:RadioButtonList>`

A web control can have several attributes depending on the needs. Only the id attribute and the runat attribute are required. We do not go through every web control tool, but give one example to explain the use of web controls, as listed in Listing 6.8.

Listing 6.8: Example of ASP.NET Web Controls (ShippingCost.aspx)

```
1 <%@ Page Language="VB" %>
2 <script runat="server">
```

```
 3 Public Sub Page_Load()
-3 End Sub

 4 Public Sub ShippingCost(sender as Object, e as EventArgs)
 5  DropDownList1.visible=false
 6  RadioButtonList1.visible=false
 7  Button1.visible=false
 8  label1.text="Ship to " & _
 9        DropDownList1.SelectedItem.text & " by " & _
10        RadioButtonList1.SelectedItem.text
11  label2.text="Shipping Cost is: $" & _
12               (Val(DropDownList1.SelectedItem.value) * _
13                Val(RadioButtonList1.SelectedItem.value))
-4 End Sub
-2 </script>

14 <html><head><title></title></head>
15 <body>
16 <form id="form1" method="post" runat="server">
17   <asp:DropDownList id="DropDownList1" runat="server">
18    <asp:ListItem Value="0" Selected="True">
-18       Select Country</asp:ListItem>
10    <asp:ListItem Value="50">Canada</asp:ListItem>
20    <asp:ListItem Value="100">USA</asp:ListItem>
-17   </asp:DropDownList>
21    <br />
22   <asp:RadioButtonList id="RadioButtonList1" runat="server">
23    <asp:ListItem Value="2" Selected="True">Express</asp:ListItem>
24    <asp:ListItem Value="1">Regular</asp:ListItem>
-22   </asp:RadioButtonList>
25    <br />
26   <asp:Button id="Button1" onclick="ShippingCost" runat="server"
27              Text="Find Shipping Cost" />
28    <br />
29   <asp:Label id="label1" runat="server" />  <br />
30   <asp:Label id="label2" runat="server" />
-16 </form>
-15 </body>
-1 </html>
```

The ASP.NET program in Listing 6.8 (`ShippingCost.aspx`) provides information for the consumer to find out the cost of a shipping transaction. The user is allowed to select a shipping destination and choose a shipping class, and then click on the button to get an answer. Lines **17** through **-17** define the dropdown list web control (`DropDownList`). There are a number of list items (`ListItem`) within the dropdown list. The `Value` attribute of `ListItem` assigns a value to the selected item that will be used for processing. The `Selected="True"` attribute means the default choice. Lines **22** through **-22** define a radio button list (`RadioButtonList`). The features of the `RadioButtonList` web control are similar to those of the `DropDownList` web control. Line **26** triggers the `ShippingCost` subroutine declared in line **5**. Lines **5–7** make the dropdown list, the radio button list, and the command button invisible (i.e., set the object's attribute to `visible=false`) when the calculated shipping cost is displayed.

6.2.5 Validation Controls

ASP.NET provides various validation control tools that validate the user's input. In ASP.NET, all validations are performed on the server side. Listing 6.9 lists the important validation controls.

Listing 6.9: Important Validation Controls

RequiredFieldValidator	Ensure that a field fills with data
CompareValidator	Compare the values of two entries
RangeValidator	Ensure that an entry falls within a defined range
RegularExpressionValidator	Ensure that an entry follows a particular pattern
CustomValidator	Validate user's input using a program subroutine

Listing 6.10 is an example of validation controls. In this example, the user is allowed to select merchandise to buy and input a number for the purchase quantity. The ASP.NET web page validates the user's input to ensure that the user has chosen an item and that the quantity is an integer and its value is no greater than 10.

Listing 6.10: Examples of Validation Control (`Validation.aspx`)

```
  1 <%@ Page Language="VB" %>
  2 <html><head><title></title></head>
  3 <body>
  4 <form id="form1" method="post" runat="server">
  5  Choose to buy:
  6 <asp:RequiredFieldValidator id="RequiredFieldValidator1"
  7     runat="server" ControlToValidate="RadioButtonList1"
  8     ErrorMessage="You must select one!" forecolor="Red">
 -6 </asp:RequiredFieldValidator>
  9 <br />
 10 <asp:RadioButtonList id="RadioButtonList1" runat="server"
 11     RepeatDirection="Horizontal">
 12  <asp:ListItem Value="CD">CD</asp:ListItem>
 13  <asp:ListItem Value="DVD">DVD</asp:ListItem>
 14  <asp:ListItem Value="TV">TV</asp:ListItem>
-10 </asp:RadioButtonList>
 15 <br />
 16  Quantity to buy:
 17 <asp:TextBox id="TextBox1" runat="server"></asp:TextBox> <br />
 18 <asp:CompareValidator id="CompareValidator1"  runat="server"
 19     ErrorMessage="Input must be an integer." forecolor="Red"
 20     ControlToValidate="TextBox1" Operator="DataTypeCheck"
 21     Type="Integer">
-18 </asp:CompareValidator> <br />
 22 <asp:RangeValidator id="RangeValidator1" runat="server"
 23     MinimumValue="0" MaximumValue="10"
 24     ControlToValidate="TextBox1" Type="Integer"
 25     ErrorMessage="Must be no more than 10." forecolor="Red">
-22  </asp:RangeValidator> <br />
 26  <asp:Button id="Button" runat="server" Text="Buy"></asp:Button>
 27 </form></body></html>
```

As shown in Listing 6.10 (`Validation.aspx`), no VB.NET program is needed in this example. The ASP.NET program contains three validation controls: `RequiredFieldValidator` (line **6**) for validating whether the required fields are filled, `CompareValidator` (line **18**) for validating the data type of the input, and `RangeValidator` (line **22**) for validating the range of the data. Each validation control must have required attributes including `id`, `ControlToValidate`, and `ErrorMessage`. Some attributes, such as `Operator` and `Type`, are only required for some validation controls.

You might remember that JavaScript is commonly used to validate a user's input on the client side. Compared with JavaScript, ASP.NET validation controls are slow since they are executed on the server side. However, ASP.NET programs are more secure since the code is invisible on the client side.

6.2.6 The Code-Behind Programming Framework

The ASP.NET framework supports code-behind programming that allows the programmer to reuse a separate code file. By doing so, the ASP.NET program contains the user interface implemented by a series of HTML and ASP.NET tags only and calls an independent VB.NET program for data processing. Listing 6.11(a) is an example of a code-behind programming ASP.NET program (`Greeting.aspx`). It allows the user to input her or his name and calls a VB.NET program named `Greeting.vb` to post a greeting message in a green color on the client side.

Listing 6.11(a): Example of Code-Behind Programming (Greeting.aspx)

```
<%@ Page Language="VB" Inherits="DisplayMessage"
    CodeFile="Greeting.vb" %>
<html><head><title></title></head>
<body>
 <form runat="server">
  Name:
  <input id="textbox1" type="text" runat="server" /> <br />
  <input id="submit1" type="submit" value="Submit"
     runat="server" onserverclick="Greeting" />  <br />
  <asp:Label id="label1" runat="server"
       forecolor="Green"></asp:Label>
 </form>
</body></html>
```

The VB.NET code (`Greeting.vb`) used by `Greeting.aspx` is listed in Listing 6.11(b).

Listing 6.11(b): VB.NET Code (`Greeting.vb`) Called by `Greeting.aspx`

```
Imports System
Public Class DisplayMessage
  Inherits System.Web.UI.Page
```

```
Public Sub Greeting(sender As Object, e As EventArgs)
    label1.Text = "Hello, " & textbox1.value & "!"
End Sub
End Class
```

Compare Listings 6.11(a) (ASP.NET code) and 6.11(b) (VB.NET code) by noting the highlighted connection elements. In the ASP.NET heading tag, the `Inherits` attribute specifies the class name (`DisplayMessage` in this example) that must also be used in the `Public Class` statement of the VB.NET program. The `CodeFile` attribute specifies the name of the VB.NET part. Even in this simple example, there are many parameters that connect the ASP.NET web page and the VB.NET program, including `Greeting` (for the subroutine), `label1` (for the label), `textbox1` (for the textbox), and `submit1` (for the submit button).

An advantage of code-behind programming is that the user interface is separated from the procedural codes. The programmer may change only the codes in the VB.NET part without touching the user interface in the `.aspx` part. However, in the example of Listings 6.11(a) and 6.11(b), if the programmer wants to change the subroutine name `Greeting` to, say, **ABC**, then she has to make changes in both `.aspx` and `.vb` parts. One can avoid such hassles by using `AutoEventWireup`, as shown in Listings 6.12(a) and 6.12(b).

Listing 6.12(a): Code-Behind Programming Using AutoEventWireup (Greeting2.aspx)

```
1  <%@ Page Language="VB" Inherits="DisplayMessage"
2  CodeFile="Greeting2.vb" AutoEventWireup="False" %>
3  <html><head><title></title></head>
4  <body>
5  <form runat="server">
6   Name:
7   <input id="textbox1" type="text" runat="server" /> <br />
8   <input id="submit1" type="submit" value="Submit"
9      runat="server" />   <br />
10  <asp:Label id="label1" runat="server"
11       forecolor="Green"></asp:Label>
12 </form>
13 </body></html>
```

Listing 6.12(b): VB.NET Code (Greeting2.vb) Called by Greeting2.aspx

```
1  Imports System
2  Public Class DisplayMessage
3   Inherits System.Web.UI.Page
4   Public Sub ABC(sender As Object, e As EventArgs) Handles _
5        submit1.ServerClick
6    label1.Text = "Hello, " & textbox1.value & "!"
7   End Sub
8  End Class
```

In Listing 6.12(a) (`Greeting2.aspx`), the `AutoEventWireup` attribute is set to `False` in line **2**. The default value of `AutoEventWireup` is `True`. When `AutoEventWireup` is set to `False`, ASP.NET will rely only on the `Handles` keyword in the .vb part to connect the event to the event handler subroutine, as shown in lines **4** and **5** of Listing 6.12(b) (`Greeting2.vb`). Line **5** is the continuation of line **4**, and it specifies that the `ServerClick` event of the `submit1` button will be handled by the subroutine `ABC`. Correspondingly, we do not specify any subroutine name in the `Greeting2.aspx` part.

6.2.7 Server-Side File Processing

One of the advantages of server-side programming is the data processing on the web server to allow the client to process information over the Internet. In this subsection, we examine how ASP.NET programs access and update data files that are stored on the web server. We use an example of an ASP.NET program that allows the user to input his or her e-mail address to join a group. The e-mail address will be added to the e-mail list that is permanently stored on the disk of the web server. After the user adds the e-mail address, the entire group e-mail list is then displayed on the screen for the user to view. The ASP.NET program (`FileProcess.aspx`) is shown in Listing 6.13.

Listing 6.13: ASP.NET Program (`FileProcess.aspx`)
for Writing and Reading Data File Stored on Server

```
 1 <%@ Page Language="VB" %>
 2 <%@ import Namespace="System" %>
 3 <%@ import Namespace="System.IO" %>
 4 <script runat="server">
 5 Public Sub Page_Load()
-5 End Sub

 6 Public Sub WriteAndRead(sender As Object, e As EventArgs)
 7    WriteToFile()
 8    ReadFromFile()
-6 End Sub

 9 Public Sub WriteToFile()
10   Dim StreamWriter1 As StreamWriter
11   Dim FileName As String = Request.MapPath("InputOutput.txt")
12   Dim FileInfo1 As FileInfo = New FileInfo(FileName)
13   If FileInfo1.Exists = False Then
14       StreamWriter1 = File.CreateText(FileName)
15       StreamWriter1.WriteLine(Textbox1.Text)
16   Else
17       StreamWriter1 = File.AppendText(FileName)
```

```
 18         StreamWriter1.WriteLine(Textbox1.Text)
-13  End If
 19  StreamWriter1.Close()
 -9 End Sub

 20 Public Sub ReadFromFile()
 21  Dim StreamReader1 As StreamReader
 22  Dim FileName As String = Request.MapPath("InputOutput.txt")
 23  Dim FileInfo2 As FileInfo = New FileInfo(FileName)
 24  ListBox1.Items.Clear
 25  If FileInfo2.Exists = True Then
 26         StreamReader1 = File.OpenText(FileName)
 27         Do While StreamReader1.Peek() > 0
 28             ListBox1.Items.Add(StreamReader1.ReadLine())
-27         Loop
 29         StreamReader1.Close()
 30  Else
 31         MsgBox("Unexpected error!", , "Error")
-25  End If
-20 End Sub
 -4 </script>

 32 <html><head><title></title></head>
 33 <body>
 34  <form id="form1" method="post" runat="server">
 35    Add your email address to join the group:
 36    <br />
 37    <asp:TextBox id="TextBox1" runat="server">
-37    </asp:TextBox>
 38    <br />
 39    <asp:Button id="Button1" onclick="WriteAndRead" runat="server"
 40               text="View the email list of the group">
-39    </asp:Button>
 41    <br />
 42    <asp:ListBox id="ListBox1" runat="server"
 43               forecolor="Red">
-42    </asp:ListBox>
-34  </form>
-33 </body>
-32 </html>
```

After the client loads the ASP.NET program (FileProcess.aspx) in Listing 6.13, the browser displays one textbox (line **37**), one button (line **39**), and one list box (line **42**). The textbox accepts the user's input. Note that the textbox is defined as a web control here, and its Text property (equivalent to the Value property of an HTML textbox control) is used in lines **15** and **18**. The list box displays the e-mail list of the entire group. When the user clicks on the button (line **39**), the WriteAndRead() subroutine (line **6**) is called. This subroutine in turn calls two subroutines: WriteToFile(), for writing data to the server file, and ReadFromFile() for reading data from the server file.

As shown in lines **10–12** and **21–23**, three variables are generally needed for processing a disk file on the server:

1. The first variable is `StreamWriter` (line **10**) or `StreamReader` (line **21**), depending on whether the process is writing or reading, which represents the disk data file.

2. The second variable is `FileName` (lines **11** and **22**), which defines the file name on the server. In this example, the physical name of the file is `InputOutput.txt`, a plain text file. If you place the data file with the ASP.NET program, `Request.MapPath()` (lines **11** and **22**) is applied without specifying the access path of the data file.

3. The third variable is `FileInfo` (lines **12** and **23**), which holds information about the data file, such as whether it exists, to avoid errors.

To create these three variables, the ASP.NET program needs to import two namespaces: the `System` namespace and the `System.IO` namespace, as shown in lines **2** and **3**.

In the `WriteToFile()` subroutine, lines **13** through **-13** are an if-then-else statement, which means that if the file does not exist, then the program creates the file on the disk and writes the e-mail address received from the textbox to the disk on the server; otherwise, the program appends the e-mail address to the existing group list. After the process, the file must be closed (line **19**).

In the `ReadFromFile()` subroutine, line **24** clears anything in the list box that might be left over from the previous operation. Lines **25** through **-25** are an if-then-else statement to handle an exceptional case where the data file does not exist. Line **26** opens the file for reading. Lines **27** through **-27** are a do-loop to make actions as long as the data file has not reached the end. As the result of the action (line **28**), the server reads a record from the data file and adds it to the list box. Line **29** closes the file. Line **31** signals an error message when the data file does not exist.

If the original `InputOutput.txt` file contains the following e-mail list, the execution result of `FileProcess.aspx` appears similar to that shown in Figure 6.5.

Figure 6.5 Write and read data file stored on server (`FileProcess.aspx`).

```
who@abc.com
some@bcd.net
swang@umassd.edu
```

Flat text file is the simplest form of data set. However, processing a flat text file could be tedious. Flat text files are fine for simple record keeping (e.g., retaining logs), but are poor for searching or updating. To deal with a relational database directly from ASP.NET, one must apply a database connection, as discussed later in this section.

6.2.8 Accessory Features

In this subsection, we introduce several other useful features of ASP.NET.

6.2.8.1 Sending E-mail Message   ASP.NET supports email sending in a simple way. Listing 6.14 provides a template of an ASP.NET program that allows the user to type an e-mail receiver's address and send a message. Note that Listing 6.14 (EmailTemplate. aspx) is not an operational program. To make EmailTemplate.aspx work, the e-mail server must be valid and set properly.

Listing 6.14: Template (`EmailTemplate.aspx`) for Sending E-mail

```
<%@ Page Language="VB" %>
<script runat="server">
 Public Sub Page_Load()
 End Sub

 Public Sub SendEmail(sender As Object, e As EventArgs)
  'Textbox1.text must not be empty
  'There are two parameters for MailMessage:
  '             From address and To address
 Dim myMsg As New _
     System.Net.Mail.MailMessage("sender@provider.com", TextBox1.text)
 Dim mySmtpClient As New System.Net.Mail.SmtpClient()
  myMsg.Subject = "Email subject ..."
  myMsg.Body = "Email message body ..."
  'set your own email smtp server here
  mySmtpClient.Host = "smtp.smu.ca"
  mySmtpClient.Send(myMsg)
 End Sub
</script>

<html><head><title></title></head>
<body>
<form id="form1" method="post" runat="server">
 <p>
 Email Address:
 <asp:TextBox id="TextBox1" runat="server"></asp:TextBox>
 </p>
 <p>
 <asp:Button id="Button1" onclick="SendEmail" runat="server"
                Text="Send Email"></asp:Button>
 </p>
</form></body></html>
```

6.2.8.2 Calendar ASP.NET has the calendar web control that displays the calendar. The example in Listing 6.15 (`Calendar.aspx`) allows the user to click a date on the calendar and view the date in the long date string format (see Figure 6.6). The date information generated by the calendar web control can be useful for many business applications, such as hotel reservations and event planning.

Listing 6.15: ASP.NET Program (`Calendar.aspx`) for Showing Calendar

```
<%@ Page Language="VB" %>
<script runat="server">
  Public Sub Page_Load()
  End Sub

  Public Sub CalendarDate(sender As Object, e As EventArgs)
    label1.text = Calendar1.SelectedDate.ToLongDateString()
  End Sub
</script>

<html><head><title></title></head>
<body>
 <form id="form1" method="post" runat="server">
  <br />
  <asp:Calendar id="Calendar1" runat="server" forecolor="Blue" />
  <br />
  <asp:Button id="button1" runat="server" onclick="CalendarDate"
       text="Find Long Date String" />
  <br />
  <asp:Label id="label1" runat="server" forecolor="Red" />
</form></body></html>
```

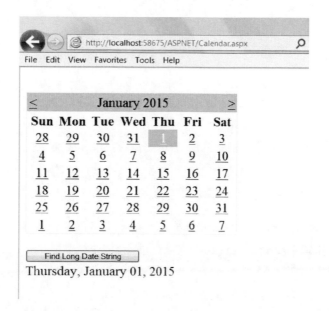

Figure 6.6 Example of calendar web control (`Calendar.aspx`).

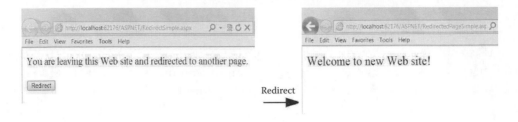

Figure 6.7   Execution result of `RedirectSimple.aspx`.

6.2.8.3 Redirect Method   As demonstrated in the previous examples, an ASP.NET program allows the user to work on the dynamic web page interactively. However, if the application redirects the user to another ASP.NET program or a new website, the `Redirect` method must be applied. Listing 6.16 (`RedirectSimple.aspx`) shows an example of the `Redirect` method, which is a method of the `Response` object. The instruction `Response.Redirect("RedirectedPageSimple.aspx")` redirects the user on the client side to another ASP.NET program, named `RedirectedPageSimple.aspx`, which is listed in Listing 6.17. Figure 6.7 shows the execution results. A URL of the website can be used for the redirected destination.

Listing 6.16: Example of `Redirect` Method (`RedirectSimple.aspx`)

```
<%@ Page Language="VB" %>
<script runat="server">
 Public Sub Page_Load()
  label1.text="You are leaving this Web site and redirected to another page."
 End Sub
 Public Sub RedirectTo(sender As Object, e As EventArgs)
    Response.Redirect("RedirectedPageSimple.aspx")
 End Sub
</script>

<html><head><title></title></head>
<body>
 <form id="form1" method="post" runat="server">
  <asp:Label id="label1" runat="server"></asp:Label> <br />
  <br />
  <input type="submit" id="submit1" value="Redirect"
         runat="server" onserverclick="RedirectTo" />
 </form>
</body>
</html>
```

Listing 6.17: `RedirectedPageSimple.aspx` Used by `RedirectSimple.aspx`

```
<%@ Page Language="VB" %>
<script runat="server">
 Public Sub Page_Load()
   label1.text="Welcome to new Web site!"
 End Sub
</script>
```

```
<html><head><title></title></head>
<body>
 <form id="form1" method="post" runat="server">
   <asp:Label id="label1" runat="server" font-size="20"
      ></asp:Label>
 </form></body></html>
```

Note that the simple redirect approach demonstrated here does not pass any parameter from the source web page to the directed web page. More often, the application needs to pass information from the source web page to the directed web page. For example, the directed web page might want to know the validated user ID, which has been input on the source web page so that it can follow up a specific process.

There are several techniques for passing parameters when using the Redirect method. The use of query string is an easy technique. Originally, a query string is the part of a URL that contains data to be passed to web applications. ASP.NET uses this approach to implement the parameter transfer between the source program and the directed program. Listing 6.18 (RedirectWithPara.aspx) shows an example of the Redirect method with passing a parameter. In this example, the user inputs the user's name and redirects to the target web page. The source web page passes the user name (in SenderName) to the directed program, named RedirectedPagePara.aspx. Note the syntax of line **7** for passing a parameter.

Listing 6.18: Example of Redirect Method with Passing Parameter (RedirectWithPara.aspx)

```
1 <%@ Page Language="VB" %>
2 <script runat="server">
3 Public Sub Page_Load()
4 label1.text="You are redirected to another page."
5 End Sub

6 Public Sub RedirectTo(sender As Object, e As EventArgs)
7   Response.Redirect("RedirectedPagePara.aspx?SenderName=" + textbox1.value)
8 End Sub
9 </script>

10 <html><head><title></title></head>
11 <body>
12 <form id="form1" method="post" runat="server">
13  <asp:Label id="label1" runat="server"></asp:Label> <br />
14  <br />
15  Your Name:
16  <input type="text" id="textbox1" runat="server" />
17  <br />
18  <input type="submit" id="submit1" value="Redirect"
19         runat="server" onserverclick="RedirectTo" />
20 </form></body></html>
```

Listing 6.19 (RedirectedPagePara.aspx) is the redirected program that receives the data passed from RedirectWithPara.aspx. Note the syntax of line **5** for the communication between the two programs. Figure 6.8 shows the execution

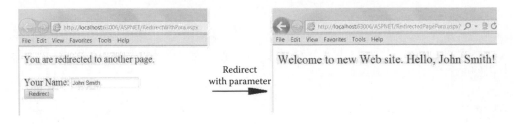

Figure 6.8 Execution result of `RedirectWithPara.aspx`.

result of `RedirectWithPara.aspx`. In this example, the user's name is passed to the new web page.

Listing 6.19: `RedirectedPagePara.aspx` Used by `RedirectWithPara.aspx`

```
1 <%@ Page Language="VB" %>
2 <script runat="server">
3 Public Sub Page_Load()
4  Dim Sender As String
5  Sender = Request.QueryString("SenderName")
6  label1.text="Welcome to new Web site.  Hello, " + Sender + "!"
7 End Sub
8 </script>

9 <html><head><title></title></head>
10 <body>
11 <form id="form1" method="post" runat="server">
12   <asp:Label id="label1" runat="server" font-size="20"></asp:Label>
13 </form></body></html>
```

6.2.8.4 Security Security is an important issue in web applications. At the communication level, encryption technologies are used to encrypt communication between a web client and a web server. Secure sockets layer (SSL) is one of the popular encryption technologies to transmit private or sensitive information between the authenticated client and the web server. Both the web client and the web server must have certificates that are installed on the computers. To access a page through SSL, the user simply types the URL with a preceding "`https://`" instead of "`http://`." At the application level, authentication and authorization ensure the application security. Authentication is the process that enables the determination of a user's identity by asking the user to prove it. A user's name and password and or IP address are commonly used in authentication. Authorization is the process that determines which resources an authenticated user can access and how those resources can be used. For example, the user must use a password to access restricted files.

ASP.NET provides various approaches to security. ASP.NET supports three types of authentication: windows authentication, passport authentication, and form authentication. When using windows authentication, the ASP.NET web page calls IIS (Internet information service) at the operating system level for authentication. The goal of windows authentication is to verify the user against the accounts on the web server.

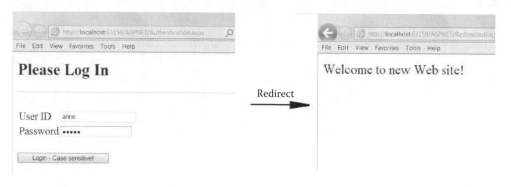

Figure 6.9   Execution result of `Authentication.aspx`.

Passport authentication is carried out through Microsoft Passport, which is maintained by Microsoft to authenticate registered users. Form authentication is the commonly used approach for authentication that uses log-in forms in web pages. ASP.NET has built-in utilities for form authentication. To use these built-in utilities, you need to specify the requirements through the `web.config` files provided by the ASP.NET development environment. For beginners, this may not be straightforward. Here, we provide a simple example that implements customized form authentication within the ASP.NET program in Listing 6.20 (`Authentication.aspx`). To simplify the program, the user IDs and passwords are stored in the program. Practically, they should be stored in the database, and SQL is used for processing, as discussed later in this section. Note that, in Listing 6.20, `textmode="password"` is used for `textbox2` for password mode. Figure 6.9 shows an example of the execution result of `Authentication.aspx`.

Listing 6.20: Example of Form Authentication (`Authentication.aspx`)

```
<%@ Page Language="VB" %>
<script runat="server">
 Public Sub PasswordCheck(sender As Object, e As EventArgs)
   If (((textBox1.text="anne") AND (textBox2.text="12345")) OR _
       ((textBox1.text="john") AND (textBox2.text="23456")) OR _
       ((textBox1.text="peter") AND (textBox2.text="34567"))) Then
      Response.Redirect("RedirectedPageSimple.aspx")
   Else
    label1.Text = "Your ID and password do not match. Try again!"
   End If
 End Sub
</script>

<html><head><title></title></head>
<body>
 <form id="form1" method="post" runat="server">
  <h2>Please Log In</h2>
  <hr /><br />
  <table>
   <tr>
   <td>User ID</td>
   <td><asp:TextBox id="textBox1" runat="server" /></td>
   </tr>
```

```
<tr>
<td>Password</td>
<td><asp:TextBox id="textBox2" runat="server" textmode="password"/></td>
</tr>
</table>
<br />
<asp:Button id="button1" onclick="PasswordCheck" runat="server"
      Text="Login - Case sensitive!"></asp:Button>
<br /><br />
<asp:Label id="label1" runat="server" />
</form></body></html>
```

6.2.9 Web Application Design

There are many types of web applications, including

- Information presentation
- Access authentication
- Information search
- Business transaction
- Notification, reporting, or confirmation
- User interaction, etc.

To facilitate web application design, we use scenario design diagram as a tool to articulate the web application project in the aspects of

1. Features of each of the web pages
2. Interaction between the client and the web server
3. Data on the server
4. Logic of the entire process
5. Major outcomes of the process

In this section, we present an example of toy-scale web application to explain the use of scenario design diagram and the implementation of a web application project using ASP.NET. The example is a hotel reservation system. In this example, the home page introduces the user to making a reservation. The user is allowed to search the prices of different types of rooms. The data used for search are stored on the server. When the user decides to make a reservation, she can input her contact information and reservation request on the form and send the form back to the server. The reservation data are recorded on the server for the hotel for further processing.

Figure 6.10 shows a scenario design diagram for the preceding example. Apparently, the diagram in Figure 6.10 includes screenshots of the execution results of the programs. Practically, the program designer draws a draft for the design of the application before writing the programs.

Listing 6.21(a) is the home page (`ReservationHome.html`), which triggers `Search.aspx` (see Listing 6.21(b)). The `Search.aspx` program allows the user to

Web Application Scenario Design – Hotel Reservation

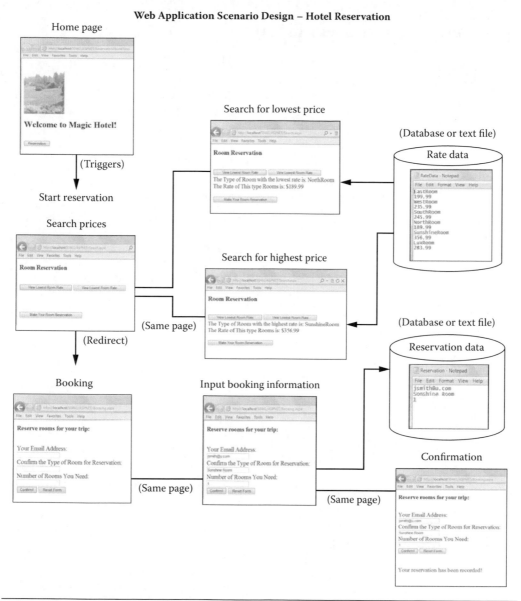

Figure 6.10   Example of scenario design.

find the room types with the lowest price or the highest price. This search process uses a data file on the server named `RateData.txt` (see Listing 6.21(c)). The `Search.aspx` program also allows the user to make a reservation by redirecting the user to the `Book.aspx` program. The `Book.aspx` program (Listing 6.21(d)) allows the user to input contact information and booking information to reserve rooms. These data of contact information and booking information are sent back to the server and are stored in a data file named `Reservation.txt`. Upon the completion of the booking transaction, the user will receive a confirmation message on the screen.

Listing 6.21(a): Example of Application Design: Home Page (`ReservationHome.html`)

```html
<html>
<head>
    <title>Online Hotel Reservation</title>
</head>
<body>
    <img alt="HotelPicture" src="Hotel.png"
        width="150" height="200" />
    <h2>Welcome to Magic Hotel!</h2>
    <br />
    <form action="Search.aspx" method="post">
      <input type="submit" value="Reservation" />
    </form>
</body>
</html>
```

Listing 6.21(b): Example of Application Design: Search (`Search.aspx`)

```vb
<%@ Page Language="VB" %>
<%@ import Namespace="System" %>
<%@ import Namespace="System.IO" %>
<script runat="server">
  Public Sub Page_Load()
  End Sub

  Private Sub LowestRate(sender as Object, e as EventArgs)
   Dim SR As StreamReader
   Dim RateFile As String = Request.MapPath("RateData.txt")
   Dim FI As FileInfo = New FileInfo(RateFile)
   Dim RoomType, LowestRoomType As String
   Dim Rate, LowestRate As Double
   LowestRate = 999
        LowestRoomType = ""
   If FI.Exists = True Then
      SR = File.OpenText(RateFile)
      Do While SR.Peek() > 0
         RoomType=SR.ReadLine()
         Rate = SR.ReadLine()
          If (Rate<LowestRate) Then
           LowestRate = Rate
           LowestRoomType = RoomType
          End If
      Loop
      SR.Close()
   Else
      MsgBox("Unexpected error!", , "Error")
   End If
   label1.text = "The Type of Room with the lowest rate is:  " & _
                 LowestRoomType
   label2.text = "The Rate of This type Rooms is: $" & LowestRate
  End Sub

  Private Sub HighestRate(sender as Object, e as EventArgs)
   Dim SR As StreamReader
   Dim RateFile As String = Request.MapPath("RateData.txt")
   Dim FI As FileInfo = New FileInfo(RateFile)
```

```
    Dim RoomType, HighestRoomType As String
    Dim Rate, HighestRate As Double
    HighestRate = 0
        HighestRoomType = ""

    If FI.Exists = True Then
        SR = File.OpenText(RateFile)
        Do While SR.Peek() > 0
           RoomType=SR.ReadLine()
           Rate = SR.ReadLine()
            If (Rate>HighestRate) Then
             HighestRate = Rate
             HighestRoomType = RoomType
            End If
        Loop
        SR.Close()
    Else
        MsgBox("Unexpected error!", , "Error")
    End If
    label1.text = "The Type of Room with the highest rate is:  " & _
                HighestRoomType
    label2.text = "The Rate of This type Rooms is: $" & HighestRate
    End Sub

    Private Sub Booking(sender as Object, e as EventArgs)
     Response.Redirect("Booking.aspx")
    End Sub
</script>
<html><head><title></title></head>
<body>
<h3>Room Reservation</h3>
  <form id="form1" method="post" runat="server"> <br />
     <asp:Button id="button1" onclick="LowestRate"
         runat="server" text="View Lowest Room Rate"></asp:Button>
      <asp:Button id="button2" onclick="HighestRate"
         runat="server" text="View Lowest Room Rate"></asp:Button> <br />
    <asp:Label id="label1" runat="server"></asp:Label> <br />
    <asp:Label id="label2" runat="server"></asp:Label> <br /><br />
    <asp:Button id="button3" onclick="Booking" runat="server"
         text="Make Your Room Reservation"></asp:Button><br />
  </form>
</body></html>
```

Listing 6.21(c): Example of Application Design: Data on Server (`RateData.txt`)

```
EastRoom
199.99
WestRoom
235.99
SouthRoom
245.99
NorthRoom
189.99
SunshineRoom
356.99
LuxRoom
283.99
```

Listing 6.21(d): Example of Application Design: Transaction (`Booking.aspx`)

```
<%@ Page Language="VB" %>
<%@ import Namespace="System" %>
<%@ import Namespace="System.IO" %>
<script runat="server">
 Public Sub Page_Load()
 End Sub

 Public Sub MakeReserve (sender As Object, e As EventArgs)
  Dim SR As StreamWriter
  Dim ReserveFile As String = Request.MapPath("Reservation.txt")
    SR = File.AppendText(ReserveFile)
    SR.WriteLine(textbox1.Text)
    SR.WriteLine(textbox2.Text)
    SR.WriteLine(textbox3.Text)
    SR.Close()
    label1.Text = "Your reservation has been recorded!"
 End Sub

</script>
<html><head><title></title></head>
<body>
<h4>Reserve rooms for your trip:</h4>
 <form id="form1" method="post" runat="server"><br />
   Your Email Address: <br />
   <asp:TextBox id="textBox1" runat="server"></asp:TextBox><br />
   Confirm the Type of Room for Reservation: <br />
   <asp:TextBox id="textBox2" runat="server"></asp:TextBox><br />
   Number of Rooms You Need:  <br />
   <asp:TextBox id="textBox3" runat="server"></asp:TextBox><br />
   <asp:Button id="button1" onclick="MakeReserve"
        runat="server" text="Confirm!"></asp:Button>
   <input type="reset" value="Reset Form" />
   <br /><br /><br />
   <asp:Label id="label1" forecolor="blue" runat="server"></asp:Label>
   <br />
 </form>
</body></html>
```

6.2.10 ADO.NET—Server-Side Database Processing

A practical web application can deal with relational databases directly from a web page. One may create an ASP.NET web application project in the Microsoft Visual Studio environment and use the default SQL server connection and predeveloped modules and resources to practice database processing in a limited scope. To understand the concept of database connection and database processing on a large scale, one needs to create her or his own database.

To make a connection to databases, database connection software must be integrated into the web application development tool. ASP.NET has the `<asp:SqlDataSource>` control that allows the ASP.NET program to connect to a database and to use the tblStudent

	StudentID	StudentNam	StudentAddr	StudentEnrol	Click to Add
+	01234567	John	285 Westport	2015	
+	02345678	Anne	287 Eastport	2016	
+	03456789	Robert	324 Northport	2017	

Figure 6.11 Sample data sheet of `tblStudent` for ADO.NET examples.

database in a simple way. However, in the Microsoft .NET framework, ADO.NET (ADO stands for ActiveX Data Objects) provides a general framework for database connection and manipulation for any databases in a variety of platforms. The ADO.NET framework is considered to be more flexible than the `<asp:SqlDataSource>` control, although they can do similar jobs for simple applications. In fact, the `<asp:SqlDataSource>` control inside ASP.NET uses ADO.NET classes to interact with any database supported by ADO.NET. In this section, we study ADO.NET to learn a broad view of the .NET framework relating to database processing. In the next section of ASP.NET with C#.NET, we will discuss the use of the `<asp:SqlDataSource>` control. We assume students have basic knowledge of database and SQL for studying this section. The subject of SQL is discussed in detail in Chapter 9.

In this section, as an example, a Microsoft Access database named `StudentDB.accdb` is used for the ASP.NET program. This database has a table named `tblStudent` that has four attributes:

```
tblStudent
    StudentID (Key, Text)
    StudentName (Text)
    StudentAddress (Text)
    StudentEnrolYear (Number).
```

A sample data sheet of the table is shown in Figure 6.11.

A database used by ASP.NET must be created by using the database management system (DBMS), although the database could be empty, so ASP.NET is to use databases through SQL.

6.2.10.1 Database Connection and SQL in ASP.NET Listing 6.22 (`ADOAccess.aspx`) is an example of web application that uses SQL to access the Microsoft Access database in the ADO.NET environment. In this example, the Access database is named `StudentDB.accdb` and is stored in the same folder as this ASP.NET web page. Particular lines that are relevant to the database connection and SQL are highlighted in bold.

Listing 6.22: Access Database Using ADO.NET (`ADOAccess.aspx`)

```
 1 <%@ Page Language="VB" %>
 2 <%@ import Namespace="System.Data.OleDb" %>
 3 <script runat="server">

 4 Public Sub Page_Load()
 5  Dim sql As String
 6  Dim dbconn=New OleDbConnection _
 7   ("Provider=Microsoft.ACE.OLEDB.12.0; data source=" & _
 8     server.mappath("StudentDB.accdb"))
 9  dbconn.Open()

10  sql="SELECT * FROM tblStudent"

11  Dim dbcomm=New OleDbCommand(sql,dbconn)
12  Dim dbread=dbcomm.ExecuteReader()
13  tblStudent.DataSource=dbread
14  tblStudent.DataBind()
15  dbread.Close()
16  dbconn.Close()
-4 End Sub
-3 </script>

17 <html><head><title></title></head>
18 <body>
19 <form runat="server">
20  <h3>Student Records</h3>
21  <asp:Repeater id="tblStudent" runat="server">
22  <HeaderTemplate>
23   <table border="1" width="100%">
24   <tr>
25   <th>Student ID</th>
26   <th>Student Name</th>
27   <th>Student Address</th>
28   <th>Student Year</th>
-24   </tr>
-22 </HeaderTemplate>
29  <ItemTemplate>
30   <tr>
31   <td><%#Container.DataItem("StudentID")%></td>
32   <td><%#Container.DataItem("StudentName")%></td>
33   <td><%#Container.DataItem("StudentAddress")%></td>
34   <td><%#Container.DataItem("StudentEnrolYear")%></td>
-30   </tr>
-29 </ItemTemplate>
35  <FooterTemplate>
-23   </table>
-35 </FooterTemplate>
-21 </asp:Repeater>
-19 </form>
36 </body></html>
```

In Listing 6.22, lines **1** and **2** are heading lines of the ASP.NET program that claims to use VB.NET and ADO.NET. Lines **3** through **-3** are the VB.NET part. Line **5** defines a variable for the SQL string. Lines **6–8** are a single sentence that makes the database connection. The database name is specified in line **8.** When editing the

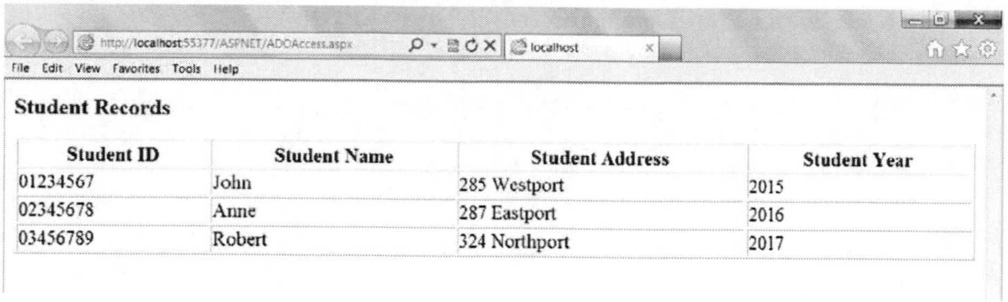

Figure 6.12 Web application with ADO.NET and SQL (ADOAccess.aspx).

program in practice, try to avoid any line break and type the sentence in a single line without the line break sign. Line **9** opens the database connection. Apparently, a beginner of ADO.NET may simply follow these lines except for the database name.

Line **10** is the SQL for this example that selects all fields from the table tblStudent. Note the quotation marks for the SQL string. Lines **11–14** read the table using the SQL and make data binding. Lines **15** and **16** stop the access and close the database connection. Again, a beginner might use these lines for a simple application except for the database name in line **8** and the table name in lines **13** and **14**.

In the web page part, line **21** specifies database connection control. Commonly, there are two connection control methods in ASP.NET: Repeater and DataList. In this example, the Repeater control is applied. The table of the database is also declared here. Lines **23** through -**23** create an HTML table to present the data to the client. Lines **31–34** place the data items into the table cells. The syntax of the ASP.NET sentences in these lines looks unfamiliar. Again, a beginner may simply follow these sentences but specify the particular data item names here. Another new feature is the templates defined in lines **22**, -**22**, **29**, -**29**, **35**, and -**35**. Without including these templates, the table does not work. Figure 6.12 shows the execution result of ADOAccess.aspx.

6.2.10.2 Search Database The program in Listing 6.23 (ADOSearch.aspx) is an extension of ADOAccess.aspx and allows the client to input a student number to search a specific student record. Note the SQL string in bold and the use of the quotation marks in particular. An example of a database search is shown in Figure 6.13.

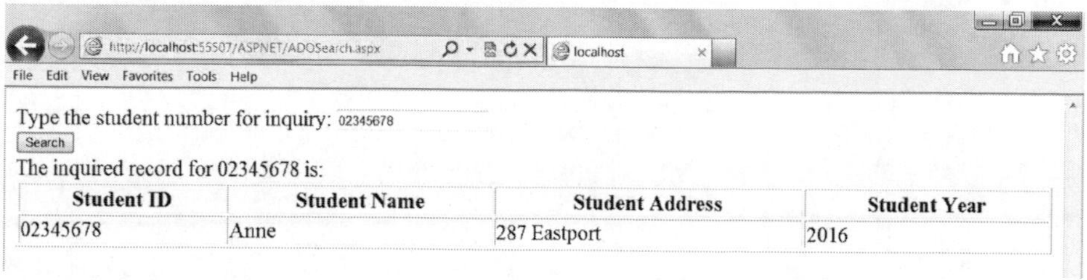

Figure 6.13 Search database (ADOSearch.aspx).

Listing 6.23: Search Database Using ADO.NET (`ADOSearch.aspx`)

```
<%@ Page Language="VB" %>
<%@ import Namespace="System.Data.OleDb" %>
<script runat="server">
 Public Sub Page_Load()
 End Sub

 Public Sub SearchStudent(sender As Object, e As EventArgs)
   label1.text="The inquired record for " + textbox1.value + " is:"
   Dim StudentID As String
   StudentID=textbox1.value

   Dim sql As String
   Dim dbconn=New OleDbConnection _
     ("Provider=Microsoft.ACE.OLEDB.12.0; data source=" & _
       server.mappath("StudentDB.accdb"))
   dbconn.Open()

   sql="SELECT * FROM tblStudent WHERE StudentID=" & "'" & StudentID & "'"

   Dim dbcomm=New OleDbCommand(sql,dbconn)
   Dim dbread=dbcomm.ExecuteReader()
   tblStudent.DataSource=dbread
   tblStudent.DataBind()
   dbread.Close()
   dbconn.Close()
 End Sub
</script>
<html><head><title></title></head>
<body>
 <form runat="server">
  Type the student number for inquiry:
  <input id="textbox1" type="text" runat="server" /> <br />
  <input id="submit1" type="submit" value="Search" runat="server"
        onserverclick="SearchStudent" /> <br />
  <asp:Label id="label1" runat="server"></asp:Label>
  <asp:Repeater id="tblStudent" runat="server">
  <HeaderTemplate>
  <table border="1" width="100%">
   <tr>
   <th>Student ID</th>
   <th>Student Name</th>
   <th>Student Address</th>
   <th>Student Year</th>
   </tr>
  </HeaderTemplate>
  <ItemTemplate>
   <tr>
   <td><%#Container.DataItem("StudentID")%></td>
   <td><%#Container.DataItem("StudentName")%></td>
   <td><%#Container.DataItem("StudentAddress")%></td>
   <td><%#Container.DataItem("StudentEnrolYear")%></td>
   </tr>
  </ItemTemplate>
  <FooterTemplate>
    </table>
  </FooterTemplate>
```

```
  </asp:Repeater>
  </form>
 </body></html>
```

6.2.10.3 Update Database   Listing 6.24 (ADOUpdate.aspx) is an example of database updating using ASP.NET with ADO.NET. Again, note the SQL string in bold and the use of the quotation marks in particular.

Listing 6.24: Update Database Using ADO.NET (ADOUpdate.aspx)

```
<%@ Page Language="VB" %>
<%@ import Namespace="System.Data.OleDb" %>
<script runat="server">
 Public Sub Page_Load()
 End Sub

 Public Sub Updating(sender As Object, e As EventArgs)
  Dim StudentID As String
  Dim NewAddress As String
  StudentID = textbox1.Value
  NewAddress = textbox2.Value
  Dim sql As String
  Dim dbconn=New OleDbConnection _
    ("Provider=Microsoft.ACE.OLEDB.12.0; data source=" & _
     server.mappath("StudentDB.accdb"))
  dbconn.Open()

  sql = "UPDATE tblStudent SET StudentAddress=" & _
        "'" & NewAddress & "'" & " " & _
        "WHERE StudentID=" & "'" & StudentID & "'"

  Dim dbcomm=New OleDbCommand(sql,dbconn)
  Dim dbread=dbcomm.ExecuteReader()
  dbread.Close()
  dbconn.Close()
  label1.Text = "Thank you for updating ...."
 End Sub
</script>
<html><head><title></title></head>
<body>
  <form runat="server">
   Type the student number for updating:
   <input id="textbox1" type="text" runat="server" /> <br />
   Type the new address for the student:
   <input id="textbox2" type ="text" runat ="server" /> <br />
   <input id="submit1" type="submit" value="Change" runat="server"
          onserverclick="Updating" /><br />
   <asp:Label id="label1" runat="server"></asp:Label>
 </form></body></html>
```

6.2.10.4 Use Data of Database for Decision   Listing 6.25 (ADODecision.aspx) is an example to demonstrate the use of data in the database for decision making. In this application, the system can help the decision maker to make an action of the graduation auditing process depending on the enrollment year of a particular student.

Listing 6.25: Use Database for Decision Making (`ADODecision.aspx`)

```
<%@ Page Language="VB" %>
<%@ import Namespace="System.Data.OleDb" %>
<script runat="server">
  Public Sub Page_Load()
  End Sub

  Public Sub Decision(ByVal sender As Object, ByVal e As EventArgs)
   Dim sql As String
   Dim StudentID As String
   Dim StudentYear As Integer
   StudentID = textbox1.Value
   Dim dbconn=New OleDbConnection _
       ("Provider=Microsoft.ACE.OLEDB.12.0; data source=" & _
       server.mappath("StudentDB.accdb"))
   dbconn.Open()

   sql = "SELECT * FROM tblStudent WHERE StudentID =" & _
       "'" & StudentID & "'"

   Dim dbcomm=New OleDbCommand(sql,dbconn)
   Dim dbread=dbcomm.ExecuteReader()

   While dbread.Read()
      StudentYear = Val(dbread("StudentEnrolYear").ToString())
   End While

   dbread.Close()
   dbconn.Close()

   If (StudentYear = 0) Then
     label1.Text = " "
     label2.Text = "Sorry, the record is not found.... Try again...."
   Else
     If (StudentYear < 2016) Then
        Option1()
     Else
        Option2()
     End If
   End If
 End Sub

 Public Sub Option1()
   label1.Text = "This student is subject to graduation auditing!"
   label2.Text = " "
 End Sub

 Public Sub Option2()
   label1.Text = " "
   label2.Text = "This student is not graduating!"
 End Sub
</script>
<html><head><title></title></head>
<body>
 <form runat="server">
   Type the student number for process:
   <input id="textbox1" type="text" runat="server" /> <br />
```

```
<input id="submit1" type="submit" value="Find Action" runat="server"
       onserverclick="Decision" /> <br />
<asp:Label id="label1" ForeColor="Red" runat="server"></asp:Label> <br />
<asp:Label id="label2" ForeColor="Green" runat="server"></asp:Label>
</form></body></html>
```

6.3 ASP.NET with C#.NET

This section introduces ASP.NET with C#.NET (or C#). One can edit, compile, and execute an ASP.NET with C#.NET program in the Microsoft Visual Studio environment. The interested reader is referred to the part of ASP.NET with VB.NET for the steps of the general procedure of editing an ASP.NET with a C#.NET program and viewing the execution result. Note that the name of the folder storing the ASP.NET programs must not contain the # sign.

Alternatively, when the application project is large, one might want to create a website project for the application in the Microsoft Visual Studio programming environment to involve various resources. Figure 6.14 shows the instruction to use the Microsoft Visual Studio environment to create and to view the execution result of a website application of ASP.NET with C#.NET.

6.3.1 C# Programming with ASP.NET Web Controls

The structure of ASP.NET programs with C# is the same as that with VB.NET. In Microsoft Visual Studio, the user interface design/creation for ASP.NET programs with C# is the same as for ASP.NET programs with VB.NET. The concept of HTML control and web control discussed in ASP.NET with VB.NET is applicable to ASP.NET with C#. The only difference is that the actual code is C# instead of VB.NET.

Listing 6.26 is the C# version of HelloWorld.aspx in Listing 6.1.

Listing 6.26: Example of ASP.NET with C# (HelloWorld.aspx)

```
1   <%@ Page Language="C#" %>
2   <script runat="server">

3       public void Page_Load()
4       {
5           label1.Text="Hello World - ASP.NET with C#.NET!";
6       }

7   </script>
8   <html><head><title></title></head>
9   <body>
10      <form id="form1" method="post" runat="server">
11          <asp:Label id="label1" runat="server"></asp:Label>
12      </form>
13  </body>
14  </html>
```

Start Microsoft Visual Studio

Click on [File]

Choose [New Web Site...]
    or [Open Web Site...]
    for an existing Web Site

In New Web Site Window:
    choose [Visual C#]

choose [ASP .NET Web Site]

specify your folder for the Web Site
    or use the default name;
    click on [OK].

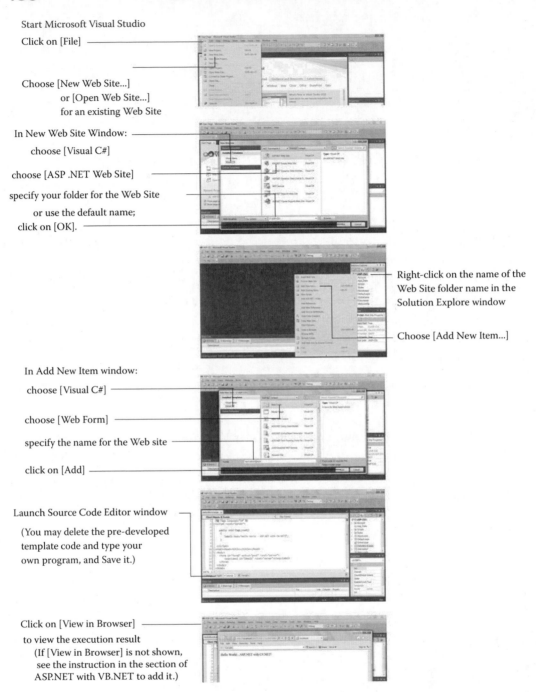

Right-click on the name of the
Web Site folder name in the
Solution Explore window

Choose [Add New Item...]

In Add New Item window:
    choose [Visual C#]

    choose [Web Form]

    specify the name for the Web site

    click on [Add]

Launch Source Code Editor window

(You may delete the pre-developed
template code and type your
own program, and Save it.)

Click on [View in Browser]

to view the execution result
    (If [View in Browser] is not shown,
    see the instruction in the section of
    ASP.NET with VB.NET to add it.)

Figure 6.14 Create and execute website application of ASP.NET with C#.NET.

The main differences between the C# version in Listing 6.26 and the VB.NET version in Listing 6.1 are:

1. In Listing 6.26, the first line, <%@ Page Language="C#" %>, indicates that the programming language to be used is C#. In Listing 6.1, the first line, <%@ Page Language="VB" %>, indicates the programming language is VB.NET.
2. The Page _ Load() defined in Listing 6.26 runs every time when the page, which is defined by the HTML block, is loaded. The C# Page _ Load() in Listing 6.26 is a void function, while the VB.NET Page _ Load() in Listing 6.1 is a subroutine.
3. In Listing 6.26, the letters "P" and "L" in "Page _ Load" in line **3** and the letter "T" in "Text" in line **5** must be capital letters. In ASP.NET with C#, the first letter of all control properties must be uppercase. This rule is not for VB.NET.

Listing 6.27 is the C# version of the example in Listing 6.2.

Listing 6.27: ASP.NET Program (SubmitButton.aspx) with HTML Submit Button Control

```
1    <%@ Page Language="C#" %>
2    <script runat="server">
3       public void Page_Load()
4       {
5       }

6       public void HelloWorld(Object sender, EventArgs e)
7       {
8          label1.Text="Hello World!";
9       }

10   </script>
11   <html><head><title></title></head>
12   <body>
13   <form id="form1" method="post" runat="server">
14   <input id="submit1" type="submit" value="Greeting"
15          runat="server" onserverclick="HelloWorld" />
16   <asp:Label id="label1" font-names ="Forte"
17             font-size ="48" runat="server"></asp:Label>
18   </form>
19   </body>
20   </html>
```

In line **6** of Listing 6.27, the function corresponding to the button-click of the button "Greeting" must be the fixed arguments (Object sender, EventArgs e). The name of the function in line **6** must be identical to the value of the onserverclick attribute in line **15.** Since the Page _ Load() function in lines **3–5** is empty, it is optional.

Listing 6.28 shows an example of ASP.NET with C# that involves various HTML controls, including the HTML submit button, textbox, checkbox, and radio button controls. As a comparison, Listing 6.29 shows a similar example that employs various web controls, including the `Button`, `TextBox`, `CheckBoxList`, and `RadioButtonList` web controls. It demonstrates that web controls can have more advanced features than HTML controls do.

Listing 6.28: ASP.NET Program (`Coffee1.aspx`) with HTML Controls

```
<%@ Page Language="C#" %>
<script runat="server">

public void Order(Object sender, EventArgs e)
{
 label1.Text = "Thank you! " + textbox1.Value + ". ";

 if ((chk1.Checked) && (chk2.Checked))
 { label1.Text = label1.Text + "You have ordered coffee with sugar and milk.";}
 else if (chk1.Checked)
      { label1.Text = label1.Text + "You have ordered coffee with sugar. ";}
      else if (chk2.Checked)
           {label1.Text = label1.Text + "You have ordered coffee with milk. ";}
           else
           {label1.Text = label1.Text + "You have ordered black coffee. ";}

 if (rad1.Checked)
 {label1.Text = label1.Text + "You will pay with cash.";}
 else if (rad2.Checked)
      {label1.Text = label1.Text + "You will pay with debit card.";}
      else
      {label1.Text = label1.Text + "You will pay with other method.";}
}

</script>
<html><head><title></title></head>
<body>
  <form id="form1" method="post" runat="server">
  <p>
  Name:
  <input id="textbox1" type="text" runat="server" />
  </p>
  <p>
  How do you like your coffee:
  <input id="chk1" type="checkbox" name="checkbox1" runat="server" />
  With sugar
  <input id="chk2" type="checkbox" name="checkbox1" runat="server" />
  With milk
  </p>
  <p>
  Payment Methods:
  <input id="rad1" type="radio" name="radio1" runat="server" />
  Cash
  <input id="rad2" type="radio" name="radio1" runat="server" />
  Debit card
  </p>
  <p>
  <input id="submit1" type="submit" value="Submit" runat="server"
```

```
      onserverclick="Order" />
   </p>
   <p>
   <asp:Label id="label1" runat="server"></asp:Label>
   </p>
  </form>
</body>
</html>
```

Listing 6.29: ASP.NET Program (`Coffee2.aspx`) with Web Controls

```
<%@ Page Language="C#" %>
<script runat="server">

public void Order(Object sender, EventArgs e)
{
 TextBox1.Visible = false;
 Label2.Visible = false;
 CheckBoxList1.Visible = false;
 Label3.Visible = false;
 RadioButtonList1.Visible = false;
 Button1.Visible = false;

 Label1.Text = "Thank you! " + TextBox1.Text + ". ";

 if ((CheckBoxList1.Items[0].Selected) &&
   (CheckBoxList1.Items[1].Selected))
 {Label1.Text = Label1.Text + "You have ordered coffee with sugar and milk.";}
 else if (CheckBoxList1.Items[0].Selected)
      {Label1.Text = Label1.Text + "You have ordered coffee with sugar. ";}
      else if (CheckBoxList1.Items[1].Selected)
          {Label1.Text = Label1.Text + "You have ordered coffee with milk. ";}
          else
             {Label1.Text = Label1.Text + "You have ordered black coffee. ";}

  Label1.Text = Label1.Text + "You will pay with " +
                RadioButtonList1.SelectedItem.Text + ".";
}

</script>
<html><head><title></title></head>
<body>
  <form id="form1" method="post" runat="server">
  <p>
  <asp:Label id="Label1" runat="server">Name:</asp:Label>
  <asp:TextBox id="TextBox1" runat="server"></asp:TextBox>
  </p>

  <p>
  <asp:Label id="Label2" runat="server">How do you like your coffee:
  </asp:Label>
  <asp:CheckBoxList id="CheckBoxList1" runat="server">
   <asp:ListItem Value="Sugar">Sugar</asp:ListItem>
   <asp:ListItem Value="Milk">Milk</asp:ListItem>
  </asp:CheckBoxList>
  </p>
  <p>
  <asp:Label id="Label3" runat="server">Payment Methods:
```

```
  </asp:Label>
  <asp:RadioButtonList id="RadioButtonList1" runat="server">
   <asp:ListItem Value="cash" Selected="True">Cash</asp:ListItem>
   <asp:ListItem Value="debit card">Debit Card</asp:ListItem>
  </asp:RadioButtonList>
  </p>
  <p>
  <asp:Button id="Button1" onclick="Order" runat="server" Text="Button">
  </asp:Button>
  </p>
 </form>
</body>
</html>
```

In Listing 6.29, once the user clicks on the button, the Order function, which is specified in the onclick attribute of the Button control, will be executed. In the Order function, all web controls, except for Label1, have the Visible property set to false to make them invisible. Label1 will display the user's selections for the CheckBoxList and RadioButtonList controls. Each list item in the CheckBoxList control can be accessed through an array index, such as [0] and [1]. Each list item includes the Selected property, the Text property, and the Value property. The SelectedItem object of the RadioButtonList control corresponds to the selected list item in the RadioButtonList list and includes the Selected property, which is always true; the Text property; and the Value property. For all list items of the CheckBoxList and RadioButtonList controls, the property Selected="True" means the default choice. For a RadioButtonList control, at most one list item can be set to the default choice (Selected="True").

As with ASP.NET with VB.NET, validation controls can be used in the same fashion in ASP.NET with C#.

6.3.2 Code-Behind Programming

Currently, C# only supports ASP.NET code-behind programming for the ASP. NET default setting AutoEventWireup="True". Code-behind programming separates the user interface and the C# source codes. The user interface design is specified in the .aspx file and the corresponding C# source code is in the .cs file. Listing 6.30(a) shows an example of the .aspx file for code-behind programming, and Listing 6.30(b) shows the corresponding .cs file.

Listing 6.30(a): Example of Code-Behind Programming (Greeting2.aspx)

```
<%@ Page Language="C#" Inherits="DisplayMessage"
    CodeFile="Greeting2.cs" %>
<html><head><title></title></head>
<body>
 <form runat="server">
  Name:
  <input id="textbox1" type="text" runat="server" /> <br />
  <input id="submit1" type="submit" value="Submit"
```

```
            runat="server" onserverclick="Greeting" />   <br />
        <asp:Label id="label1" runat="server"
            forecolor="Green"></asp:Label>
    </form>
</body></html>
```

Listing 6.30(b): C# Code (`Greeting2.cs`) Called by `Greeting2.aspx`

```
1 using System;
2 public partial class DisplayMessage: System.Web.UI.Page
3 {
4     public void Greeting(object sender, EventArgs e)
5     {
6         label1.Text = "Hello, " + textbox1.Value + "!";
7     }
8 }
```

The `Greeting2.aspx` program is almost identical to the `Greeting.aspx` program in Listing 6.12(a), except that the `Page Language` attribute in the first line is C#. In the first line of the `Greeting2.aspx` program, the `CodeFile` attribute specifies the file name of the C# source code, and the `Inherits` attribute specifies the class name defined in C#. As shown in line **2** of the `Greeting2.cs` program, the class `DisplayMessage` must be `public` as well as `partial`, and it must inherit the class `System.Web.UI.Page` in the `System` namespace. Line **1** of the `Greeting2.cs` program indicates the `System` namespace will be used in this program. The function named `Greeting` specified in the `onserverclick` attribute of the submit button in the `Greeting2.aspx` program must be a `public` method of the class defined in the `Greeting2.cs` program.

The main advantage of code-behind programming is that the user interface is separated from the C# source codes. The programmer may change the C# source codes only, without touching the user interface.

6.3.3 Server-Side File Processing

Server-side programming often involves data processing on the web server. In this subsection, we examine how ASP.NET with C# accesses and updates data files stored on the web server. We use an example of an ASP.NET program that allows the user to input feedback on a web page and to view the summary of all previous feedback stored in a data file. The ASP.NET program (`Feedback1.aspx`) is shown in Listing 6.31.

Listing 6.31: ASP.NET Program of Server-Side File Processing (`Feedback1.aspx`)

```
1  <%@ Page Language="C#" %>
2  <%@ import Namespace="System" %>
3  <%@ import Namespace="System.IO" %>
4  <script runat="server">

5      public void WriteToFile(Object sender, EventArgs e)
6      {
```

```
7     // Set the file folder to that of this .aspx file
8     string folder = AppDomain.CurrentDomain.BaseDirectory;

9     // Open file, write user's feedback to file, and close file
10    StreamWriter write_file;
11    string file_name = folder + "feedback.txt";
12    FileInfo file_info = new FileInfo(file_name);
13    if (file_info.Exists == false)
14    {
15        write_file = File.CreateText(file_name);
16    }
17    else
18    {
19        write_file = File.AppendText(file_name);
20    }
21    write_file.WriteLine("Time:" + DateTime.Now.ToString());
22    write_file.WriteLine("Feedback Type:" +
          RadioButtonList1.SelectedItem.Text);
23    write_file.WriteLine("Name:" + TextBox1.Text);
24    write_file.WriteLine("Email:" + TextBox2.Text);
25    write_file.WriteLine("Message:");
26    write_file.WriteLine(TextBox3.Text);
27    write_file.WriteLine("---------------------------");
28    write_file.Close();

29    // Display the confirmation message and hide all other controls
30    Label2.Visible = false;
31    Label3.Visible = false;
32    Label4.Visible = false;
33    Label5.Visible = false;
34    Label6.Visible = false;
35    RadioButtonList1.Visible = false;
36    TextBox1.Visible = false;
37    TextBox2.Visible = false;
38    TextBox3.Visible = false;
39    Button1.Visible = false;
40    Button2.Visible = false;
41    Label1.Text = "Thank you for your feedback! " +
42    "Your following feedback has been recorded:<br />" +
43    "Name:" + TextBox1.Text + "<br />" + "Email:" + TextBox2.Text + "<br />" +
44    "Feedback Type:" + RadioButtonList1.SelectedItem.Text + "<br />" +
45    "Message:<br />" + TextBox3.Text;
46  }

47  public void ReadFromFile(Object sender, EventArgs e)
48  {
49      // Set the file folder to that of this .aspx file
50      string folder = AppDomain.CurrentDomain.BaseDirectory;

51      // Open the file, read all users' feedbacks from the file,
52      // Display only time and feedback type of each feedback message
53      StreamReader read_file;
54      string file_name = folder + "feedback.txt";
55      FileInfo file_info = new FileInfo(file_name);
56      string line;
57      if (file_info.Exists == true)
58      {
59          read_file = File.OpenText(file_name);
```

```
60              Label1.Text = "";
61              while (read_file.Peek() > 0)
62              {
63                  line = read_file.ReadLine();
64          if (line.StartsWith("Time:") || line.StartsWith("Feedback Type:"))
65                  {
66                      Label1.Text = Label1.Text + line + "<br />";
67                  }
68              }
69              read_file.Close();
70          }

71      // Hide all other controls
72      Label2.Visible = false;
73      Label3.Visible = false;
74      Label4.Visible = false;
75      Label5.Visible = false;
76      Label6.Visible = false;
77      RadioButtonList1.Visible = false;
78      TextBox1.Visible = false;
79      TextBox2.Visible = false;
80      TextBox3.Visible = false;
81      Button1.Visible = false;
82      Button2.Visible = false;
83  }

84  </script>
85  <html>
86  <head><title></title></head>
87  <body>
88    <form method="post" runat="server">
89        <asp:Label ID="Label1" runat="server" Text="Feedback Form"
              Font-Size="Large">
90        </asp:Label>
91        <br />
92        <asp:Label ID="Label2" runat="server" Text="Your feedback is very
93              important to us and we read every message that we receive."
                Font-Size="Large">
94        </asp:Label>
95        <br />
96        <asp:Label ID="Label3" runat="server" Text="Feedback Type:">
97        </asp:Label>
98        <asp:RadioButtonList ID="RadioButtonList1" runat="server"
99              RepeatDirection="Horizontal">
100              <asp:ListItem>Request</asp:ListItem>
101              <asp:ListItem>Complaint</asp:ListItem>
102              <asp:ListItem>Comment</asp:ListItem>
103      </asp:RadioButtonList>
104      <br />
105      <asp:Label ID="Label4" runat="server" Text="Name:">
106      </asp:Label>
107      <asp:TextBox id="TextBox1" runat="server">
108      </asp:TextBox>
109      <br />
110      <asp:Label ID="Label5" runat="server" Text="Email:">
111      </asp:Label>
112      <asp:TextBox ID="TextBox2" runat="server">
113      </asp:TextBox>
```

```
114        <br />
115        <asp:Label ID="Label6" runat="server" Text="Message:">
116        </asp:Label>
117        <br />
118        <asp:TextBox ID="TextBox3" runat="server" Columns="50" Rows="10"
119            TextMode="MultiLine">
120        </asp:TextBox>
121        <br />
122        <asp:Button id="Button1" onclick="WriteToFile" runat="server"
123            Text="Submit Feedback">
124        </asp:Button>
125        <asp:Button id="Button2" onclick="ReadFromFile" runat="server"
126            Text="Display Previous Feedback Summary">
127        </asp:Button>
128    </form>
129 </body>
130 </html>
```

After the client loads the ASP.NET program (Feedback1.aspx) in Listing 6.31, the browser displays the interface in Figure 6.15 for the user to input. When the user clicks the Submit Feedback button (lines **122–124**), the subroutine WriteToFile() (line **5**) is called. This subroutine writes the user's input to the file and displays a confirmation message while hiding all other controls, as shown in Figure 6.16. The data stored in the file include the time and type of the user feedback as well as the user's name, e-mail, and message. When the user clicks on the Display Previous Feedback Summary button (lines **125–127**), the subroutine

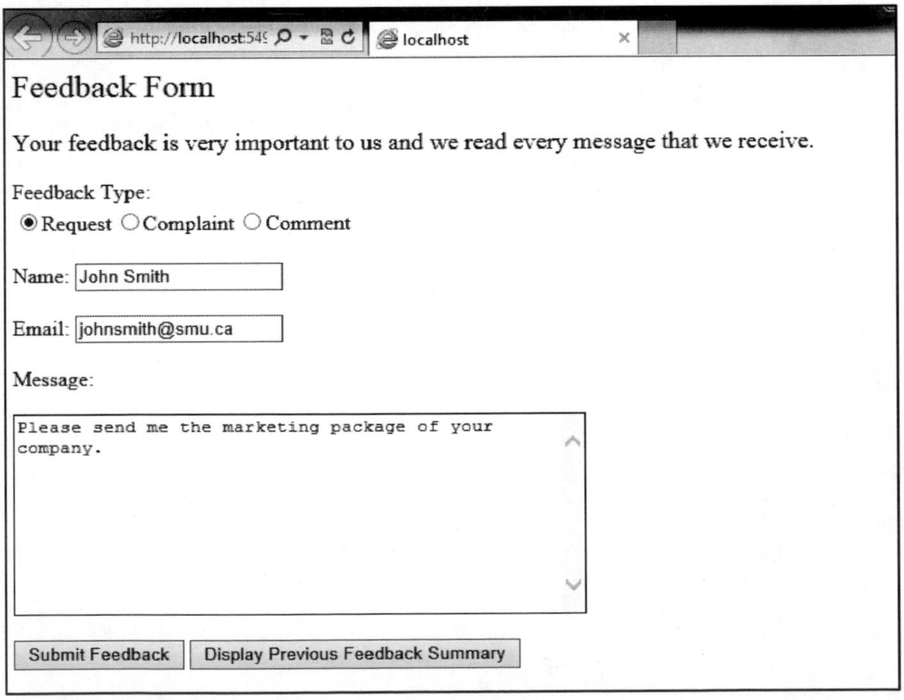

Figure 6.15 User interface of Feedback1.aspx.

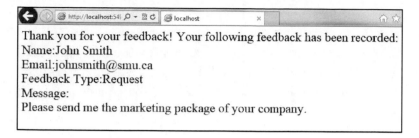

Figure 6.16 Output of Feedback1.aspx after the user clicks on the Submit Feedback button.

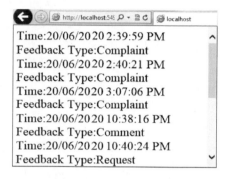

Figure 6.17 Output of Feedback1.aspx when the user clicks on the Display Previous Feedback Summary button.

ReadFromFile() (line **47**) is called. This subroutine reads all previous users' feedback from the file and displays the feedback type and time, as shown in Figure 6.17.

As shown in lines **5–83**, four classes are needed for server-side file processing.

- Classes StreamWriter (line **10**) and StreamReader (line **53**) represent the data file for writing and reading, respectively. The WriteLine() method of StreamWriter (lines **21–28**) writes a line to the file. The ReadLine() method of StreamReader (line **63**) reads a line from the file. Before calling the ReadLine() method, the Peek() method (line **61**) must be called to make sure that the end of the file has not already been reached.

- Class File (lines **15, 19,** and **59**) defines the operations for opening the data file. The File.CreateText() method (line **15**) creates the file for writing if it does not exist. The File.AppendText() method (line **19**) opens the file for appending, where the existing content of the file will be kept and new content will be written at the end of the file. The File.OpenText() method (line **59**) opens the file for reading. All of these three methods require the full file path of the file to be opened. The folder where the ASP.NET program Feedback1.aspx and data file locate can be obtained from AppDomain. CurrentDomain.BaseDirectory (lines **8** and **50**).

- Class FileInfo (lines **12** and **25**) holds information about the data file, such as whether it exists, to avoid errors.

To access these four classes, the ASP.NET program needs to import the System namespace and the System.IO namespace, as shown in lines **2** and **3**.

Listings 6.32(a) and 6.32(b) are the code-behind version of the ASP.NET program Feedback1.aspx. The ASP.NET program Feedback2.aspx shown in Listing 6.32(a) contains the user interface and calls the source code in Feedback2.cs, shown in Listing 6.32(b).

Listing 6.32(a): Code-Behind: User Interface for Server-Side File Processing (Feedback2.aspx)

```
<%@ Page Language="C#" Inherits="FileProcessingClass"
   CodeFile="feedback2.cs" %>
<html>
<head><title></title></head>
<body>
    <form method="post" runat="server">
        <asp:Label ID="Label1" runat="server" Text="Feedback Form"
           Font-Size="Large">
        </asp:Label>
        <br />
        <asp:Label ID="Label2" runat="server" Text="Your feedback is very
           important to us and we read every message that we receive."
           Font-Size="Large">
        </asp:Label>
        <br />
        <asp:Label ID="Label3" runat="server" Text="Feedback Type:">
        </asp:Label>
        <asp:RadioButtonList ID="RadioButtonList1" runat="server"
              RepeatDirection="Horizontal">
              <asp:ListItem>Request</asp:ListItem>
              <asp:ListItem>Complaint</asp:ListItem>
              <asp:ListItem>Comment</asp:ListItem>
        </asp:RadioButtonList>
        <br />
        <asp:Label ID="Label4" runat="server" Text="Name:">
        </asp:Label>
        <asp:TextBox id="TextBox1" runat="server">
        </asp:TextBox>
        <br />
        <asp:Label ID="Label5" runat="server" Text="Email:">
        </asp:Label>
        <asp:TextBox ID="TextBox2" runat="server">
        </asp:TextBox>
        <br />
        <asp:Label ID="Label6" runat="server" Text="Message:">
        </asp:Label>
        <br />
        <asp:TextBox ID="TextBox3" runat="server" Columns="50" Rows="10"
              TextMode="MultiLine">
        </asp:TextBox>
        <br />
        <asp:Button id="Button1" onclick="WriteToFile" runat="server"
              Text="Submit Feedback">
        </asp:Button>
        <asp:Button id="Button2" onclick="ReadFromFile" runat="server"
```

```
                    Text="Display Previous Feedback Summary">
            </asp:Button>
        </form>
    </body>
    </html>
```

Listing 6.32(b): C# Code (Feedback2.cs) Called by Feedback2.aspx

```csharp
using System;
using System.IO;

public partial class FileProcessingClass: System.Web.UI.Page
{
    public void Page_Load()
    {
    }

    public void WriteToFile(Object sender, EventArgs e)
    {
        // Set the file folder to that of this .aspx file
        string folder = AppDomain.CurrentDomain.BaseDirectory;

        // Open file, write user's feedback to file, and close file
        StreamWriter write_file;
        string file_name = folder + "feedback.txt";
        FileInfo file_info = new FileInfo(file_name);
        if (file_info.Exists == false)
        {
            write_file = File.CreateText(file_name);
        }
        else
        {
            write_file = File.AppendText(file_name);

        }
        write_file.WriteLine("Time:" + DateTime.Now.ToString());
        write_file.WriteLine("Feedback Type:" +
           RadioButtonList1.SelectedItem.Text);
        write_file.WriteLine("Name:" + TextBox1.Text);
        write_file.WriteLine("Email:" + TextBox2.Text);
        write_file.WriteLine("Message:");
        write_file.WriteLine(TextBox3.Text);
        write_file.WriteLine("----------------------------");
        write_file.Close();

        // Display the confirmation message and hide all other controls
        Label2.Visible = false;
        Label3.Visible = false;
        Label4.Visible = false;
        Label5.Visible = false;
        Label6.Visible = false;
        RadioButtonList1.Visible = false;
        TextBox1.Visible = false;
        TextBox2.Visible = false;
        TextBox3.Visible = false;
        Button1.Visible = false;
        Button2.Visible = false;
        Label1.Text = "Thank you for your feedback! "+
```

```
                "Your following feedback has been recorded:<br />" +
                "Name:" + TextBox1.Text + "<br />" + "Email:" + TextBox2.Text +
                "<br />" + "Feedback Type:" + RadioButtonList1.SelectedItem.Text
                + "<br />" + "Message:<br />" + TextBox3.Text;
        }

        public void ReadFromFile(Object sender, EventArgs e)
        {
            // Set the file folder to that of this .aspx file
            string folder = AppDomain.CurrentDomain.BaseDirectory;

            // Open the file, read all users' feedbacks from the file,
            // Display only time and feedback type of each feedback message
            StreamReader read_file;
            string file_name = folder + "feedback.txt";
            FileInfo file_info = new FileInfo(file_name);
            string line;
            if (file_info.Exists == true)
            {
                read_file = File.OpenText(file_name);
                Label1.Text = "";
                while (read_file.Peek() > 0)
                {
                    line = read_file.ReadLine();
                    if (line.StartsWith("Time:") ||
                      line.StartsWith("Feedback Type:"))
                    {
                        Label1.Text = Label1.Text + line + "<br />";
                    }
                }
                read_file.Close();
            }

            // Hide all other controls
            Label2.Visible = false;
            Label3.Visible = false;
            Label4.Visible = false;
            Label5.Visible = false;
            Label6.Visible = false;
            RadioButtonList1.Visible = false;
            TextBox1.Visible = false;
            TextBox2.Visible = false;
            TextBox3.Visible = false;
            Button1.Visible = false;
            Button2.Visible = false;
        }
    }
```

6.3.4   <asp:SqlDataSource> *Control for Database Processing*

In the ASP.NET with VB.NET section, we have introduced ADO.NET for database processing. Clearly, ADO.NET can also be incorporated in an application of APS.NET with C#.NET. To avoid unnecessary replications of features of APS. NET, we discuss the <asp:SqlDataSource> control for database processing in this section. This control uses ADO.NET to interact with any database supported by ADO.NET. The `<asp:SqlDataSource>` control allows the programmer to develop an ASP.NET application to access and manipulate the database for simple applications without using ADO.NET explicitly. The default DBMS used for the `<asp:SqlDataSource>` control is the SQL server. The Microsoft Visual Studio environment might have built in limited components of the SQL server for demonstrative practices, but does not support its essential features unless the SQL server DBMS (database management system) is fully installed. In this section, we use a Microsoft Access database as an example to explain the use of the `<asp:SqlDataSource>` control because Microsoft Access is commonly available in comparison with the SQL server. As Microsoft Access is not the default DBMS of ASP.NET, one needs to set the connection specifically for a Microsoft Access database. Clearly, the knowledge learned here can be applied to setting connections for any other DBMS.

The Microsoft Access database used in the present example is the one used in Subsection 6.2.10 and is displayed in Figure 6.11. This small database is named `StudentDB.accdb` and contains a table of student data named `tblStudent`. The following are the steps to creating an ASP.NET application with the `<asp:SqlDataSource>` control to access the Microsoft Access database:

Step 1. Create a website project, say, `ASP-CS`, following the procedure shown in Figure 6.14.

Step 2. In the `Solution Explorer` window of the website project, find the `App _ Data` directory. Right-click on the `[App _ Data]` directory and choose `[Open Folder in Windows Explorer]`. You can add your Microsoft Access database, say, `StudentDB.accdb`, as illustrated in Figure 6.18.

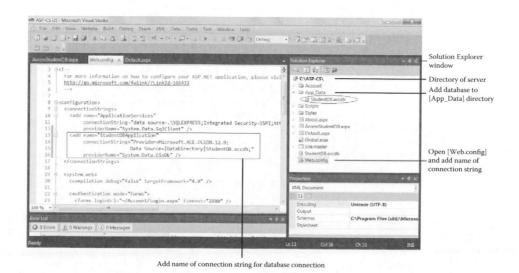

Add name of connection string for database connection

Figure 6.18   Set and connect database for `<asp:SqlDataSource>` control.

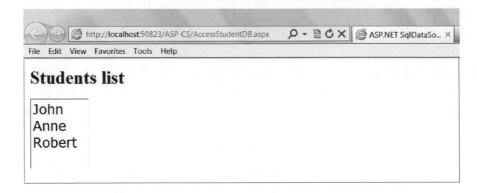

Figure 6.19 Execution result of `AccessStudentDB.aspx`. (The sample data of the Access database are displayed in Figure 6.11.)

Step 3. In the `Solution Explorer` window of the website project, find the `Web.config` file (see Figure 6.18) and double-click on it to open it. Find the `<connectionStrings>` tag and insert the program shown in Listing 6.33 to set the database connection. If the `<connectionStrings>` tag is not found, you can add one along with its closing tag.

Step 4. Right-click on the root directory of the project (`C:\ASP-CS\` in this example) in the `Solution Explorer` window, choose [`Add New Item...`], and add your ASP.NET program, say, `AccessStudentDB.aspx`, as listed in Listing 6.34.

Step 5. View the execution result of the ASP.NET program by clicking on [`View in Browser`]. The result of this example is shown in Figure 6.19.

Listing 6.33: Edit `Web.config` File to Set Connection to Microsoft Access Database

```
1 <connectionStrings>

2   <add name="StudentDBApplication"
3       connectionString="Provider=Microsoft.ACE.OLEDB.12.0;
4                        Data Source=|DataDirectory|StudentDB.accdb;"
5       providerName="System.Data.OleDb" />

6 </connectionStrings>
```

Listing 6.34: Example of `<asp:SqlDataSource>` Control (`AccessStudentDB.aspx`)

```
1 <%@ Page language="C#" %>
2 <html>
3 <head>
4   <title>ASP.NET SqlDataSource Example</title>
5 </head>
6 <body>
7 <form id="form1" runat="server">
```

```
 8  <asp:SqlDataSource
 9  ID="StudentDB"
10  runat="server"
11  ConnectionString="<%$ ConnectionStrings:StudentDBApplication%>"
12  ProviderName="<%$ ConnectionStrings:StudentDBApplication.ProviderName %>"
13  SelectCommand="SELECT * FROM tblStudent">
14  </asp:SqlDataSource>

15  <h2>Students list</h2>

16  <asp:ListBox
17      id="ListBox1"
18      runat="server"
19      Font-Names="Verdana" Font-Size="18pt" ForeColor="Blue"
20      DataTextField="StudentName"
21      DataSourceID="StudentDB">
22  </asp:ListBox>
23 </form></body></html>
```

Listing 6.33 is to configure a `SqlDataSource` control. Line **2** adds the name of a `connectionStrings` element. This allows any ASP.NET program in the project to use the `connectionStrings` element. In this example, the element is named `StudentDBApplication`. Lines **3** and **4** are a single sentence to set the value of `connectionString` for the Microsoft Access database. Here, `StudentDB.accdb` is the name of the Microsoft Access database used for the `SqlDataSource` control. Finally, line **5** sets the value of `providerName` to `System.Data.OleDb` for a Microsoft Access database.

Listing 6.34 is the ASP.NET program with the `<asp:SqlDataSource>` control, which is configured as `StudentDBApplication` in the `Web.config` file. Line **9** declares the data source ID (`StudentDB` in this example), which is used in line **21** for data access. Lines **11** and **12** apply the name of the `connectionStrings` element stored in the `Web.config` file. Line **13** declares the SQL code for the program. In this example, the `tbleStudent` table is retrieved. As a simple example, this ASP.NET program uses the `<asp:ListBox>` control to present a list of the student names that are retrieved by the SQL code. Line **20** declares the attribute name (`StudentName`) of the data table for the data presentation. Other lines of the program are rather straightforward.

6.4 Debugging

Debugging ASP.NET programs is a little different from that for other languages as both server controls and VB.NET/C#.NET are involved. In addition, debugging an ASP.NET program in the Microsoft Visual Studio environment is not easy for beginners.

Common syntax errors include:

- Typos or misspelling a word
- Omitting a symbol (e.g., missing one side of parentheses)

- Violating format
- Using an undefined user-defined variable

Logical errors or runtime errors often occur when the computer performs wrong operations or does not perform as expected. To debug logical errors, you should use data samples to test the program based on the output of the program:

1. Ensure the setting of the data file and database used in the program is correct.
2. Exercise every possible option to check the computer outputs to see if the program does only as expected. Examine all if-statements to find possible options.
3. If a program is "dead," you must terminate it by closing the web page. This is more likely caused by an endless loop. You should check for loop and if-statements.
4. When debugging ASP.NET as server-side programs, you need to save your programs once you make changes to the program and reopen it. In Microsoft Internet Explorer, you might need to delete browsing history from time to time.

Chapter 6 Exercises

1. Fill blanks in the following ASP.NET program and sketch the screenshots of the page and its execution:

```
1  <%@ Page _____>
2  <script _____="server">
3    Public Sub Page_Load()
4    End Sub

5    Public Sub _____(sender As Object, e As EventArgs)
6        Dim TotalPrice As Integer
7        label1.text = ""
8        if (_____.checked) then
9            TotalPrice = TotalPrice + 10
10       end if
11       if (_____.checked) then
12            TotalPrice = TotalPrice + 20
13       end if
14       if (_____.checked) then
15            TotalPrice = TotalPrice + 30
16       end if
17       label1.text="Total Price is:  $" & TotalPrice
18   End Sub
19   _____

20 <html><head><title></title></head>
21 <body>
22    <form id="form1" method="post" runat="server">
23        Select:
24        <input id="check1" type="checkbox" name="checkbox1"
25                runat="server" />
```

```
26        Computer
27        <input id="check2" type="checkbox" name="checkbox1"
28              runat="server" />
29        Printer
30        <input id="check3" type="checkbox" name="checkbox1"
31              runat="server" />
32        Laptop
33        <br />
34        <input id="submit1" type="submit"
35              value="Submit to view the total price"
36              runat="server" onserverclick="abc" />
37        <br />
38        <asp:Label id="_____" runat="server"></asp:Label>
39   _____
40  </body>
41  </html>
```

2. Fill blanks in the following ASP.NET program and the called VB.NET code
   and sketch the screenshots of the page and its execution:

```
1  <%@ Page Language="VB" Inherits="_____"
2       CodeFile="_____" %>
3  <html><head><title></title></head>
4  <body>
5       <form id="form1" method="post" runat="server">
6       <br />
7       Add your email address to join the group:
8       <br />
9       <_____ id="TextBox1" runat="server" />
10      <br />
11      <asp:Button id="Button1" onclick="joingroup"
12                  runat="server"
13                  text="Join the group" />
14      <br />
15      <asp:Label id="Label1" runat="server" forecolor="Red" />
16      </form>
17  </body>
18  </html>
```

```
1  Imports System
2  _____ Class JoinGroup
3                    _____ System.Web.UI.Page
4      Public Sub _____ (sender As Object, e As EventArgs)
5         Textbox1.visible=false
6         Button1._____=false
7         Label1._____="The email address " & _
8             Textbox1._____ & "has been added " & _
9             "to the group"
10     End Sub
11  _____
```

3. Use ASP.NET with VB.NET or C#.NET to develop the following web application project for hotel reservations.

Online Reservation

Reservation Information

Check-In Date: [Should be the ASP.NET Calendar Control]

Check-Out Date: [Should be the ASP.NET Calendar Control]

Number of Guests: 1 ▾

Number of Rooms: 1 ▾

Contact Information

Last Name: _____

First Name: _____

Street Number: _____

City: _____

Province/State: ____

Country: Canada ▾

Postal Code _____

Phone Number: _____

E-mail Address: _____

Credit Card Information

Credit Card: ◯ Visa   ◯ MasterCard   ◯ American Express   ◯ Discover

Name on Credit Card: _____

Credit Card Number: _____ (No spaces or dashes, please)

Expiration Date: _____ (MM/YYYY)

[Submit Form]   [Clear Form]

The following server-based validations will be performed on the user input of this form when the "submit form" button is clicked:

- All fields on the form must be entered (i.e., all fields are required).
- The check-out date should be greater than the check-in date.
- The last name, first name, city, province/state, and credit card holder's name should not contain the following characters:

    ; : ! @ # $ % ^ * + ?

- The country should be either Canada or the United States.
- If the country is Canada, then the postal code must be a valid Canadian postal code.
- If the country is the United States, then the postal code must be a valid US zip code.
- The phone number is a valid US/Canadian phone number.
- The e-mail address is a valid Internet e-mail address.
- The type of the credit card must be selected.
- The credit card number should consist of digits only and must have the following properties:

CREDIT CARD	PREFIX	LENGTH
MasterCard	51–55	16
Visa	4	16
American Express	34 or 37	15
Discover	6011	16

- The format of the expiration date should be MM/YYYY, where MM means month and YYYY means year. Both M and Y represent a single digit. The range of MM is between 01 and 12, and YYYY is between 2017 and 2027 (inclusively).
- All validations described here should be server based (i.e., these validations are performed on the server side).
- When the form is validated and submitted, a new web page will be generated to display the customer's input and ask for the customer's confirmation. Once the customer confirms, another new web page will be generated to inform the customer that the reservation is being processed, and the reservation information will be recorded in a file on the server to allow the hotel manager to process the reservation. Draw a scenario design diagram before writing the programs.

4. Search the Internet to learn the features of ASP.NET beyond the examples in this chapter.
5. Using ASP.NET with C#, rewrite the ASP.NET with VB.NET program in Listing 6.13.
6. Follow question 5 and employ code-behind programming to separate the C# source from the user interface design in the .aspx file.
7. Use ASP.NET with VB.NET or C#.NET to develop a web application project for the online auction of a precious gemstone. The user interface should allow users to input their e-mail addresses and bid for the gemstone. If the user's bid is currently the highest bid, then an indication message will be displayed to the user. All users' bids will be recorded in a file or a database on the server. For simplicity, there is no ending time for this online auction.

8. Develop a web application project (using either ASP.NET with VB.NET, or ASP.NET with C#). The minimum requirements are:
   - An HTML home page starts an ASP.NET program, followed by at least three times of interaction between the client and server implemented by ASP.NET
   - Use the `Redirect` method at least one time.
   - Use at least three validation controls.
   - At least one data file (.txt file) and one database table (MS Access) are used for the programs for data storage, search, and updating.

This project emphasizes the interaction between the client and server, but de-emphasizes the static web page itself (such as hyperlinks, client-side calculations, and image manipulations through JavaScript). The project report should include:
   - Description of your project
   - Scenario design diagram
   - Artifact of the project (html document, asp.net programs, text files and ms access database, and images)

7
PHP

7.1 Introduction to PHP and PHP Development Environment

PHP script was developed in 1994. Originally it was called personal home page, and now it is referred to as PHP hypertext preprocessor. As a server-side programming tool, PHP script can print dynamic web pages in HTML. A dynamic web page is different from a static web page in that a dynamic web page does not reside at a URL and its contents can vary depending on the request of a user or a computer program. PHP has been popular for several major reasons. First, PHP is easy to use. Its syntax is similar to C language. Second, PHP is free software. Supported by the Apache Software Foundation, <http://www.apache.org>, an open source software development community, PHP can be downloaded for free from the PHP Group at <http://www.php.net>. Third, PHP can be installed on different platforms, including UNIX, Windows, and others. Fourth, the PHP community has developed many PHP library programs for MySQL, an open-source DBMS (database management system). This makes PHP even more popular for small or medium-sized organizations.

In terms of the roles of web applications, PHP is not much different from other server-side programming tools such as ASP.NET. Figure 7.1 shows a general process for a web application supported by PHP. The user on the client side sends a request, which might include data, over the Internet to the server. The request and data received by the web server are used as input for a PHP program. The PHP program processes the request and generates a dynamic web page in HTML. The web server then sends the dynamic web page back to the client side, where it is shown on the client computer by the web browser.

To build a PHP web application, you need a server to run PHP. You can install a PHP server by using free software packages provided by PHP (<http://www.php.org> and Apache <http://www.apache.org>) websites. With a PHP server, you can upload PHP programs to the server and run them though the Internet. However, installation of a real server may not be feasible for students. Alternatively, it is more feasible to download a free PHP development environment software package that is able to create a local server on your personal computer for testing PHP applications. In this book, EasyPHP, a PHP development environment software package from <http://www.easyphp.org>, is used for examples. EasyPHP is not a production server, but rather is a developing server to test web applications in PHP before moving them on

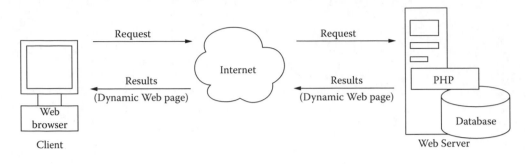

Figure 7.1 Execution cycle of PHP program.

a web hosting server. EasyPHP is able to install a personal server on your computer that emulates a real server to test PHP programs. EasyPHP can be easily installed by following the instructions provided by its website. The following steps are the general procedure of editing a PHP program and viewing the execution result in EasyPHP:

1. Install EasyPHP on your computer. Find the local server folder in the folder of EasyPHP (e.g., E:\EasyPHP\www, or E:\EasyPHP\data\localweb, depending on the version). This folder will contain all PHP applications for the default server.
2. Open Notepad, edit your PHP program (see Listing 7.1 for an example), and then save it to the local server folder as *FileName*.php (e.g., HollowWorld. php). Make sure that you choose [All Files] for [Save as type] before you save the file in Notepad.
3. Start the EasyPHP environment (e.g., E:\EasyPHP\EasyPHP.exe).
4. Once EasyPHP is launched, you can see the EasyPHP Window (see Figure 7.2). Click on the logo icon and a menu shows up that allows you to start and stop the local server and other procedures.
5. On the menu, select [Local Web]. You will see the local server (see Figure 7.2), which is supposed to be <http://localhost/> or <http:// *PortNumber*/>; this contains all programs and data stored on the local server. If Microsoft Internet Explorer is the browser for testing PHP programs, you often need to delete [Browsing history] under [Tools] and then [Internet option].
6. Select the PHP program or the web page on the local server (e.g., HollowWorld.php); you will see the execution result presented by the browser on the client side.

7.2 Format of PHP Program

We present a simple PHP program, named HelloWorld.php, in Listing 7.1. The line numbers are added for explanation and should not be included in the program.

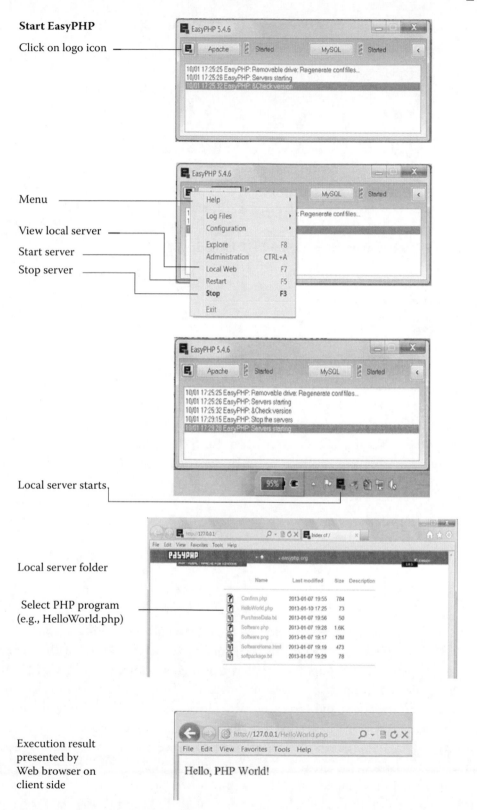

Figure 7.2 EasyPHP development environment.

Listing 7.1: Example of PHP Program (`HelloWorld.php`)

```
1 <html>
2 <body>
3 <?php print("Hello, PHP World!");
4 ?>
5 </body>
6 </html>
```

If you installed the PHP system correctly, the execution result of Listing 7.1 presented in the web browser for the client is shown in Figure 7.2.

There are a number of formats of PHP program. Instead of using <? and ?>, you may use <script> tag for a PHP script, as shown in Listing 7.2.

Listing 7.2: Use `<script>` Tag for PHP Program

```
<html>
  <body>
   <script language="PHP">
       print("Hello again, PHP World!");
   </script>
  </body>
</html>
```

The format of Listing 7.2 makes PHP look similar to JavaScript, but, actually, PHP may not be embedded within HTML. Rather, PHP can print HTML documents as other server-side programming tools do. Listing 7.3 shows another format of PHP. This format shows the major characteristics of PHP that a PHP program responds the client's request by simply printing an HTML document for the client. In the remaining part of this chapter, we use this format for all PHP programs.

Listing 7.3: Standard Format of PHP

```
<?php
     print("<html><body>");
     print("Again, hello, PHP World!");
     print("</body></html>");
?>
```

In principle, every time a dynamic web page printed by PHP is sent back to the client, the web browser on the client side repaints the screen to present the dynamic web page. Apparently, in comparison with the postback feature of ASP.NET, PHP is simple, but does not support postback automatically. This weakness makes the interactions between the client and server look discontinuous unless the programmer does more programming or uses a certain PHP library. For example, suppose the client fills a form with data and requests a PHP program to process it. If the PHP program is simple, it sends merely the processed result back to the client. The client can see the processed result, but is unable to see the original form that has been filled before sending the request because the screen has been repainted. To keep the original form along with the processed result for the client, the programmer must add code to reprint the original form along with the original form data in the PHP program. We will return to this issue later in this chapter and demonstrate examples.

7.3 Structure of PHP Program

To explain the structure of a PHP program, Listing 7.4 shows an example (Date. php) that displays the current date in several formats (Figure 7.3).

Listing 7.4: Example of PHP Program (Date.php)

```
 1 <?php
 2     print("<html><body>");

 3 // This is to show the day of month
 4     $day=date("d");
 5     print("Day=$day");
 6     print("<br>");

 7 // This is to show the current month of year
 8     $month=date("M");
 9     print("Month=$month");
10     print("<br>");

11 // This is to show today date
12     print(date("F d, Y"));
13     print("</body></html>");
14 ?>
```

The syntax and structure of PHP is similar to those of C language. A PHP statement ends with a semicolon ";". "//" indicates a comment line. The first character of a user-defined variable name must be the dollar sign "$." In Listing 7.4, $day and $month are user-defined variables. PHP is a function-oriented language that has many built-in functions. The general syntax of a PHP built-in function is

```
function_name( arguments )
```

In Listing 7.4, print() is a built-in function, and its argument is a string. date() is also a built-in function, and its argument is the format of the date, including many

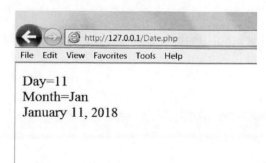

Figure 7.3   Execution result of Date.php.

formats such as d for numerical day of month, D for day of week, M for current month in short form, F for current month in long form, m for current month in number, Y for current year, etc.

7.4 Activate PHP in Web Page and Process Form Data on Server

In this section, we present an example to show how a PHP program responds to a request sent from the client side by a form. Listing 7.5 is an HTML web page (Request.html). On the web page, the user is allowed to input data, including delivery weight, days needed for transportation, and location, and to send the form to the server to find out the delivery charge. Listing 7.6 is a PHP program, named **DeliveryCharge.php**, that responds to the form input and prints a dynamic web page for the client.

Listing 7.5: Web Page to Activate PHP Program (Request.html)

```
1   <HTML>
2   <HEAD>
3   <TITLE> Delivery Charge Calculation </TITLE>
4   </HEAD>
5   <BODY>
6   <H2>Find the delivery charge.</H2>
7   <FORM ACTION="DeliveryCharge.php"  METHOD="POST">
8   <P> Input the weight of package for the delivery:
9   <INPUT TYPE=TEXT SIZE=10 NAME="Weight"> lb<BR>
10  </P>
11  <P>Input the days needed for transportation:
12  <INPUT TYPE=TEXT SIZE=10  NAME="Days"><BR>
13  </P>
14  <P>Choose the destination State:</P>
15  <INPUT TYPE=RADIO NAME="State"
16       VALUE="Yes" checked>In State<BR>
17  <INPUT TYPE=RADIO NAME="State" VALUE="No">Out State
18  <BR></P>
19  <INPUT TYPE="SUBMIT" VALUE="Find Out Delivery Charge">
20  <INPUT TYPE="RESET"  VALUE="Reset">
21  </FORM>
22  </BODY>
23  </HTML>
```

Listing 7.6: PHP Program (DeliveryCharge.php) Activated by Request.html

```
1   <?php
2   print("<html><body>");
3   print("Thank you for your request! <br>");

4   $Weight=$_POST["Weight"];
5   $Days=$_POST["Days"];
6   $State=$_POST["State"];

7   $Charge=CalculateCharge($State, $Weight, $Days);

8   print("The delivery charge is: $ $Charge");
```

```
 9    print("</body></html>");

10    function CalculateCharge($ST, $WT, $DS)  {
11      if ($ST=="Yes")
12        { $CH=$WT * $DS * 1; }
13      else
14        { $CH=$WT * $DS * 2; };
15      return($CH);
16      }
17    ?>
```

This example is quite similar to the example of Listing 3.7 of JavaScript in Chapter 3. The difference between JavaScript and PHP in this case is that JavaScript performs calculations on the client side, while the PHP script performs calculations on the server side.

In Listing 7.5 (Request.html), line **7** specifies the action when the user clicks on the submit button on the form. It instructs the server to activate the PHP program DeliveryCharge.php. In this example, the PHP program and the HTML web page are placed in the same folder on the server so that a directory path name is not needed; otherwise, you must define the access path here. Line **7** also instructs the POST method used by the web browser to send the data back to the server. Actually, POST is always used for the method attribute for server-side programs.

In Listing 7.6 (DeliveryCharge.php), lines **4–6** receive the values from the form that activates the PHP program. Note that, to improve the PHP performance, the PHP version of EasyPHP uses $ _ POST["*variable-name*"] to receive the input values from the corresponding variables on the form through the POST method. This rule may not be applied in many other versions of PHP, where the global variable in the form of $*variable-name* is used directly. You need to check the reference manual of a particular version of PHP to learn how to pass the values of form data from the web page to the PHP program. Line **7** calls the CalculateCharge() function for calculation. Lines **10–16** are the user-defined function CalculateCharge(). The structure of user-defined functions is similar to that of C. There is an if-statement in lines **11–14**. We explain them in detail in the following section.

Figure 7.4 shows the execution results of Request.html and DeliveryCharge. php. It also shows the code of the dynamic web page on the client side. Apparently, this dynamic web page is simple without postback of the original form. To include the original filled form on the dynamic web page, the PHP program needs to print the form, as demonstrated in an example later in this chapter.

7.5 Programming in PHP

7.5.1 PHP Functions

The general syntax of a PHP built-in function is

Function-name(arguments)

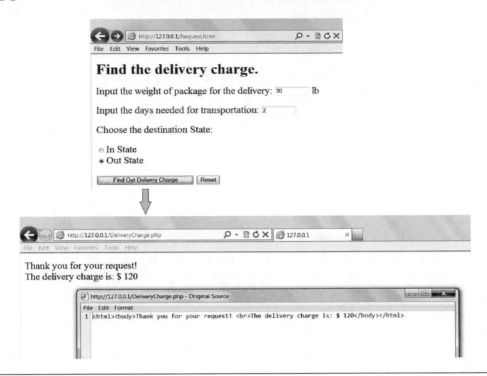

Figure 7.4   Execution results of `Request.html` and DeliveryCharge.php.

As shown in the previous examples of PHP program, `print()` is a built-in function, and its argument is a string. The `print()` function is probably the most used function in PHP programs. Note that single and double quotation marks have different outcomes if there is a variable with the $ sign in the printed string. Single quotes will print the variable name, while double quotes will print the value of the variable.

You will see the `echo()` function later in some examples of PHP programs. `echo()` does the same job as `print()` does, although their internal implementations are different. `date()` is also a built-in function. Other commonly used PHP functions and their arguments include:

- `rand(`*low limit, high limit*`)`—generating random numbers in the defined range
- `substr(`*string, start position, end position*`)`—extracting a portion of the characters from the defined string
- `trim(`*string*`)`—removing blanks from the beginning and end of the defined string

The syntax of the user-defined function is

```
function function-name( arguments )
{ [actions] ;
return( variable ); }
```

For example, in function **CalculateCharge**($ST, $WT, $DS), **CalculateCharge**() is a user-defined function, and ($ST, $WT, $DS) are the function arguments. The location of the user-defined function is not important; in other words, the programmer can place a user-defined function anywhere in the PHP program.

7.5.2 if-*Statement*

The syntax of if-statement of PHP is similar to C; that is,

```
if ( [condition] ) { [action_1] ; }
else             { [action_2] ; };
```

PHP also provides an if-elseif controlling statement, which could be confusing for beginners.

7.5.3 *Read Data File from Server*

In this subsection, we present an example of how a PHP program reads data from a file on the server. Listing 7.7 shows a brief HTML web page, named Travel.html, for travelers to check air-ticket prices on the server through the Internet.

Listing 7.7: Web Page (Travel.html) to Access Server Data

```
<HTML><BODY>
<FORM ACTION="Airticket.php" METHOD=POST>
<H2>Welcome to Spring Travel Agency!</H2>
<INPUT TYPE=SUBMIT VALUE="Check the Prices">
</FORM></BODY></HTML>
```

Suppose there has been a text file (ASCII file), named Airticket.txt, on the server disk, as shown in Listing 7.8. The PHP program, named Airticket.php, is supposed to read the disk file and to send the requested data back to the client.

Listing 7.8: Text Data File (Airticket.txt) Used for Airtickets.php

```
New York - Boston
$99.90
Toronto - Las Vegas
$155.50
Halifax - Providence
$109.50
```

The PHP program Airticket.php activated by **Travel.html** to access the server data of air-ticket prices is listed in Listing 7.9.

Listing 7.9: PHP Program (`Airticket.php`) Reads Data File on Server

```php
1   <?php
2   print("<html><body>");
3   print("<h3>Airticket Price Table</h3>");
4   $FileName='Airticket.txt';
5   $File=fopen($FileName, 'r') or die("Cannot open file!");
6   print("<table border=1>");

7   while(!feof($File)) {
8       $line1=fgets($File, 120);
9       $line2=fgets($File, 120);
10      print("<tr><td>$line1</td><td>$line2</td></tr>");
11  };

12  fclose($File);
13  print("</table>");
14  print("</body></html>");
15  ?>
```

In Listing 7.9 (`Airticket.php`), line **4** stores the name of the external data file on the server (`Airticket.txt`) to a variable for the external file name (`$FileName`). Line **5** opens the data file for read-only. It uses the variable of external data file name (`$FileName`) and defines the internal file name (`$File`) for the program. Lines **6** and **13** define a table to present the data to the client. Lines **7** through **11** are a while-loop. Line **7** means that, although the data file has not reached the end, execute the instructions included in the loop. For each time of the loop, lines **8** and **9** read two lines from the disk file (`Airticket.php`), and line **10** prints them into the table. Here, 120 is the size (in bytes) of the buffer to hold the data read from the server. Once the process reaches the end of the file, line **12** closes the file. Several important PHP functions are described next.

7.5.4 `fopen()` and `fclose()`

The `fopen()` function is to open a disk file on the server using the external file name (or the variable that stores the external file name), and the `fclose()` function is to close the opened file using the internal file name. The syntax of these functions is

```php
fopen($VariableOfExternalFileName, 'open mode');
fclose($InternalFileName);
```

Note that, in PHP, the external data file name and the internal file name are different, as shown in Listing 7.9 (`Airticket.php`). The file open mode could be `'r'` for read-only, `'w'` for overwrite-only, `'r+'` for read and write, `'a'` for append, or `'a+'` for read and append. The `die()` function often follows `fopen()` and gives instructions when the open process fails (e.g., the file is missing on the server).

7.5.5 feof() *and* fgets()

The feof() function indicates the end of a file. Its argument is the internal file name. (!feof($*InternalFileName*)) is often used for the condition that the file has not been reached to the end.

The fget() function reads one line from the disk file. Its syntax is

```
fgets($InternalFileName, maximum bytes);
```

7.5.6 while-*loop*

while implements a loop to execute a set of instructions repeatedly while the specified condition is true. The syntax of a while-loop is

```
while( condition ) { actions; };
```

The condition could contain operators such as ! for NOT, && for AND, and || for OR.

7.5.7 *Write Data File to Server and* fputs()

In this subsection we show how PHP saves the data sent by a form and writes them to the server disk. Listing 7.10 is an HTML web page (Order.html) that contains the user's input and activates a PHP program to save the data. Listing 7.11 is the PHP program (SaveForm.php) that receives the data of the form and appends them to the disk file on the server.

Listing 7.10: Web Page (Order.html) to Save Data on Server

```
1    <HTML> <BODY>
2    <H3> PHP saves data of FORM, and write them to a file </H3>
3    <FORM ACTION="SaveForm.php" METHOD=POST>
4    Your Last Name: <BR>
5    <INPUT TYPE=TEXT NAME="LName" SIZE=50> <BR>
6    Your First Name: <BR>
7    <INPUT TYPE=TEXT NAME="FName" SIZE=50> <BR>
8    Your Email Address: <BR>
9    <INPUT TYPE=TEXT NAME="Email" SIZE=50> <BR><BR>
10   Your Orders: <BR>
11   Item:       <INPUT TYPE=TEXT NAME="Item" SIZE=10>
12   Quantity:   <INPUT TYPE=TEXT NAME="Quantity" SIZE=5> <BR>
13   <BR>
14   <INPUT TYPE=SUBMIT VALUE="Process the data">
15   <INPUT TYPE=RESET VALUE="Start Over Again">
16   </FORM>
17   </BODY></HTML>
```

Listing 7.11: PHP Program Writes Data to Disk File on Server (SaveForm.php)

```php
1   <?php
2   print("<html><body>");
3   $lname=$_POST["LName"];
4   $fname=$_POST["FName"];
5   $email=$_POST["Email"];
6   $item=$_POST["Item"];
7   $quant=$_POST["Quantity"];

8   $FileName='FormData.txt';
9   $File=fopen($FileName, 'a+') or die("Cannot open file!");
10  fputs($File, "$lname\r\n");
11  fputs($File, "$fname\r\n");
12  fputs($File, "$email\r\n");
13  fputs($File, "$item\r\n");
14  fputs($File, "$quant\r\n");
15  fclose($File);
16  print("<h2>Thank you for sending the order form!</h2>");
17  print("</body></html>");
18  ?>
```

In Listing 7.11, lines **3** through **7** receive the values of the variables from the form. Line **8** stores the server file name to the external disk file name. After the execution of this program, you will find a disk file named FormData.txt on the server (i.e., in the local server folder of the EasyPHP environment). Line **9** opens the file in the append and read mode. Lines **10–14** write the data received from the form to the disk file. Note that \r\n indicates a return key and a new line to separate these data items in the text file. Function fputs() writes a record to the file. Its syntax is:

```
fputs($InternalFileName, "string name");
```

Finally, line **15** closes the file. The execution results of Order.html and SaveForm. php are shown in Figure 7.5.

7.6 Relay Data through Multiple Dynamic Web Pages Using Hidden Fields

When a PHP program sends a dynamic web back to the client in response to the request through a form, the data of the form might be lost if they are not stored on the server. In cases where several interactions are involved in a process, such as online shopping, it is important to pass data from one dynamic web page to another. However, if the PHP program saves these data to the server every time, then the programming becomes complicated and the execution time becomes long. In addition, some pieces of data are used for interactions but are unnecessary to be saved on the server. Here, we present a simple way to relay data through multiple dynamic web pages using hidden fields of form. The user on the client side would not see the data in the hidden fields on the web page unless its source code is viewed.

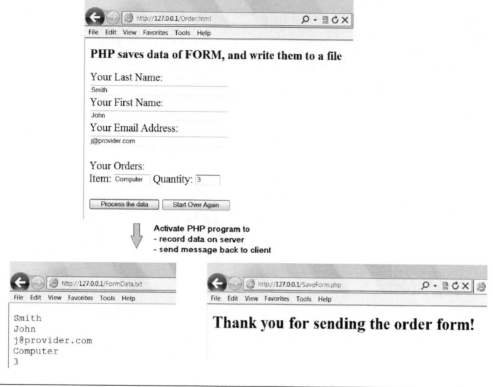

Figure 7.5 Execution results of `Order.html` and `SaveForm.php`.

The following three programs show how one can relay data through two dynamic web pages using hidden fields without interrupting a user's view. Listing 7.12 is a static web page (`Email.html`) with a form that allows the user to input her or his e-mail address. Note that line **5** catches the input and stores it in a variable named `hiddenemail`. The submit button in Listing 7.12 activates the PHP program in Listing 7.13, named `AirticketEmail.php`. This PHP program (`AirticketEmail.php`) is a variation of the PHP program in Listing 7.9 (`Airticket.php`). The difference between the two programs is shown in lines **14** through **18** in Listing 7.13.

Line **14** receives the data (e-mail address) sent by the form in Listing 7.12 (`Email. html`). Line **15** defines a new form for sending back to the client. Line **16** defines a hidden field that contains the e-mail address. This e-mail address is not displayed at this time, but is passed on to the next dynamic web page. Line **18** defines a button to activate another PHP program in Listing 7.14, named **`AirticketConfirm. php`**. In Listing 7.14, line **3** receives the e-mail address from the hidden field of the form sent by `AirticketEmail.php`, and line **5** displays it to the client. Note that the hidden field name (`hiddenemail`) should be consistent in all programs; that is, line **5** in Listing 7.12, lines **14** and **16** in Listing 7.13, and line **3** in Listing 7.14 should all use the same hidden field name `hiddenemail`. Figure 7.6 illustrates the data relay through dynamic web pages using a hidden field.

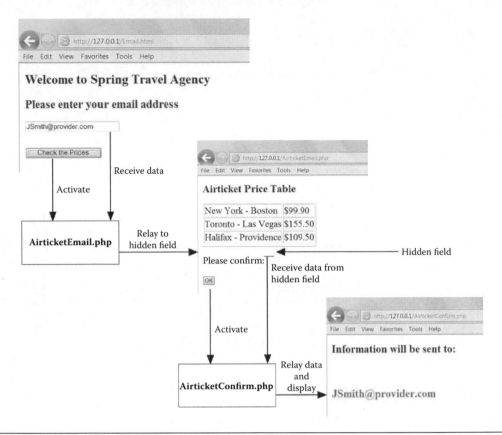

Figure 7.6   Example of data replay using hidden field.

Listing 7.12: Web Page (`Email.html`) Activates PHP Program (`AirticketEmail.php`)

```
1  <HTML><BODY>
2  <FORM ACTION="AirticketEmail.php" METHOD=POST>
3  <H3>Welcome to Spring Travel Agency</H3>
4  <H4>Please enter your email address</H4>
5  <INPUT TYPE=TEXT NAME=hiddenemail SIZE=20><BR><BR>
6  <INPUT TYPE=SUBMIT VALUE="Check the Prices">
7  </FORM></BODY></HTML>
```

Listing 7.13: PHP Program (`AirticketEmail.php`) That Uses Hidden Field to Relay Data

```
1   <?php
2   print("<html><body>");
3   print("<h3>Airticket Price Table</h3>");
4   $FileName='Airticket.txt';
5   $File=fopen($FileName, 'r') or die("Cannot open file!");
6   print("<table border=1>");
7   while(!feof($File)) {
8     $line1=fgets($File, 120);
9     $line2=fgets($File, 120);
10    print("<tr><td>$line1</td><td>$line2</td></tr>");
11  };
```

```
12   fclose($File);
13   print("</table>");
14   $e=$_POST["hiddenemail"];
15   print("<form action=AirticketConfirm.php  method=post>");
16   print("<input type=hidden name=hiddenemail value=$e>");
17   print("Please confirm:<br><br>");
18   print('<input type="submit" value="OK">');
19   print("</form></body></html>");
20   ?>
```

**Listing 7.14: PHP Program (`AirticketConfirm.php`)
That Receives and Displays the Relayed Data**

```
1  <?php
2  print("<html><body>");
3  $e=$_POST["hiddenemail"];
4  print("<h3>Information will be sent to:</h3><br><br>");
5  print("<h3><font color=red> $e</h3>");
6  print("</body></html>");
7  ?>
```

7.7 Example of Web Application Design

There are many types of web applications, including:

- Information presentation
- Access authentication
- Information search
- Business transaction
- Notification, reporting, or confirmation
- User interaction, etc.

To facilitate web application design, we use a scenario design diagram as a tool to articulate the web application project in the aspect of

1. Features of each of the web pages
2. Interaction between the client and the web server
3. Data on the server
4. The logic of the entire process
5. Major outcomes of the process

In this section, we present an example of a toy-scale web application to explain the use of a scenario design diagram and the implementation of a web application project using PHP. The example is an online software shopping system. In this example, the home page introduces the user to search the prices of software packages. The user is allowed to type in the name of a software package and the version for the search. The data used for search are stored on the server. The server of the online store makes a response to the user by notifying her whether the online shop has the requested software package or not. To make the search easy, the original form with the user's inputs

Web Application Scenario Design – Online Software Store

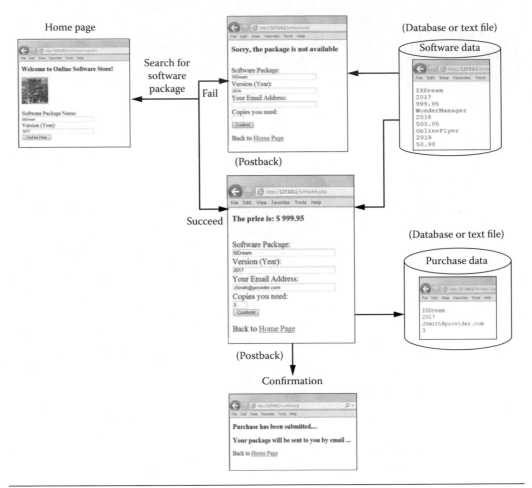

Figure 7.7   Example of scenario design.

must appear on the screen on the client side, along with the response. In other words, the PHP program has to make the "postback" feature. Once the user finds the right software package to purchase, she can input her e-mail address along with other purchasing data and click on a button to make a purchase. All data used for the purchase are recorded on the server for the online store for further processing.

Figure 7.7 shows a scenario design diagram. Apparently, the diagram in Figure 7.7 includes screenshots of the execution results of the programs. Practically, the program designer draws a draft for the design of the application before writing the programs.

Listing 7.15(a) is the home page (SoftwareHome.html), which activates Software.php (see Listing 7.15b). The Software.php program allows the user to search a software package. This search process uses a data file on the server, named Softpackage.txt (see Listing 7.15c). The Software.php program searches the data file on the server and makes a response to the client's request depending on the search outcome. If the search fails, Software.php sends a message back to the user and allows the user to go back to the home page to redo the search. If the search succeeds, it posts a form that contains the user's original inputs back to the client side and asks the user to input additional purchasing data, including contact information and copies of the software package. The command button on the postback form activates `Confirm.php` program. The `Confirm.php` program (Listing 7.15(d)) receives all purchasing data from the client and writes them to a data file named `PurchaseData.txt` on the server. The data file can be used by the online store for further processing. Upon the completion of the purchasing transaction, the client receives a confirmation message on the screen.

Listing 7.15(a): Example of Application Design: Home Page (SoftwareHome.html)

```
<HTML><HEAD><TITLE>Online Software Store</TITLE></HEAD>
<BODY><H3> Welcome to Online Software Store! </H3>
 <IMG ALT="Software" SRC="Software.png"
        width="100" height="100" />
 <FORM ACTION="Software.php"  METHOD=POST>
 Software Package Name:<BR>
 <INPUT TYPE=TEXT NAME="SoftwarePackage" SIZE=50><BR>
 Version (Year):<BR>
 <INPUT TYPE=TEXT NAME="VersionYear" SIZE=50><BR>
 <INPUT TYPE=SUBMIT  VALUE="Find the Price">
 </FORM></BODY></HTML>
```

Listing 7.15(b): Example of Application Design: Search (Software.php)

```
<?php
  print("<html><body>");
   $Package = $_POST["SoftwarePackage"];
   $Version = $_POST["VersionYear"];

  $PackageFile='Softpackage.txt';
  $File=fopen($PackageFile, 'r') or die("Cannot open file!");

  $record=fgets($File, 120);
  $pg="";
  $vy="";
  $pc="";
  $Price="";
  $Found="no";
    while (!feof($File)) {
      $pg = trim($record);
      //trim() function deletes spaces before and after a string
      $vy = trim(fgets($File, 120));
      $pc = trim(fgets($File, 120));

     if (($pg==$Package)&&($vy==$Version))
        { $Found = "yes";
          $Price=$pc;
          $record = "";
        }
     else { $record=fgets($File, 120); };
```

```
    };
   if ($Found=="no")
   {print("<H3>Sorry, the package is not available</H3>"); }
    else {
    print("<H4>The price is:  $ $Price </H4>");
      };
   print("<br>");
   fclose($File);

   print("<form action=Confirm.php method=post>");
   print("Software Package: <br>");
   print("<input type=text name=SoftwarePackage size=50 value=$Package>");
   print("<br>");
   print("Version (Year): <br>");
   print("<input type=text name=VersionYear size=50 value=$Version>");
   print("<br>");
   print("Your Email Address: <br>");
   print("<input type=text name=email size=50>");
   print("<br>");
   print("Copies you need:  <br>");
   print("<input type=text name=Copies size=3>");
   print("<br>");
   print("<input type=submit value=Confirm!>");
   print("</form>");
   print("<p>Back to <a href=SoftwareHome.html>Home Page</a>");
   print("</body></html>");
?>
```

Listing 7.15(c): Example of Application Design: Data on Server (`Softpackage.txt`)

```
ISDream
2017
999.95
WonderManager
2018
505.05
OnlineFlyer
2019
50.98
```

Listing 7.15(d): Example of Application Design: Transaction (`Confirm.php`)

```
<?php

   $Package = $_POST["SoftwarePackage"];
   $Version = $_POST["VersionYear"];
   $email = $_POST["email"];
   $Copies = $_POST["Copies"];

     if (strlen($email)>0)
     //strlen() function determines the length of a string
      {print("<h3>Purchase has been submitted....</h3>");

     $PurchaseFile='PurchaseData.txt';
     $File=fopen($PurchaseFile, 'a+') or die("Cannot open file!");
```

```
    fputs($File,  "$Package\r\n");
    fputs($File,  "$Version\r\n");
    fputs($File,  "$email\r\n");
    fputs($File,  "$Copies\r\n");
    fclose($File);
    print("<h3>Your package will be sent to you by email ...</h3>");
    }
    else { print("Missing email address...."); };

    print("<p>Back to <a href=SoftwareHome.html>Home Page</a>");
?>
```

7.8 PHP and MySQL Database

Practical web applications deal with relational databases directly from a web page. MySQL is the most used open source relational database management system. PHP and MySQL is a common combination for web application development. First, both are open-source software systems and are platform independent. Second, many development tools, such as the EasyPHP used for this chapter, have integrated PHP and MySQL into the development environments. Thus, no substantial work for database connection setting would be required for the web application development stage. Third, the PHP community has developed many PHP libraries for MySQL already. This makes the combination of PHP and MySQL even stronger in the future. Because of these reasons, we use MySQL for PHP in this book for learning web application development with databases. We assume students have basic knowledge of database and SQL (structured query language) for studying this section. The subject of SQL is discussed in detail in Chapter 9.

7.8.1 Set MySQL Database

PHP programs can use databases, but cannot create a database. A database used by PHP must be created by using the DBMS, although the database could be empty (i.e., with no data). The EasyPHP development environment is able to create a MySQL database that can be connected to PHP without a need for database connection setting at the operating system level. Figure 7.8 demonstrates the steps to setting an empty MySQL database, named studentdb, in EasyPHP that will be used for the PHP programs to create tables and to access the tables from the database within the development environment. When setting a database in EasyPHP, the [Local Web] window must be closed.

To make sure the database has been created by the EasyPHP [Administration] window, you can check the data folder on the local server (e.g., E:\EasyPHP\ mysql\data) on your computer, as shown in the last step in Figure 7.8.

Again, if the browser is Microsoft Internet Explorer, you need to delete browsing history from time to time in order to run PHP programs in EasyPHP.

Start EasyPHP

Click on logo icon

Select [Administration]

Administration Home window:

Click on [Open] in MODULES

MODULES window:

Select [Databases]

Databases window:

Type in database name

Click on [Create]

EasyPHP server: (E:\EasyPHP)

\mysql\data folder

Database created

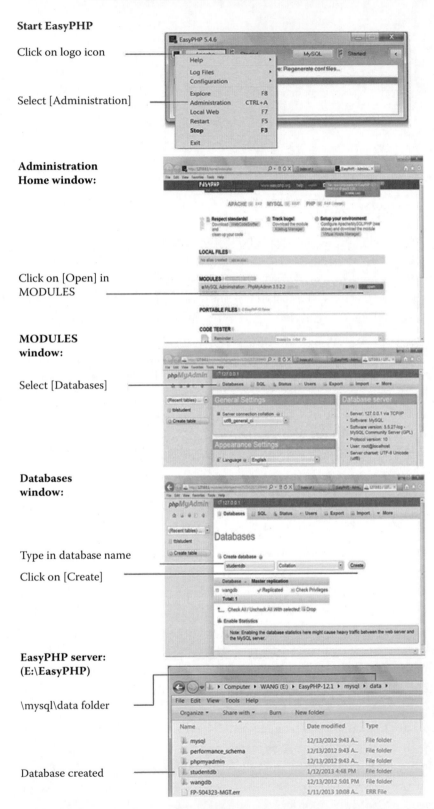

Figure 7.8   Set MySQL database (studentdb) in EasyPHP.

7.8.2 Create and Delete Table in PHP Using SQL

One may create tables in the EasyPHP [Administration] window directly. However, we have found it easy to use PHP programs to create and delete tables. Listing 7.16 is a PHP program (CreateTable.php) to create a table named tblStudent. The tblStudent table has four attributes:

```
tblStudent
    StudentID (Key, 8 char)
    StudentName (30 char)
    StudentAddress (40 char)
    StudentEnrolYear (4 integer)
```

In Listing 7.16 (CreateTable.php), line **3** connects to the server. Here, "root" is the default user, and "" means there is no password. You may change these parameters in the MySQL setting. Line **4** selects the database used for this program. Line **5** shows a message to indicate the database has been connected successfully. The echo() function does the same job as print() does. We use a simple programming convention here: echo() is used for displaying messages for the programmer, and print() is used for print lines for the client. Lines **7–12** are the SQL part, which is straightforward, given Chapter 9. Line **13** executes the SQL. Line **14** closes the server connection.

Listing 7.16: PHP Program (CreateTable.php) Creates Table in MySQL Database

```
 1  <?php
 2  // Make a MySQL connection and select database
 3  $conn=mysql_connect("localhost", "root", "") or die(mysql_error());
 4  mysql_select_db("studentdb") or die(mysql_error());
 5  echo("studentdb has been selected!");
 6  echo("<br>");

 7  $sql="CREATE TABLE tblStudent
 8     (StudentID char(8) NOT NULL,
 9      StudentName char(30) NOT NULL,
10      StudentAddress char(40) NOT NULL,
11      StudentYear int(4) NOT NULL,
12      PRIMARY KEY (StudentID))";
13  mysql_query($sql);
14  mysql_close($conn);
15  echo("Table tblStudent has been created!");
16  ?>
```

Listing 7.17 is a PHP program (DeleteTable.php) to delete the tblStudent table. The logic of this program is similar to that for CreateTable.php.

Listing 7.17: PHP Program (DeleteTable.php) Deletes Table

```
<?php
// Make a MySQL connection and select database
```

```
$conn=mysql_connect("localhost", "root", "") or die(mysql_error());
mysql_select_db("studentdb") or die(mysql_error());
echo("studentdb has been selected!");
echo("<br>");

$sql="DROP TABLE tblStudent";
mysql_query($sql);
mysql_close($conn);
echo("Table tblStudent has been deleted!");
?>
```

7.8.3   Insert Data to Table

Once the table is created, you can add data to the table by using PHP programs. Listing 7.18 is an example of a PHP program (InsertData.php) to insert three records of student data in the tblStudent table. The mysql_query() function is used to process the SQL script. The script used here is slightly different from the standard format in that the attributes of the table are listed here (see lines **9, 13,** and **17**).

Listing 7.18: PHP Program (InsertData.php) Inserts Data to Table

```
1  <?php
2  // Make a MySQL Connection and select database
3  $conn=mysql_connect("localhost", "root", "") or die(mysql_error());
4  mysql_select_db("studentdb") or die(mysql_error());
5  echo("studentdb has been selected!");
6  echo("<br>");

7  // Insert rows of information into tblStudent
8  mysql_query("INSERT INTO tblStudent
9  (StudentID, StudentName, StudentAddress, StudentYear)
10   VALUES('01234567', 'John', '285 Westport', 2015)")
11 or die(mysql_error());

12 mysql_query("INSERT INTO tblStudent
13 (StudentID, StudentName, StudentAddress, StudentYear)
14   VALUES('02345678', 'Anne', '287 Eastport', 2016)")
15 or die(mysql_error());

16 mysql_query("INSERT INTO tblStudent
17 (StudentID, StudentName, StudentAddress, StudentYear)
18   VALUES('03456789', 'Robert', '324 Northport', 2017)")
19 or die(mysql_error());

20 mysql_close($conn);
21 echo ("Data Inserted!");
22 ?>
```

7.8.4 Access Database

Listing 7.19 is a PHP Program (StudentData.php) to access the MySQL database and place the data into a table for the client. In PHP, the mysql_query() function (line **6**) returns the query result in the form of a single long string. The

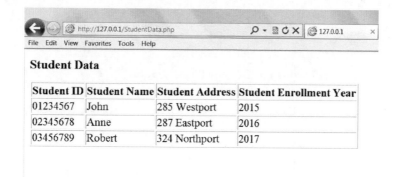

Figure 7.9   PHP program (StudentData.php) to access MySQL database.

mysql_fetch_assoc() function (line **14**) is used to process the long string by extracting a row from the long string as an associative array. The while-loop (line **14** through line **21**) generates all rows extracted from the long string. Lines **16–19** print these rows to the table. Note that the attribute names of the table are used for the associate array. The dot sign "." used in the print() function (see line **16**) links the strings for printing. Figure 7.9 is the execution outcome of StudentData.php given the data inserted by InsertData.php.

Listing 7.19: PHP Program (StudentData.php) to Access MySQL Database

```
 1  <?php
 2  // Make a MySQL connection and select database
 3  $conn=mysql_connect("localhost", "root", "") or die(mysql_error());
 4  mysql_select_db("studentdb") or die(mysql_error());

 5  print("<h3>Student Data</h3>");

 6  $Result=mysql_query("SELECT * FROM tblStudent");

 7  print("<table border='1'>
 8    <tr>
 9    <th>Student ID</th>
10    <th>Student Name</th>
11    <th>Student Address</th>
12    <the>Student Enrollment Year</th>
13    </tr>");

14  while ($row = mysql_fetch_assoc($Result)) {
15    print("<tr>");
16    print("<td>" . $row['StudentID'] . "</td>");
17    print("<td>" . $row['StudentName'] . "</td>");
18    print("<td>" . $row['StudentAddress'] . "</td>");
19    print("<td>" . $row['StudentYear'] . "</td>");
20    print("</tr>");
21  }
22  print("</table>");
23  mysql_close($conn);
24  ?>
```

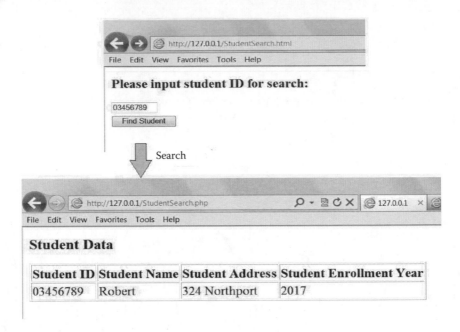

Figure 7.10   Search MySQL database using PHP (`StudentSearch.php`).

7.8.5 Search Database

The client might want to search the database using a search criterion. Listing 7.20 is a web page (`StudentSearch.html`) that allows the user to input a student ID number to search the database. Listing 7.21 is the PHP program (`StudentSearch.php`) used by the web page to perform the search task. The logic of the program is straightforward. Figure 7.10 shows an example of search.

Listing 7.20: Web Page (`StudentSearch.html`) to Activate PHP Program (`StudentSearch.php`)

```
<HTML>
<BODY>
<H4>Please input student ID for search:</H4>
<FORM ACTION="StudentSearch.php" METHOD="POST">
<INPUT TYPE=TEXT SIZE=10 NAME="StudentID"><BR>
<INPUT TYPE="SUBMIT" VALUE="Find Student">
</FORM></BODY></HTML>
```

Listing 7.21: PHP Program (`StudentSearch.php`) to Search MySQL Database

```
<?php
// Make a MySQL connection and select database
$conn=mysql_connect("localhost", "root", "") or die(mysql_error());
mysql_select_db("studentdb") or die(mysql_error());

$StID=$_POST["StudentID"];
print("<h3>Student Data</h3>");
```

```
$Result=mysql_query("SELECT * FROM tblStudent
                        WHERE StudentID=$StID");

print("<table border='1'>
 <tr>
 <th>Student ID</th>
 <th>Student Name</th>
 <th>Student Address</th>
 <th>Student Enrollment Year</th>
 </tr>");

while ($row = mysql_fetch_assoc($Result)) {
  print("<tr>");
  print("<td>" . $row['StudentID'] . "</td>");
  print("<td>" . $row['StudentName'] . "</td>");
  print("<td>" . $row['StudentAddress'] . "</td>");
  print("<td>" . $row['StudentYear'] . "</td>");
  print("</tr>");
}
print("</table>");
mysql_close($conn);
?>
```

7.8.6 Use ODBC Connection

As PHP and MySQL is a commonly applied combination for web application development, PHP has built-in MySQL database process functions such as `mysql _ connect()`. More generally, one may use ODBC (open database connectivity) for other database systems of the Windows platform (such as Microsoft SQL Server). The syntax of functions used for ODBC-related processes is slightly different from that shown in the preceding programs with MySQL. Listing 7.22 (which is not a production program) shows a simple template for ODBC-related database processes.

Listing 7.22: Template of Database Processing through ODBC

```
<?php
$v1=odbc_connect("DatabaseName", "User", "Password");
$v2="SELECT * FROM TableName";
$v3=odbc_exec($v1, $v2);

while(odbc_fetch_row($v3))
{
 $v4=odbc_result($v3, "AttributeName");
 print($v4);
}
odbc_close($v1);
?>
```

7.9 Debugging

Since PHP is simple, the debugging task is not difficult. When you run a PHP program in the development environment (e.g., EasyPHP), you will see the PHP running error messages on the screen if the program has errors. Common syntax errors include:

- Typos or misspelling a word
- Omitting a symbol (e.g., missing one side of parentheses)
- Violating format
- Using an undefined user-defined variable or function

Logical errors or runtime errors often occur when the computer performs wrong operations or not as expected. To debug logical errors, you should use data samples to test the program based on the output of the program:

1. Exercise every possible option to check the computer outputs to see if the program does only as expected. Examine all if-statements to find possible options.
2. If a program is "dead," you must terminate it by closing the web page. This is most likely caused by an endless loop. You should check while-loop and all if-statements.

Chapter 7 Exercises

1. Fill blanks in the following PHP program and sketch the screenshot of its execution results:

```
1   <?php
2   _____("<html>_____");
3   print("Example");

4   $Weight=$_____["Weight"];
5   $Days=$_POST["Days"];
6   $State=$_POST["State"];

7   $_____=_____($State, $Weight, $Days);

8   print("The payment is: $ $Payment");
9   print("</body></html>");

10  function CalPayment($ST, $WT, $DS)  {
11    if ($ST=="Yes")
12    { $CH=$WT * $DS * 1; }
13    else
14    { $CH=$WT * $DS * 2; };
15    return($CH);
16  _____
17  _____>
```

2. Fill blanks in the following PHP program and sketch the screenshots of the page and its execution result:

```
1   <?php
2   print("<html><body>");
3   print("<h3>Airticket Price Table</h3>");
4   $_____='air-tickets.txt';
```

```
 5   $File=_____($FileName, 'r') or die("Cannot open file!");
 6   print("<table border=1>");

 7   while(!feof($_____)) {
 8       $line1=fgets($_____, 120);
 9       $line2=_____($_____, 120);
10       print("<tr><td>$line1</td><td>$line2</td></tr>");
11   };

12   fclose($_____);
13   print("_____");
14   print("</body></html>");
15   ?>
```

3. Develop a web-based application project by using PHP, with a scenario design diagram for the project. The project has a web page with a form. On the client side, the user can submit the form with input data. On the server side, the submitted data are stored and cumulated on a disk file. This disk file is further processed by Excel in batch.

4. Develop a web-based application project by using PHP to pass data through three forms using hidden fields.

5. Implement the following scenario using PHP:

   a. The company has its website (home page in HTML) on the server and allows any clients to access the website using its URL.

   b. The home page is a log-in page that asks the client to enter her or his user ID (e-mail address) and password. After the client enters the user ID and password and clicks the log-in button, the server will check the user ID and password on the server to see whether the user is permitted to enter the system.

   c. The client will receive an error message if the user ID and password do not match. Otherwise, the client will see an online auction window with a greeting message and the auction item image. The dynamic web page is generated by PHP.

   d. After the client enters the online auction by clicking a button, a window that tells the current highest bid will show up. The client is allowed to enter his or her bid.

   e. After bidding, the server will record the bidding data on the disk and send back a confirmation message to the client.

   The requirements of this project include:

   • Application scenario design diagram
   • At least one text file used
   • At least one table of a MySQL database used
   • Programmed "postback" feature for the client

6. Discuss the advantages and disadvantages of PHP compared with ASP.NET.

8
XML

8.1 Introduction to XML

XML (extensible markup language) is a computer language designed to provide a standard information description framework used for Internet computing. XML and HTML both are derived from the standard generalized markup language (SGML), which was defined in 1986 as an international standard for document markup. XML was completed in early 1998 by the World Wide Web Consortium (W3C). However, the implementation of the XML standard is far from over and depends upon the progress of the entire information technology industry. Also, the XML technology is somehow more complicated than any other computer language because several companion languages must be applied in order to use XML correctly. Two major reasons why XML is needed are discussed here: HTML documents are difficult to process by computers, and different databases need a common data format.

8.1.1 HTML Documents Are Difficult to Process

HTML has been discussed earlier in this book. Web pages written in HTML can be presented by a web browser for human users. However, HTML documents are difficult to use for data processing by computers. Specifically, information hiding in HTML documents is hard for computers to extract. We use an example to illustrate this. Suppose we have the HTML document in Listing 8.1 for online auctions.

Listing 8.1: Example of HTML Document

```
<HTML>
<HEAD>
<TITLE>Online Auction</TITLE>
</HEAD>
<BODY>
<H2>ABC Online Auction Web Page</H2>
<TABLE BORDER=1>
  <TR><TD>Merchandise on Auction</TD>
      <TD>Current Highest Bid</TD>
  </TR>
  <TR><TD>ThinkPad</TD>
      <TD>$200</TD>
  </TR>
  <TR><TD>HP Laser Printer</TD>
      <TD>$100</TD>
  </TR>
```

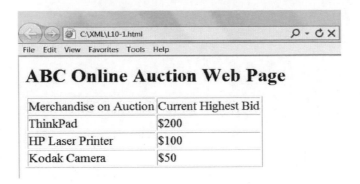

Figure 8.1   The presentation of the HTML document.

```
  <TR><TD>Kodak Camera</TD>
      <TD>$50</TD>
  </TR>
 </TABLE>
 </BODY>
 </HTML>
```

Figure 8.1 shows the presentation of this HTML document. This presentation is perfect for the user to read.

Suppose one wants to use a computer program to extract the bidding information from the HTML documents every hour, and then store the data on computers without retyping. The extracting task for the programmer is quite tedious and difficult. A programmer might consider that the bidding data start from line 11 in the HTML document. However, if the auctioneer's web master changes the HTML document format, such an extracting method will not work. Another programmer might consider that the tag <TABLE> is a reference point to find these bidding data. However, if another table is added to this HTML document, the programmer must redo the programming. The issue raised here is the so-called independence of data and presentation. Later we will see that XML provides a uniform data format for web documents so that documents circulated on the Internet can be searched and processed by computers easily and accurately. The cost for achieving this objective is that the data documents must be formatted in XML, and additional techniques for presentation are needed as discussed in this chapter.

8.1.2 Databases Need Common Data Format to Exchange Data

The second major reason why we need XML is the requirement for a uniform data format for different databases. There have been many database systems commonly used in the information industry. Although SQL (structured query language) is a standard language for processing databases, the data formats are all platform dependent. To transfer data from one database to another, usually one needs an interface implemented by programs to describe the data format (see Figure 8.2a). To make data transfers on the Internet efficient, we need a common data format description

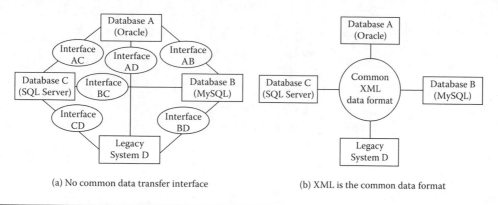

(a) No common data transfer interface   (b) XML is the common data format

Figure 8.2   Databases need common data format for data transfer.

framework so that each database can understand exactly what is requested or what is received from the Internet. The cost for this is that each database must support the XML standard (so-called XML-enabled database) to exchange data in the common XML format (see Figure 8.2b).

Furthermore, traditional relational databases are typically used for processing numerical data and character data. However, the formats of data available on the Internet are rich, including audio, video, complex documents, and international characters. Using XML, these rich data formats can be easily implemented.

8.2 XML Documents Are Data Sheets

For simplicity, we use Notepad (or Notepad++) for editing XML programs. However, there are many commercial XML editors with more functions. These editors can help programmers to format and validate the programs.

8.2.1 XML Instance Documents

Use Notepad to edit the XML document in Listing 8.2. In Notepad, click [File], [Save As], choose file type [All files], and save the document of Listing 8.2 as *file-name*.**xml**—say, greeting.xml—in the user's folder.

Listing 8.2: First XML Example (greeting.xml)

```
<?xml version="1.0" standalone="yes"?>
<GREETING>
Hello, XML World!
</GREETING>
```

Using Microsoft Internet Explorer, open the XML document file to view it (Figure 8.3). You will find that the browser simply displays the document, but does not show a meaningful presentation. This means that XML makes data independent of presentation. An XML document containing data is called an instance document

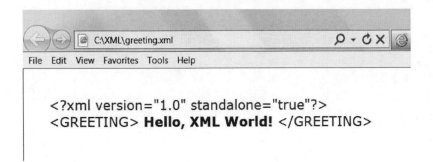

Figure 8.3   XML instance document is viewed in the web browser.

and is stored on the computer with extension `.xml`. To present an instance document in a meaningful form, a program, called style sheet, must be applied, as discussed later in this chapter.

8.2.2 Declaration

The first line of an XML instance document is a processing instruction, enclosed by pair `<?` and `?>`. The first word `xml` after `<?` is the name of the instruction. In this case, the first line of the document is XML declaration. A declaration statement always starts at the first column without any space before it.

8.2.3 Tags and Element

XML uses tags to describe data. For example, `<GREETING>` is a start tag, and `</GREETING>` is an end tag. Unlike HTML, XML tags are named by the programmer for the data items. A pair of tags defines an element. In this example, the pair of tags defines the `GREETING` element, and "`Hello, XML World!`" is the content of this element. A well-formed XML document represents data in a tree structure, and the tree must have one root element. The root element contains every other element in the document. Later we will learn more about how XML tags are used to designate a tree data structure.

8.2.4 Attribute

An XML element can have attributes and their values—for example:

```
<CAR COLOR="Red">
</CAR>
```

`COLOR` is the attribute of the `CAR` element, and `"Red"` is the unique value of the `COLOR` attribute. In principle, one can use either an attribute or an element (e.g., `<COLOR>Red</COLOR>`) to contain a piece of data. However, the value of an attribute is unique for the element, while an element can be repeated with different contents.

Thus, using attributes, one can describe the element in a concise way, as seen in the examples later in this chapter.

8.2.5 *Comment Line and Editorial Style*

Like HTML, a comment line in the XML program is delimited by `<!--` and `-->`. However, XML is case sensitive. A good programmer applies a consistent programming style of uppercase and lowercase for the XML document.

8.3 Cascading Style Sheets

To instruct the web browser on how the contents of XML tags (or the data) are displayed, one may use cascading style sheets (CSS). CSS is well supported by web browsers. As an exercise of CSS, open Notepad and type the following CSS document:

Listing 8.3: Example of CSS (`greeting.css`) for the XML Document in Listing 8.2

```
GREETING {display: block; font-size: 30pt; font-weight: bold;}
```

Save the CSS program in Listing 8.3 as *file-name*.css—say, **greeting. css**—in the same folder with **greeting.xml**. Reopen **greeting.xml** in Notepad, re-edit it as shown in Listing 8.4, and save it as **greetingcss.xml**. Note the bold lines for processing instructions that associate the XML document with the CSS document.

Listing 8.4: XML Document (`greetingcss.xml`) Associated to the CSS (`greeting.css`)

```
<?xml version="1.0" standalone="yes"?>
<?xml-stylesheet type="text/css" href="greeting.css"?>
<GREETING>
Hello, XML World!
</GREETING>
```

Open **greetingcss.xml** in Internet Explorer. The content of the XML document is presented as instructed by **greeting.css**, as shown in Figure 8.4.

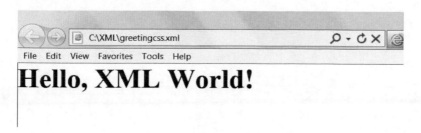

Figure 8.4 Present `greetingcss.xml` with `greeting.css`.

8.4 Extensible Style Language

One can also use extensible style language (XSL), instead of CSS, to detail instructions on how to display the contents of XML tags. XSL has two specific technologies: XSL formatting objects (XSL-FO) and XSL transformation (XSLT). XSLT enables the programmer to use HTML to present data, to reorder elements in the XML document, and to add additional contents. XSL-FO enables the programmer to define a powerful view of the document as pages by specifying appearance and layout of the page. XSLT is discussed in this chapter.

As an exercise, edit the XSLT style sheet of Listing 8.5 in Notepad. The line numbers are used for explanation only and must not be typed in the program. Also, the first line always starts at the first column without any spacing.

Listing 8.5: Example of XSLT Style Sheet (`greeting.xsl`) for XML Document in Listing 8.2

```
 1 <?xml version="1.0" ?>
 2 <xsl:stylesheet
 3   xmlns:xsl="http://www.w3.org/1999/XSL/Transform" version="1.0">
 4     <xsl:template match="/GREETING">
 5       <HTML>
 6         <BODY>
 7           We are learning XML and XSLT!
 8           <H2>
 9           <xsl:value-of select="."/>
10           </H2>
11         </BODY>
12       </HTML>
13     </xsl:template>
14 </xsl:stylesheet>
```

Save this XSLT style sheet as *file-name*.xsl—say, greeting.xsl—in the same folder with **greeting.xml**.

Reopen **greeting.xml** in Notepad, re-edit it as shown in Listing 8.6, and save it as **greetingxsl.xml**. Note the bold line that associates the XML document with the XSLT style sheet.

Listing 8.6: XML Document (`greetingxsl.xml`) Associated to the XSLT Program (`greeting.xsl`)

```
<?xml version="1.0" standalone="yes"?>
<?xml-stylesheet type="text/xsl" href="greeting.xsl"?>
<GREETING>
Hello, XML World!
</GREETING>
```

Open **greetingxsl.xml** in Internet Explorer, and you will see the presentation as shown in Figure 8.5, which is slightly different from Figure 8.4 in that a line is added by the XSLT program for presentation.

Now, we examine the XSLT program in Listing 8.5.

Figure 8.5   Present `greetingxsl.xml` with `greeting.xsl`.

8.4.1 `<xsl:stylesheet>`

XSLT performs its tasks with numerous elements and their attributes. The syntax of the XSLT element is `<xsl:[element-name] [attribute]=value>`.

The very first element in an XSLT style sheet is `<xsl:stylesheet>` (see the tag pair lines **2** and **14** in Listing 8.5). It indicates that the document is an XSLT style sheet. The element has a mandatory attribute: a namespace declaration for the XSLT namespace (see line **3** in Listing 8.5). Namespace is a technique that ensures that the element names are unique and will not lead to confusion.

8.4.2 `<xsl:template>`

The data contained in the XML document are organized into a tree. The data tree has a root and many nodes. To match the data tree, we need a template. Every style sheet must contain a template, which is declared with the `<xsl:template>` element (see lines **4** and **13** in Listing 8.5). This element has attributes, and the match attribute is almost always necessary. In line **4,** the / character is shorthand for the root of the tree. Thus, the value of the match attributes is "/" (or "/*root*"; e.g., "/GREETING" in this example).

8.4.3 *HTML Presentation*

When transforming an XML document for presentation, XSLT uses HTML's features to control the appearance of the data on the screen. See lines **5** and **12**, lines **6** and **11,** and lines **8** and **10** for the HTML tag pairs in Listing 8.5.

8.4.4 `<xsl:value-of>`

To display the value of a data item as a string, the element `<xsl:value-of>` along with its attribute `select` is used. Its general syntax is

```
<xsl:value-of select="expression" />
```

In the example of Listing 8.5, the expression "." represents the current data node (i.e., <GREETING>). The slash character in the tag is used for the empty tag.

8.4.5 Empty Tag

If an element has no content, one can use an empty tag as short cut. An empty tag does not have a corresponding end tag, but ends with /> instead of just >. For example, <xsl:value-of select="*expression*" /> is an empty tag.

8.4.6 <xsl:for-each>

The example of Listing 8.5 is so simple that it contains only one data item. For a complex XML document, a *<xsl:for-each>* element can be used to implement a loop to avoid repeating a search path for the *<xsl:value-of>* element. It operates on a collection of nodes of the data tree designated by the expression of its select attribute. The selected node becomes the current node. Examples of the <xsl:for-each> element will be shown later in the chapter.

8.5 XML Data Tree

The structure of an XML data document can be represented by a tree model. Figure 8.6 shows an example of a simple data tree. A data tree has one root element and one or many subelements (or nodes). A subelement can have its subelement(s). An element can have attribute(s). A plus sign (+) means that the subelement can have one or more instances.

Listing 8.7 is an example of an XML document that is represented by the data tree in Figure 8.6.

Listing 8.7: XML Document (`Message.xml`) Represented by the Data Tree in Figure 8.6

```
<?xml version="1.0" standalone="yes"?>
<Message From="XML">
  <Greeting>
  Hello, World!
```

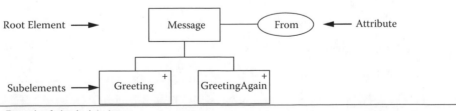

Figure 8.6   Example of simple data tree.

```
      </Greeting>
      <GreetingAgain>
      Hello Again!
      </GreetingAgain>
    </Message>
```

In Listing 8.7, Message is the root element with attribute From. The root contains two elements: Greeting and GreetingAgain.

8.6 CSS Versus XSLT

CSS can only change the format of a particular element based on the chosen tag. In other words, CSS implements styles on an element-wide basis, but does not change these elements. On the other hand, XSLT can choose style based on tag, contents and attributes of tag, position of tag in the document relative to other elements, and so on. XSLT can rearrange and reorder the data, and it can incorporate HTML tags for enhanced presentation. The relationships between XML, XSLT, and HTML for XML data presentations are summarized in Figure 8.7. Apparently, XSLT is more flexible in defining and controlling the presentation.

The following two examples are exercised to further compare CSS and XSLT in presenting XML data with the tree structure. Open Message.xml in Listing 8.7 in Notepad, add <?xml-stylesheet type="text/css" href="message.css"?> after the first line, and save the new XML document as Messagecss.xml. Open Notepad and edit the CSS document in Listing 8.8 and save it as **message.css**. In Listing 8.8, the first line means "display the content in the From attribute before the contents of the elements Greeting and GreetingAgain." The rest of Listing 8.8 is straightforward. Open Messagecss.xml in Internet Explorer; the presentation is shown in Figure 8.8.

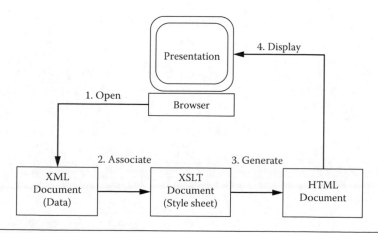

Figure 8.7 XML, XSLT, HTML, and data presentation.

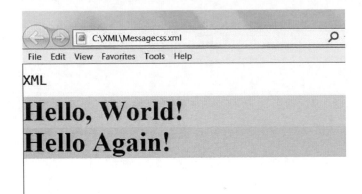

Figure 8.8   Present `messagecss.xml` with `message.css`.

Listing 8.8: CSS (`message.css`) for `Messagecss.xml`

```
Message:before { content: attr(From); font-family:Consolas;
   line-height:3;}

Greeting {display: block; font-size: 30pt;
         background: pink; color: green; font-weight: bold;}

GreetingAgain {display: block; font-size: 30pt;
         background: lightblue; color: red; font-weight: bold;}
```

Open Message.xml in Listing 8.7 in Notepad, add `<?xml-stylesheet type="text/xsl" href="message.xsl"?>` after the first line, and save the new XML document as `Messagexsl.xml`. Open Notepad and edit the XSLT style sheet in Listing 8.9 and save it as `message.xsl`. Note the line in bold in Listing 8.9. **`<xsl:value-of select="@From" />`** displays the data in the **From** attribute. The **@** symbol is used for an attribute. The rest is straightforward. Open `Messagecss. xml` in Internet Explorer; the presentation is shown in Figure 8.9. Apparently, XSLT makes data presentation more flexible.

Listing 8.9: XSLT (`message.xsl`) for `Messagexsl.xml`

```
<?xml version="1.0" ?>
<xsl:stylesheet
 xmlns:xsl="http://www.w3.org/1999/XSL/Transform" version="1.0">
  <xsl:template match="/">
   <HTML>
      <BODY>
        <xsl:for-each select="Message">
          <H3>
          Greetings from <xsl:value-of select="@From" />
          </H3>
          <H1>
             <xsl:value-of select="Greeting"/>
          </H1>
          <H2>
```

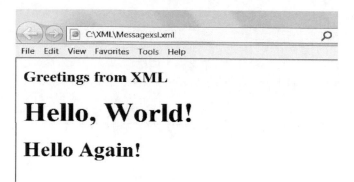

Figure 8.9   Present `Messagexsl.xml` with `message.xsl`.

```
            <xsl:value-of select="GreetingAgain"/>
         </H2>
      </xsl:for-each>
    </BODY>
  </HTML>
 </xsl:template>
</xsl:stylesheet>
```

8.7 Document Type Definition and Validation

An XML document is supposed to be used in the Internet environment for data sharing. If an XML document does not comply with the data structure (i.e., the tree) as designed, the document may contain significant errors. To ensure that people can share the data in an XML document correctly and accurately, the document must be validated before it is posted on the Internet. Two techniques can be used for XML document validation: document type definition (DTD) and XML schema. This section introduces DTD. A DTD document describes the XML data structure by providing a list of elements, attributes, notations, and entities contained in the XML document as well as their hierarchical relationships. DTD ensures the described XML document to comply with the described data structure.

A DTD document can be embedded in the corresponding XML document (called internal DTD), or it can be an independent file stored at an external URL (called external DTD). To ensure that an XML document meets the specification defined by the DTD, one must validate the document against the DTD. The validation of the XML document includes two aspects: formats and semantics. Many commercial DTD validating parsers (or validators) have been available on the software market. Open-source DTD validators are also available on the Internet (e.g., <http://www.xmlvalidation.com> and <http://validator.w3.org/>), but may not be so user friendly.

Note that web browsers do not check XML documents for validity automatically. An invalidated XML document could cause unpredictable and serious mistakes, especially when the data are going to be used for updating a database. It is ultimately the responsibility of the user of the XML document to validate it with the DTD.

8.7.1 Simple Example of Internal DTD

Open the XML document `Message.xml` in Listing 8.5. Re-edit the document, as shown in Listing 8.10, and save it as `Messagedtd.xml`. Note the DTD part in bold in Listing 8.10, which will be explained later in this section.

Listing 8.10: Example of XML Document (`Messagedtd.xml`) with Internal DTD

```
<?xml version="1.0" standalone="yes"?>

<!DOCTYPE Message  [
    <!ELEMENT Message (Greeting+, GreetingAgain+)>
    <!ELEMENT Greeting (#PCDATA)>
    <!ELEMENT GreetingAgain (#PCDATA)>
    <!ATTLIST Message
      From CDATA #IMPLIED >
]>

<Message From="XML">
  <Greeting>
  Hello, World!
  </Greeting>
  <GreetingAgain>
  Hello Again!
  </GreetingAgain>
</Message>
```

8.7.2 Simple Example of External DTD

Open the XML document `Message.xml` in Listing 8.5. Re-edit the document, as shown in Listing 8.11, and save it as `Messagedtd-ex.xml`. Note the two lines in bold in Listing 8.11. The first bold line, **standalone="no"**, declares that the current XML document is not standalone and is associated with an external DTD document—**message.dtd** in this example. The second line in bold will be explained in the next subsection.

Listing 8.11: Example of XML Document (`Messagedtd-ex.xml`) with External DTD (`message.dtd`)

```
<?xml version="1.0" standalone="no"?>

<!DOCTYPE Message SYSTEM "message.dtd">

<Message From="XML">
  <Greeting>
  Hello, World!
  </Greeting>
  <GreetingAgain>
  Hello Again!
  </GreetingAgain>
</Message>
```

Open Notepad, edit the program as shown in Listing 8.12, and save it as `message.dtd`.

> **Listing 8.12: External DTD (`message.dtd`) for XML Document `Messagedtd-ex.xml`**
>
> ```
> <!ELEMENT Message (Greeting+, GreetingAgain+)>
>     <!ELEMENT Greeting (#PCDATA)>
>     <!ELEMENT GreetingAgain (#PCDATA)>
>     <!ATTLIST Message
>       From CDATA #IMPLIED >
> ```

Clearly, the external DTD document is exactly the same as the DTD declaration body in the internal DTD document.

8.7.3 `<!DOCTYPE>`

A DTD document begins with the `<!DOCTYPE>` clause. It declares the root element of the XML document and starts the DTD declarations. The syntax of `!DOCTYPE` for internal DTD is

```
<!DOCTYPE root-element [ DTD declarations ]>
```

The syntax of `!DOCTYPE` for external DTD is

```
<!DOCTYPE root-element SYSTEM "DTD-URL">
```

`"DTD-URL"` declares the location of the DTD document, which is separated from the XML document.

8.7.4 `<!ELEMENT>`

`<!ELEMENT>` declares the name of an XML element and its permissible subelements. For example, `<!ELEMENT Message (Greeting+, GreetingAgain+)>` means that `Message` is the root element and has two subelements: `Greeting` and `GreetingAgain`. The plus sign (+), called cardinality operator, means that the subelement can have one or more instances. Note that there is no space before the + sign. If one uses `*` as the cardinality operator, it means that the subelement can have one, more than one, or no instance.

Next, an element at the lowest level in the data tree, called a leaf element, could have its data. `<!ELEMENT Greeting (#PCDATA)>` means that `Greeting` is a leaf of the data tree and has the `#PCDATA` (parsed character data) type of data. It defines that `Greeting` can have only textual data. An element could have an attribute(s), as explained next. If a leaf element does not contain data, `<!ELEMENT LeafElement EMPTY>` is applied.

8.7.5 `<!ATTLIST>`

The `<!ATTLIST>` declaration declares element attributes and their permissible values. For example, `<!ATTLIST Message From CDATA #IMPLIED >` means that `From` is an attribute of the `Message` element, its type is character data, and optional. The `#IMPLIED` keyword means optional. If `#REQUIRED` is applied, the attribute must appear. `<!ATTLIST>` declarations are placed after all `<!ELEMENT>` declarations.

8.7.6 `<!ENTITY>`

The `<!ENTITY>` declaration declares special character references, text macros, and other content from external sources. The `<!ENTITY>` declaration provides reference mechanisms for any non-ASCII characters (such as international characters) that do not have a direct input method on a keyboard. It can also provide references to prestored texts or image files. Listing 8.13 is a simple XML document with DTD entity declarations.

Listing 8.13: Example of XML Document (`Credit.xml`) with DTD Entity Declarations

```
<?xml version="1.0" standalone="yes"?>

<!DOCTYPE CREDIT  [
   <!ENTITY copy "&#x00A9;">
   <!ENTITY author "Shouhong Wang">
   <!ENTITY copyright "&copy; 2014 &author;">
<!ELEMENT CREDIT (#PCDATA)>
]>

<CREDIT>
   &copyright;
</CREDIT>
```

In Listing 8.13, the first entity declaration defines the reference to a special character © using the Unicode standard hex value. An entity reference begins with ampersand (&) and ends with semicolon (;), and it contains the Unicode code value or the cited entity's name between these two characters. The second entity declaration defines the prestored text. The third entity declaration defines the text macro named `copyright` that in turn cites the two declared entities. In the XML document part, the `copyright` entity is cited. Open this document (`Credit.xml`) without a style sheet in Internet Explorer and the entity references are expanded, as shown in Figure 8.10.

8.8 XML Schema

There have been critiques of DTD, although it is still popular and easy to use. DTD has its unique syntax. It has limited functionality. XML schema is one of the alternatives

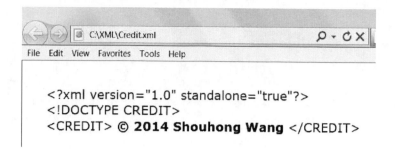

Figure 8.10 Entity references are expanded.

to DTD. XML schema standard was released by W3C in 2001 and has become a main language for XML document validation. An XML schema document is an XML document and is normally saved with extension **.xsd**. For an XML document, the way to describe the data tree using XML schema may not be unique. In the XML document, one can declare the association with the XML schema; however, such an association is not mandatory. More often, other indications for the association, which is specified by the validation parser, can be provided at the validation time.

Open Notepad, edit the XML schema program in Listing 8.14, and save it as message.xsd, which is the XML schema for the XML data tree in Figure 8.6 and the XML document in Listing 8.7 (Message.xml). Again, the line numbers in Listing 8.14 are for explanation and should not be typed in the program, and the first line always starts at the first column without any spacing.

Listing 8.14: XML Schema (`message.xsd`) for Data Tree in Figure 8.6 and `Message.xml` in Listing 8.5

```
 1  <?xml version="1.0"?>
 2  <xs:schema xmlns:xs="http://www.w3.org/2001/XMLSchema">
 3  <xs:element name="Message">
 4    <xs:complexType>
 5     <xs:sequence>
 6      <xs:element name="Greeting" type="xs:string"
 7          minOccurs="0" maxOccurs="unbounded" />
 8      <xs:element name="GreetingAgain" type="xs:string"
 9          minOccurs="0" maxOccurs="unbounded" />
-5     </xs:sequence>
10     <xs:attribute name="From" type="xs:string"/>
-4    </xs:complexType>
-3   </xs:element>
-2  </xs:schema>
```

8.8.1 Schema Element

In Listing 8.14, line **2** is the schema element. It defines the target namespace. xs: is the name of the namespace prefix. Line -**2** is the end tag.

8.8.2 Data Element, Attribute, and Data Type

The `element` tag is used to define a data element of the data tree (e.g., line **3** in Listing 8.14). The `name` attribute defines the name of the element. If the data element has its subelements, `complexType` is used to define them. If the data element has a simple data type, it is defined by the `type` attribute in the element tag (e.g., line **6**). `xs:string` means the data type is string. In fact, one can use XML schema to define specific data types, such as date, zip, etc.

8.8.3 complexType

If an element has its attribute(s) or subelement(s), then the data type of the element is `complex`. The `complexType` tags are used to describe these attributes and subelements, which are included within the tag pair (e.g., lines **4** and **-4**).

8.8.4 sequence

The `sequence` tags are a compositor that defines the ordered sequence of the subelements of the present element. Line **5** and line **-5** shows an example. Sequence could be empty if there are no subelements of the present element, but the `sequence` tags remain, as shown later in other examples.

8.8.5 Cardinality

As designed in Figure 8.6, the `Greeting` element can repeat. In the XML schema, `minOccurs` and `maxOccurs` (line **7**) are used to define its cardinality. In this example, the number of `Greeting` can range from zero to infinite.

8.8.6 Attribute

An attribute of the element is declared in an `attribute` tag. The declarations of attributes (e.g., `<xs:attribute name="From" type="xs:string"/>`) always come after the declarations of all subelements of the present element. Generally, the declarations are put right after the end tag `</xs:sequence>` (see line **-5**) and before the end tag `</xs:complexType>` for the present element (see line **-4**).

8.8.7 XML Validation

Similar to DTD, an XML schema program is used to verify that an XML document complies with the designed data structure. To ensure that the XML document meets the specification defined by the data structure, one must validate the XML document against the XML schema program. The Microsoft Visual Studio environment is able to validate an XML document against the XML schema program, as

Open File (Message.xml)

Add XML Schema (message.xsd)
in Properties pane

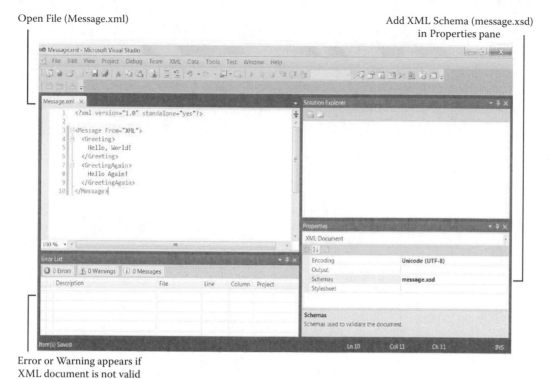

Error or Warning appears if
XML document is not valid

Figure 8.11 Validate XML document against its XML schema program in Microsoft Visual Studio.

shown in Figure 8.11. However, the validation in the Microsoft Visual Studio environment is a "one-way" validation; that is, the XML schema must be correct, and the validation is to validate the XML document against the correct XML schema. There have been many commercial and open-source (e.g., <http://xmltools.corefiling.com/schemaValidate/>) XML schema validators available on the software market. A good validator for beginners is capable of "two-way" validation; that is, the validator can detect possible errors in the XML schema program.

8.9 Summary of Application of XML

XML itself is easy to learn. However, as discussed in the previous sections, the correct use of XML is not straightforward because it involves many companion techniques. Figure 8.12 shows general relationships between XML and its companions, including data structure diagram, CSS or XSLT, and DTD or XML schema. CSS and DTD are still used in many data systems, but XSLT and XML schema have become more common since they are compatible with the style of XML.

Although XML has been with us for many years, it has unsolved problems. Generally, XML follows the hierarchical model, but databases today are relational. Theoretically, the mapping between a relational database and XML could be problematic. This issue will be further discussed later in this chapter. Also, the development of XML and its companion languages is a somewhat piecemeal style.

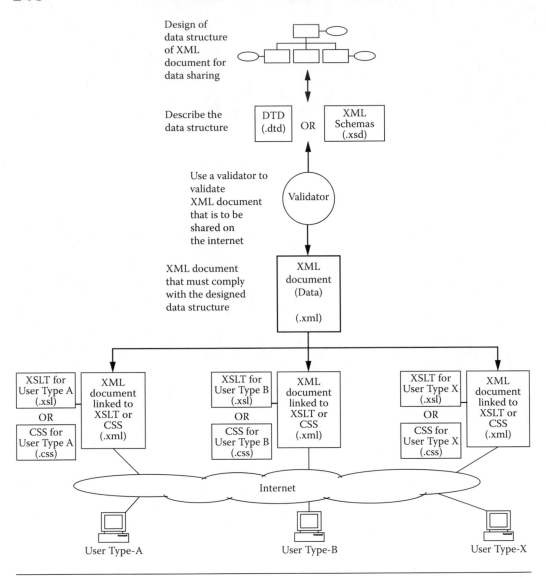

Figure 8.12   XML and companions for web applications.

8.10 An Example of XML Application

This section provides a comprehensive example of XML application that involves hierarchical data structure, DTD, XML schema, and XSLT programs. Suppose an auction house keeps all records of online auctions. Figure 8.13 shows the data tree diagram for the auction data structure. In this example, several attributes are used for the Item element because the value of each of these attributes is unique for the Item element. Listing 8.15 is an XML document with the internal DTD (in bold) that presents the data structure tree. Note that there is no content in the Item element, and thus **<!ELEMENT Item EMPTY>** is used in the DTD. In the XML document, the open tag of Item must be followed by the close tag strictly without any space between, as shown in the lines in bold in the XML document.

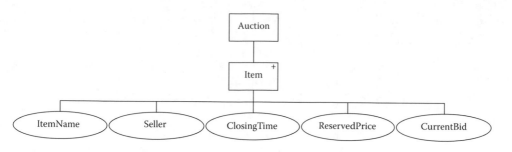

Figure 8.13   Data structure of online auction example.

Listing 8.15: XML Document (`Auction.xml`) for the Data Tree in Figure 8.13

```
<?xml version="1.0" standalone="yes"?>
     <!DOCTYPE Auction  [
     <!ELEMENT Auction (Item+)>
     <!ELEMENT Item EMPTY>
      <!ATTLIST Item
        ItemName        CDATA #REQUIRED
        Seller          CDATA #REQUIRED
        ClosingTime     CDATA #REQUIRED
        ReservedPrice CDATA #IMPLIED
        CurrentBid      CDATA #IMPLIED >
     ]>

     <Auction>
      <Item
        ItemName="Dell Computer"
        Seller="Office Equipment"
        ClosingTime="8:00pm 02/10"
        ReservedPrice="$400"
        CurrentBid="$300" ></Item>
      <Item
        ItemName="Honda Motorcycle"
        Seller="Motor Dealer"
        ClosingTime="4:00pm 01/10"
        ReservedPrice="$4000"
        CurrentBid="$4500" ></Item>
      <Item
        ItemName="Sony DVD Player"
        Seller="Best Purchase"
        ClosingTime="10:00am 03/10"
        ReservedPrice="$150"
        CurrentBid="$200" ></Item>
      <Item
        ItemName="Dartmouth Concert Ticket"
        Seller="A Charity"
        ClosingTime="8:00pm 04/10"
        ReservedPrice="$25"
        CurrentBid="$32" ></Item>
     </Auction>
```

The XML document with internal DTD in Listing 8.15 (`Auction.xml`) is validated by <http://validator.w3.org/>. For exercise, an XML schema program (`auction.xsd`) for the data tree in Figure 8.13 is also developed, as shown in Listing 8.16. `Auction.xml` is validated against `auction.xsd` in Microsoft

Visual Studio as well as the open-source validator at <http://xmltools.corefiling.com/schemaValidate/>).

Listing 8.16: XML Schema (`auction.xsd`) of the Data Structure in Figure 8.13

```
<?xml version="1.0"?>
<xs:schema xmlns:xs="http://www.w3.org/2001/XMLSchema">
  <xs:element name="Auction">
    <xs:complexType>
     <xs:sequence>
     <xs:element name="Item" minOccurs="0" maxOccurs="unbounded">
       <xs:complexType>
       <xs:sequence>
       </xs:sequence>
          <xs:attribute name="ItemName" type="xs:string"/>
          <xs:attribute name="Seller" type="xs:string"/>
          <xs:attribute name="ClosingTime" type="xs:string"/>
          <xs:attribute name="ReservedPrice" type="xs:string"/>
          <xs:attribute name="CurrentBid" type="xs:string"/>
       </xs:complexType>
     </xs:element>
     </xs:sequence>
    </xs:complexType>
  </xs:element>
</xs:schema>
```

Next, we present an illustrative example of the use of XML documents for business applications to share the XML data. Suppose the auction managers are interested in all attributes except for "seller." The XSLT style sheet in Listing 8.17 is used for the managers.

Listing 8.17: XSLT Style Sheet (`auction-manager.xsl`) for Managers

```
<xsl:stylesheet
    xmlns:xsl="http://www.w3.org/1999/XSL/Transform" version="1.0">
  <xsl:template match="/">
    <HTML>
    <BODY>
      <H2>Auction Items Listed for the Manager</H2>

      <TABLE  BORDER="1">
      <THEAD>
      <TR BGCOLOR="PINK">
      <TH>Item Name</TH>
      <TH>Closing Time</TH>
      <TH>Reserved Price</TH>
      <TH>Current Highest Bid</TH>
      </TR>
      </THEAD>

      <TBODY>
       <xsl:for-each select="Auction/Item">
        <TR>
        <TD><xsl:value-of select="@ItemName"/></TD>
```

```
        <TD ALIGN="RIGHT">
            <xsl:value-of select="@ClosingTime"/></TD>
        <TD ALIGN="RIGHT">
            <xsl:value-of select="@ReservedPrice"/></TD>
        <TD ALIGN="RIGHT"><xsl:value-of select="@CurrentBid"/></TD>
        </TR>
      </xsl:for-each>
    </TBODY>
  </TABLE>

  </BODY>
  </HTML>
  </xsl:template>
</xsl:stylesheet>
```

Clearly, to use `auction-manager.xsl` for presenting the XML data in Listing 8.15, a line like

```
<?xml-stylesheet type="text/xsl" href="auction-manager.xsl"?>
```

must be added after the first line of the XML document in Listing 8.15. Practically, the XML document associated with `auction-manager.xsl` is renamed as, say, `Auction-manager.xml`. Figure 8.14 shows the data presentation for `Auction-manager.xml` managers.

Suppose the auction bidders are not supposed to view any value of the `ReservedPrice` attribute. Accordingly, the XSLT style sheet in Listing 8.18 is applied to all bidders.

Listing 8.18: XSLT Style Sheet (`auction-bidder.xsl`) for Bidders

```
<xsl:stylesheet
    xmlns:xsl="http://www.w3.org/1999/XSL/Transform" version="1.0">
  <xsl:template match="/">
    <HTML>
    <BODY>
      <H2>Auction Items Listed for Bidders</H2>
```

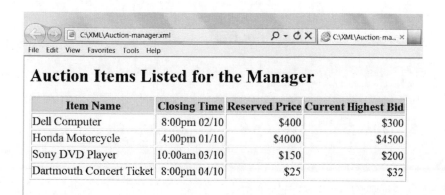

Figure 8.14   The auction data are presented for managers.

```
      <TABLE  BORDER="1">
      <THEAD>
      <TR BGCOLOR="#9acd32">
      <TH>Item Name</TH>
      <TH>Seller</TH>
      <TH>Closing Time</TH>
      <TH>Current Highest Bid</TH>
      </TR>
      </THEAD>

      <TBODY>
        <xsl:for-each select="Auction/Item">
         <TR>
         <TD><xsl:value-of select="@ItemName"/></TD>
         <TD><xsl:value-of select="@Seller"/></TD>
         <TD ALIGN="RIGHT">
               <xsl:value-of select="@ClosingTime"/></TD>
         <TD ALIGN="RIGHT"><xsl:value-of select="@CurrentBid"/></TD>
         </TR>
        </xsl:for-each>
       </TBODY>
     </TABLE>

    </BODY>
    </HTML>
  </xsl:template>
</xsl:stylesheet>
```

Again, to use `auction-bidder.xsl` for presenting the XML data in Listing 8.15, a line like

```
<?xml-stylesheet type="text/xsl" href="auction-bidder.xsl"?>
```

must be added after the first line of the XML document in Listing 8.15. Practically, the XML document associated with `auction-bidder.xsl` is renamed as, say, `Auction-bidder.xml`. Figure 8.15 shows the data presentation for `Auction-bidder.xml` managers.

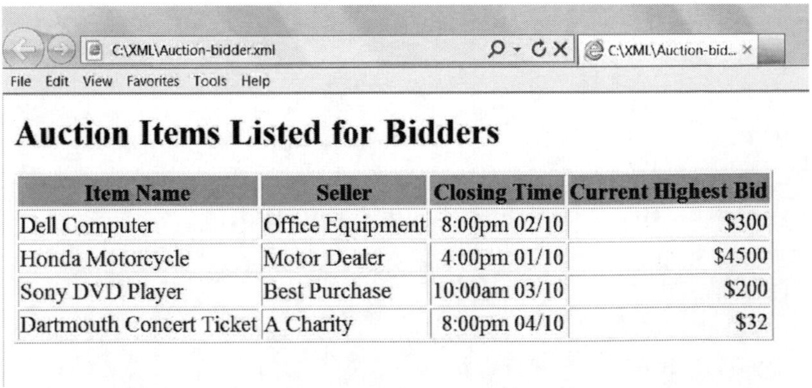
C:\XML\Auction-bidder.xml
C:\XML\Auction-bid...
File Edit View Favorites Tools Help
Auction Items Listed for Bidders
Item Name | Seller | Closing Time | Current Highest Bid
Dell Computer | Office Equipment | 8:00pm 02/10 | $300
Honda Motorcycle | Motor Dealer | 4:00pm 01/10 | $4500
Sony DVD Player | Best Purchase | 10:00am 03/10 | $200
Dartmouth Concert Ticket | A Charity | 8:00pm 04/10 | $32

Figure 8.15 The auction data are presented for bidders.

From the illustrative examples presented earlier, we can see that a single XML document can easily be used dynamically for a variety of clients. An XML document can be viewed as a database that contains numerical numbers, texts, images, and sound clips to be shared by all clients on the Internet. More advantages of XML can be observed if one incorporates XML with database technologies.

8.11 Advanced Subjects of XML

8.11.1 Conversion of Relational Database into XML Tree

Suppose we have a database of a retail company as shown by the ER (entity–relationship) diagram in Figure 8.16. The ER diagram describes the semantics of the database as follows:

- There are entities CUSTOMER, PRODUCT, ORDER, and associative entity ORDERLINE.
- Each customer can make many orders.
- Each order can contain several order lines, and each order line specifies the product ordered.

This ER diagram can be converted into an XML data tree, as shown in Figure 8.17.

A conversion from a relational database to an XML tree might not be as straightforward as thought, because the structures of the XML data tree and relational database model are incompatible. In this example, in the relational database, ORDERLINE must have OrderID, which is the foreign key from ORDER; however, in the XML tree, Orderline inherits OrderID from Order due to the explicit tree structure. Thus, it is unnecessary to repeat OrderID in Orderline. To differentiate the order lines within Orderline, OrderlineNo is then introduced as an attribute for Orderline.

Listing 8.19 shows a sample XML document for the XML data tree in Figure 8.17. Note that if an element does not have a subelements, there is nothing between the open tag and the close tag. For example, the element Customer does not have its subelements, so the close tag </Customer> follows the open tag closely without even a space.

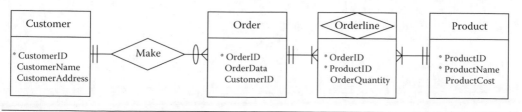

Figure 8.16   Example of relational database model.

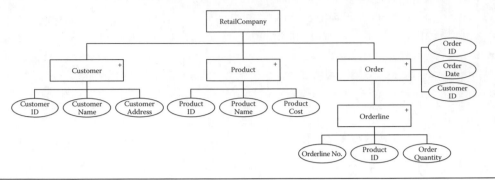

Figure 8.17 XML data tree converted from relational database represented by Figure 8.16.

Listing 8.19: A Sample XML Document of the XML Data Tree in Figure 8.17

```xml
<?xml version="1.0" standalone="yes"?>
<RetailCompany>

  <Customer
     CustomerID="001"
     CustomerName="John"
     CustomerAddress="30 Westport"></Customer>
  <Customer
     CustomerID="002"
     CustomerName="Anne"
     CustomerAddress="20 Northport"></Customer>

  <Product
     ProductID="A1"
     ProductName="Computer"
     ProductCost="1000"></Product>
  <Product
     ProductID="B1"
     ProductName="Printer"
     ProductCost="100"></Product>
  <Product
     ProductID="B2"
     ProductName="TV"
     ProductCost="500"></Product>

  <Order
     OrderID="0001"
     OrderDate="Jan.20"
     CustomerID="001">
     <Orderline
       OrderlineNo="1"
       ProductID="B2"
       OrderQuantity="3"></Orderline>

     <Orderline
       OrderlineNo="2"
       ProductID="A1"
       OrderQuantity="2"></Orderline>
  </Order>
  <Order
     OrderID="0002"
     OrderDate="Mar.18"
```

```
      CustomerID="002">
      <Orderline
        OrderlineNo="1"
        ProductID="A1"
        OrderQuantity="3"></Orderline>
      <Orderline
        OrderlineNo="2"
        ProductID="B1"
        OrderQuantity="4"></Orderline>
   </Order>

</RetailCompany>
```

Listing 8.20 is the XML schema of the XML data tree in Figure 8.17.

Listing 8.20: XML Schema of the XML Data Tree in Figure 8.17

```
 1  <?xml version="1.0"?>
 2  <xs:schema xmlns:xs="http://www.w3.org/2001/XMLSchema">

 3  <xs:element name="RetailCompany">
 4  <xs:complexType>
 5  <xs:sequence>

 6   <xs:element name="Customer" minOccurs="0"
 7                              maxOccurs="unbounded">
 8    <xs:complexType>
 9        <xs:sequence>
-9        </xs:sequence>
10        <xs:attribute name="CustomerID" type="xs:string"/>
11        <xs:attribute name="CustomerName" type="xs:string"/>
12        <xs:attribute name="CustomerAddress" type="xs:string"/>
-8    </xs:complexType>
-6   </xs:element>

13   <xs:element name="Product" minOccurs="0"
14                              maxOccurs="unbounded">
15    <xs:complexType>
16        <xs:sequence>
-16        </xs:sequence>
17        <xs:attribute name="ProductID" type="xs:string"/>
18        <xs:attribute name="ProductName" type="xs:string"/>
19        <xs:attribute name="ProductCost" type="xs:string"/>
-15    </xs:complexType>
-13   </xs:element>

20   <xs:element name="Order" minOccurs="0"
21                              maxOccurs="unbounded">
22    <xs:complexType>
23     <xs:sequence>

24       <xs:element name="Orderline" minOccurs="0"
25                                    maxOccurs="unbounded">
26         <xs:complexType>
27           <xs:sequence>
-27           </xs:sequence>
28           <xs:attribute name="OrderlineNo" type="xs:string"/>
```

```
 29          <xs:attribute name="ProductID" type="xs:string"/>
 30          <xs:attribute name="OrderQuantity" type="xs:string"/>
-26         </xs:complexType>
-24      </xs:element>

-23    </xs:sequence>
 31    <xs:attribute name="OrderID" type="xs:string"/>
 32    <xs:attribute name="OrderDate" type="xs:string"/>
 33    <xs:attribute name="CustomerID" type="xs:string"/>
-22   </xs:complexType>
-20   </xs:element>

 -5 </xs:sequence>
 -4 </xs:complexType>
 -3 </xs:element>

 -2 </xs:schema>
```

8.11.2 xlink *and* xsl:if

XML and its companion languages are still under innovation over time. In this subsection, we introduce two advanced features of XML and XSLT—xlink and xsl:if—through examples. xlink implements hyperlinks in an XML document, and xsl:if implements a data presentation condition in an XSLT style sheet.

Suppose we have a data tree for an order data system as shown in Figure 8.18. The order data system has multiple orders. Each Order has its attribute named OrderID. Each Order has subelements: CustomerName, multiple Item, and ShipTo. Each Item has its subelements: ItemID, ItemName, and Quantity. Note that ItemName has a hyperlink. For demonstration, we use the hyperlinks to access several stable URL of universities.

The schema of the data tree is listed in Listing 8.21 and is named order.xsd. Note the lines in bold for the hyperlinks modeled in the data tree.

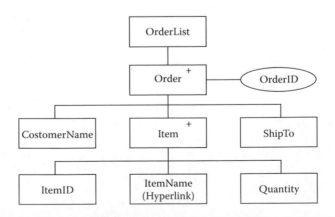

Figure 8.18　Data tree of example of order system.

Listing 8.21: Schemas (`order.xsd`) for the Data Tree in Figure 8.18

```xml
<?xml version="1.0"?>
<xs:schema
xmlns:xs="http://www.w3.org/2001/XMLSchema"
xmlns:xlink="http://www.w3.org/1999/xlink">

  <xs:element name="OrderList">
   <xs:complexType>
   <xs:sequence>
        <xs:element name="Order" minOccurs="0"
                             maxOccurs="unbounded">
         <xs:complexType>
              <xs:sequence>
              <xs:element name="CustomerName" type="xs:string"/>
              <xs:element name="ShipTo" type="xs:string"/>
              <xs:element name="Item" minOccurs="0"
                                    maxOccurs="unbounded">
              <xs:complexType>
                <xs:sequence>
                <xs:element name="ItemID" type="xs:string"/>
                <xs:element name="ItemName" xlink:type="simple"/>
                <xs:element name="Quantity" type="xs:string"/>
                </xs:sequence>
              </xs:complexType>
              </xs:element>
              </xs:sequence>
              <xs:attribute name="OrderID" type="xs:string"/>
         </xs:complexType>
        </xs:element>
     </xs:sequence>
     </xs:complexType>
   </xs:element>
 </xs:schema>
```

A sample XML document of the data tree in Figure 8.18 is listed in Listing 8.22 and is named `Order.xml`. Note the lines in bold in Listing 8.22. The `xlink` clauses in `Order.xml` allow the corresponding data items to become hyperlink entries. `Order.xml` is validated against `order.xsd` in Microsoft Visual Studio as well as the open-source validator at <http://xmltools.corefiling.com/schemaValidate/>).

Listing 8.22: An XML Document (`Order.xml`) for Data Tree in Figure 8.18

```xml
<?xml version="1.0"?>
<OrderList xmlns:xlink="http://www.w3.org/1999/xlink">
  <Order OrderID="A1234">
   <CustomerName>John Smith</CustomerName>
    <ShipTo>285 Westport</ShipTo>
    <Item>
      <ItemID>C-105</ItemID>
      <ItemName xlink:href="http://www.umassd.edu" xlink:type="simple">
               Book</ItemName>
      <Quantity>30</Quantity>
    </Item>
    <Item>
      <ItemID>T-298</ItemID>
```

```
        <ItemName xlink:href="http://www.smu.ca" xlink:type="simple">
                  Television</ItemName>
        <Quantity>50</Quantity>
      </Item>
    </Order>

    <Order OrderID="B2345">
     <CustomerName>Matt Jones</CustomerName>
      <ShipTo>120 Eastport</ShipTo>
      <Item>
      <ItemID>K-23</ItemID>
        <ItemName xlink:href="http://www.mcmaster.ca" xlink:type="simple">
                  GPS</ItemName>
        <Quantity>20</Quantity>
      </Item>
      <Item>
      <ItemID>R-101</ItemID>
        <ItemName xlink:href="http://www.uwo.ca" xlink:type="simple">
                  Cell Phone</ItemName>
        <Quantity>25</Quantity>
      </Item>
    </Order>

    <Order OrderID="C5678">
     <CustomerName>Anne Kerry</CustomerName>
      <ShipTo>45 Northport</ShipTo>
      <Item>
      <ItemID>U-200</ItemID>
        <ItemName xlink:href="http://www.unb.ca" xlink:type="simple">
                  Printer</ItemName>
        <Quantity>100</Quantity>
      </Item>
      <Item>
      <ItemID>"E-28"</ItemID>
        <ItemName xlink:href="http://www.essec.edu" xlink:type="simple">
                  iPod</ItemName>
        <Quantity>80</Quantity>
      </Item>
    </Order>
  </OrderList>
```

Suppose that the data in Order.xml are used for inventory processing, and only data about the items are presented for the application. The XSLT style sheet for this application is listed in Listing 8.23 and is named order-inventory.xsl. All special lines in bold are related to xlink presentation.

Listing 8.23: XSLT Style Sheet (order-inventory.xsl) for Order.xml

```
<xsl:stylesheet version="1.0"
                xmlns:xsl="http://www.w3.org/1999/XSL/Transform"
                xmlns:xlink="http://www.w3.org/1999/xlink"
                exclude-result-prefixes="xlink">

  <xsl:template match="/">
    <HTML>
    <BODY>
    <H3>Orders Listed for Inventory Department</H3>
```

```
<TABLE  BORDER="1">
  <THEAD>
  <TR BGCOLOR="PINK">
  <TH>Order ID</TH>
  <TH>Item ID</TH>
  <TH>Item Name</TH>
  <TH>Quantity</TH>
  </TR>
  </THEAD>

  <TBODY>
   <xsl:for-each select="OrderList/Order">

    <TR>
    <TD><xsl:value-of select="@OrderID"/></TD>
     <xsl:for-each select="Item">
     <TR>
     <TD> </TD>
     <TD><xsl:value-of select="ItemID"/></TD>
         <xsl:for-each select="ItemName">
     <TD><a href="{@xlink:href}"><xsl:value-of select="."/></a>
     </TD>
         </xsl:for-each>
     <TD ALIGN="RIGHT"><xsl:value-of select="Quantity"/></TD>
     </TR>
         </xsl:for-each>
    </TR>

   </xsl:for-each>
  </TBODY>
 </TABLE>
 </BODY>
 </HTML>
 </xsl:template>
</xsl:stylesheet>
```

To associate the `order-inventory.xsl` to the XML document, a line

```
<?xml-stylesheet type="text/xsl" href="order-inventory.xsl"?>
```

must be added to the XML document after the first line in Listing 8.22 and then the XML document saved as, say, `Order-inventory.xml`. The data presentation for `Order-inventory.xml` is shown in Figure 8.19. Click on a hyperlink on the screen; the linked website will show up.

Suppose the order system is used for shipping, and only special customers' data are presented for the delivery group. The XSLT style sheet for this application is listed in Listing 8.24 and is named `order-shipping.xsl`. All special lines in bold are related to the `<xs:if>` condition for data presentation.

Listing 8.24: XSLT Style Sheet (`order-shipping.xsl`) for `Order.xml`

```
<xsl:stylesheet version="1.0"
    xmlns:xsl="http://www.w3.org/1999/XSL/Transform">
  <xsl:template match="/">
```

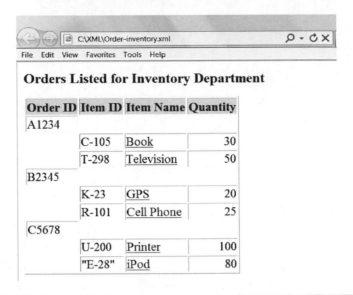

Figure 8.19   Order data with hyperlinks are presented for inventory processing.

```
<HTML>
<BODY>
<H3>Orders Listed for Shipping Department</H3>
<TABLE   BORDER="1">
  <THEAD>
  <TR BGCOLOR="Azure">
  <TH>Order ID</TH>
  <TH>Customer Name</TH>
  <TH>Shipping Address</TH>
  </TR>
  </THEAD>

  <TBODY>
    <xsl:for-each select="OrderList/Order">
  <xsl:if test="CustomerName='John Smith'">
    <TR>
    <TD><xsl:value-of select="@OrderID"/></TD>
    <TD><xsl:value-of select="CustomerName"/></TD>
    <TD><xsl:value-of select="ShipTo"/></TD>
    </TR>
  </xsl:if>
    </xsl:for-each>
  </TBODY>
  </TABLE>
  </BODY>
  </HTML>
    </xsl:template>
  </xsl:stylesheet>
```

To associate the `order-shipping.xsl` to the XML document, a line

```
<?xml-stylesheet type="text/xsl" href="order-shipping.xsl"?>
```

must be added to the XML document after the first line in Listing 8.22 and then the XML document saved as, say, `Order-shipping.xml`. The data presentation for

Figure 8.20 The order data are selected through conditions for shipping.

`Order-shipping.xml` is shown in Figure 8.20. Only the customer's data related to shipping are displayed.

8.11.2.1 xlink xlink implements hyperlinks between the data and the corresponding websites. To use `xlink`, the following steps in programming XML, schema, and XSLT style sheets are applied.

Step 1. In the schema document (`order.xsd`), specify special attribute in the `<xs:schema>` tag, as shown in Listing 8.21:

```
xmlns:xlink="http://www.w3.org/1999/xlink"
```

Step 2. In the schema document, specify special attribute in the `<xs:element>` tag for the element with hyperlink, as shown in Listing 8.21:

```
<xs:element name="ItemName" xlink:type="simple"/>
```

Step 3. In the XML document, specify the special attribute for `xlink` in the top element, as shown in Listing 8.22:

```
<OrderList xmlns:xlink="http://www.w3.org/1999/xlink">
```

Step 4. In the XML document, specify the special attribute in the element for hyperlink, as shown in Listing 8.22:

```
<ItemName xlink:href="http://www.umassd.edu" xlink:type="simple">
```

Step 5. In the XSLT style sheet, specify the special attribute for `xlink` in the `<xsl:stylesheet>`, as shown in Listing 8.23:

```
<xsl:stylesheet version="1.0"
                xmlns:xsl="http://www.w3.org/1999/XSL/Transform"
                xmlns:xlink="http://www.w3.org/1999/xlink"
                exclude-result-prefixes="xlink">
```

Step 6. In the XSLT style sheet, use `<xsl:for-each>` to select the node with hyperlink, and use the `<a>` tag to specify `xlink`, as shown in Listing 8.23:

```
<xsl:for-each select="ItemName">
<a href="{@xlink:href}"><xsl:value-of select="."/></a>
</xsl:for-each>
```

Here, `<xsl:value-of select="."/>` applies the value of the currently selected element (`ItemName` in this example).

8.11.2.2 `<xsl:if>`   The XSLT condition tag `<xsl:if>` can vary the data presentation. To use `<xsl:if>`, the following two steps are applied in programming the XSLT style sheet:

Step 1. Specify the special attribute in the `<xsl:stylesheet>` for the namespace as shown in Listing 8.24:

```
<xsl:stylesheet version="1.0"
      xmlns:xsl="http://www.w3.org/1999/XSL/Transform">
```

Step 2. Use the `<xsl:for-each>` tag to select the parent element (`OrderList/Order` in this example) of the subject element (`CustomerName` in this example) for the condition, and then use the `<xsl:if>` tag to specify the condition for the subject element (`CustomerName` in this example), as shown in Listing 8.24:

```
<xsl:for-each select="OrderList/Order">
      <xsl:if test="CustomerName='John Smith'">
         ........
      </xsl:if>
</xsl:for-each>
```

8.12 XHTML

As shown in this chapter, HTML and XML are not compatible. Nevertheless, it is quite straightforward to convert an HTML document to an XML document, since the tags in HTML can be defined as elements in XML. XHTML is such a language that keeps the feature of HTML and makes the markup document compatible with XML.

One can use structured steps to convert an HTML document to its XHTML document. For example, suppose we have an HTML document in Listing 8.25.

Listing 8.25: Example of HTML Document

```
<HTML>
<HEAD>
<TITLE>Convert HTML to XHTML</TITLE>
```

```
</HEAD>
<BODY>
<P>
<H2>Hello, XHTML!</H2>
<BR>
<IMG SRC=Book.jpg ALT="Book">
</BODY>
</HTML>
```

To convert the HTML document to an XHTML document, one performs the following steps:

Step 1. Add DOCTYPE declaration:

```
<?xml version="1.0"?>
<!DOCTYPE html PUBLIC "-//W3C//DTD XHTML 1.0 Strict//EN"
   "http://www.w3.org/TR/xhtml1/DTD/xhtml1-strict.dtd">
```

Step 2. Add the XHTML namespace to the root element:

```
<html xmlns="http://www.w3.org/1999/xhtml" xml:lang="en" lang="en">
```

Step 3. Use the following rules to create a well-formed XML document:

1. Change tags to lowercase.
2. There should be no missing close tag.
3. Make up proper syntax for empty elements.
4. There should be no missing values and quotation marks in all attributes.

The XHTML document for Listing 8.25 is listed in Listing 8.26. You can practice the preceding steps and check the conversion result.

Listing 8.26: XHTML Document for the HTML Document in Listing 8.25

```
<?xml version="1.0"?>
<!DOCTYPE html PUBLIC "-//W3C//DTD XHTML 1.0 Strict//EN"
    "http://www.w3.org/TR/xhtml1/DTD/xhtml1-strict.dtd">
<html xmlns="http://www.w3.org/1999/xhtml" xml:lang="en" lang="en">
<html>
<head>
<title>Convert HTML to XHTML</title>
</head>
<body>
<p>
<h2>Hello, XHTML!</h2>
</p>
<br />
<img src="Book.jpg" alt="Book">
</body>
</html>
```

You may use Notepad to edit the XHTML document in Listing 8.26, save it as a file with the extension .html, and then open it in the web browser to view the presentation. As shown in this example, XHTML is merely to make an HTML document well formatted and compatible with XML.

8.13 XBRL

eXtensible business reporting language (XBRL) is an extension of XML that has been defined specifically for business accounting and financial reports. Under XML, tags are applied to items of business accounting and financial data so that they can be read and processed by computers. It enables unique identifying tags to be applied to items of business data. For example, the `<tax>` tag would identify the data of `tax` in a business document. The true power of XBRL is more than simple identifiers. As XML can provide links to relative information about the data item, the XBRL can link the business data item to various sources in the business domain. More importantly, XBRL can be easily extended to meet a variety of special needs in business document processing. XBRL has been in practical use internationally and is still under development. The use of XBRL is to support all aspects of business reporting in different countries and industries.

8.13.1 Comparison of XBRL with XML

Similarly to XML, XBRL has three basic concepts: schema (taxonomy in XBRL terms), instant document of the data, and style sheets for presentation.

Compared with XML, XBRL has the following major extensions to XML:

1. XBRL provides a framework for defining and extending business data dictionaries that make business report processes and exchanges more efficient.
2. XBRL provides the ability to define and validate specific semantics (or business rules) for the business reporting domain. For instance, for the numeric accounting data set {Assets, Liability, Equity}, XBRL can validate whether "Assets = Liability + Equity." Such business domain-based semantics are beyond the XML schema.
3. XBRL provides application features such as comparison and extension. For example, a financial report from company A—say, "Assets of Fiscal Year 2014 of Company A"—can be directly compared with a financial report from company B—say, "Assets of Fiscal Year 2014 of Company B."
4. XBRL supports multiple hierarchies, such as content, calculation, and definition, while XML supports one hierarchy of content.

Because of the extensions of XBRL, XML parser or other XML software is unable to handle XBRL. One must use XBRL software to convert business reports into XBRL documents through computerized mapping processes. However, XBRL does not address formatting for presentation. The existing tools and standards for presenting data (e.g., XSLT) are intended to be used for XBRL document presentation.

8.13.2 Taxonomy

Taxonomy is an important concept of XBRL. XBRL taxonomies are the dictionaries that XBRL uses. These dictionaries define the specific tags for individual items of data (e.g., NetIncome). Since countries have different accounting documentation regulations, each country may have its own taxonomy for business reporting. The governments, industries, or even companies may also have taxonomies to meet their own business needs. Taxonomies enforce standardization of terminologies used in business reports—for instance:

```
<element name="NetIncome" />
<element name="netprofit" />
<element name="netProfit" />
```

describe the same figure of net income, but use different element names. Taxonomy is to make the meaning of data less ambiguous for processing.

8.13.3 Prepare XBRL-Based Reports

The following steps are needed to create an XBRL-based business report:

1. Select, create, or extend a taxonomy for the report.
2. Using specific software, translate the data from their current form or application to an XBRL instance document that complies with the XBRL taxonomy.
3. Validate the taxonomy and instance document against external or internal measures.
4. Create style sheets for document presentation.
5. Publish the three components (taxonomy, instance document, and style sheets) on the Internet.

To provide technical support of XBRL, many countries have established XBRL organizations. You may check the website at <http://www.xbrl.org/> and its links to find technical details of XBRL.

Chapter 8 Exercises

1. Fill the blanks in the following XML document:

```
1   <?xml version="1.0" standalone=_____ _____>
2   <?xml-stylesheet _____="text/xsl" _____="cd.xsl"?>
3   <_____>
4       <_____>
5       <Title>Soulsville<_____>
6       <Artist>Jorn Hoel<_____>
7       <Country>Norway<_____>
8       <Publisher>WEA<_____>
```

```
 9      <RegularPrice>8.90<_____>
10      <SalePrice>7.85</_____>
11      <Year>1996<_____>
12      </CD>
13      <CD>
14      <_____>Empire Burlesque</Title>
15      <_____>Bob Dylan</Artist>
16      <_____>USA</Country>
17      <_____>Columbia</Publisher>
18      <_____>11.90</RegularPrice>
19      <_____>9.99</SalePrice>
20      <_____>1985</Year>
21      <_____>
22      <CD>
23      <Title>Hide your heart</Title>
24      <Artist>Bonnie Tyler</Artist>
25      <Country>UK</Country>
26      <Publisher>CBS Records</Publisher>
27      <RegularPrice>10.90</RegularPrice>
28      <SalePrice>8.95</SalePrice>
29      <Year>1988</Year>
30      <_____>
31   </CATALOG>
```

2. Draw the data tree for the XML document in question 1.
3. Write the DTD for the XML document in question 1 and validate it.
4. Write the XML schema for the XML document in question 1 and validate it using a validation parser.
5. Fill the blanks in the following XSLT style sheet that is applied to the XML document in question 1. Applying this XSLT, what is the expected presentation output of the XML document in question 1?

```
 1   <xsl:stylesheet
 2   _____:xsl="http://www.w3.org/1999/XSL/Transform" version="1.0">
 3    <xsl:template _____="/">
 4    <_____>
 5    <BODY>
 6    <H2>Online CD Catalog</H2>
 7         <TABLE BORDER="1">
 8         <TR>
 9         <TH>Title<_____>
10         <TH>Artist<_____>
11      <TH>Price<_____>
12         </TR>
13      <xsl:for-each select="CATALOG/CD">
14         <TR>
15         <TD><xsl:_____ select="_____"/></TD>
16         <TD><xsl:_____ select="Artist"/></TD>
17         <TD><xsl:_____ select="RegularPrice"/></TD>
```

```
18          </TR>
19          <_____>
20          </TABLE>
21     </BODY>
22     </HTML>
23     <_____>
24     </xsl:stylesheet>
```

6. Change the XSLT style sheet in question 5 so that the data of `RegularPrice` are not displayed, but the data of `SalePrice` are displayed.

7. Develop an XML document and a CSS style sheet for it.

8. Develop an XML document and an XSLT style sheet for it.

9. Develop an XML document and its internal and external DTD documents with `!ELEMENT`, `!ATTLIST`, and `!ENTITY`.

10. Develop an XML document and its XML schema and use a validator for validation.

11. Develop an XML project for electronic commerce applications, including:
    • A short description of your project
    • A data tree diagram that has three levels with mixture of elements and attributes
    • XML schema for the data tree
    • A sample XML document of the data tree
    • A screenshot that indicates the validation of the XML document against the XML schema
    • Two XSL style sheets for two groups of application users. `xlink` and `<xsl:if>` might be included.

12. Convert an HTML document to an XHTML document.

13. Check the website at <http://www.xbrl.org/> to write a short essay about XBRL.

9.1 Introduction to SQL

SQL (structured query language) is a universal language for creating, updating, and querying databases. As SQL is a small language, the SQL program is often called SQL script. SQL can be used for all database management systems (DBMSs) (DB2, Oracle, MySQL, etc.) as well as all computer language platforms (PHP, .NET, etc.). SQL was developed under the name SEQUEL by IBM in the mid-1970s. That is why people pronounce SQL as "sequel" more often than as "ess-que-ell." SQL has been standardized by ANSI (American National Standard Institute).

A particular database management system can have its query development environment, the so-called QBE (query by examples), to create queries without using SQL. In the query development environments of QBE, the database management system generates the query code in SQL. This gives an impression that one might not need to write SQL code. However, there are two major reasons for learning SQL:

1. SQL integrates features of data definition languages (DDLs) and data manipulation languages (DMLs). QBE itself does not possess any features of DDL, such as CREATE and DELETE tables. Also, QBE is unable to implement sophisticated features of DML. Thus, complicated queries are always implemented by SQL.
2. QBE relies on the particular DBMS environment (e.g., Microsoft Access). When using a large computer language (such as C++ or .NET, PHP) to develop a business application program connected to databases (Oracle, MySQL, etc.), one must write SQL code that is embedded into the program in the large computer language to access and update the databases.

The syntax of SQL is quite simple. A SQL script contains a command along with needed clauses and ends with a semicolon. This chapter explains how SQL scripts can be used to define and create tables, to insert and update instances of records, retrieve data, and manipulate the data. To explain SQL, suppose we have the design of a tiny database with 4NF tables, as shown in Figure 9.1.

9.2 CREATE and DROP

CREATE TABLE is used to create a table with all attributes and their data types. For example, the SQL script in Listing 9.1 creates a table named tblStudent with

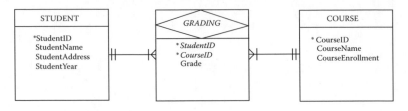

Figure 9.1   The 4NF tables for SQL examples in this chapter.

its four attributes, including the primary key. There might be variations of this SQL script depending on the specific DBMS.

> **Listing 9.1: CREATE TABLE**
>
> ```
> CREATE TABLE tblStudent
> (StudentID CHAR(9),
>  StudentName CHAR(30),
>  StudentAddress CHAR(40),
>  StudentEnrolYear INT(4),
>  PRIMARY KEY (StudentID));
> ```

Common data types used in the standard SQL are

CHAR(n)—character string (text), at most n characters long
DATE—date data
DECIMAL(p, q)—decimal number p digits long and q digits after the decimal point
INT—integer

The PRIMARY KEY clause is used to define the primary key of the table. A combination primary key could have more than one attribute—for example:

```
PRIMARY KEY (StudentID, CourseID)
```

defines the two-attribute combination key.

DROP TABLE is used to delete a table. The SQL script in Listing 9.2 deletes tblStudent.

> **Listing 9.2: DROP TABLE**
>
> ```
> DROP TABLE tblStudent;
> ```

9.3 INSERT, UPDATE, DELETE

INSERT is used to add one record to the table. The SQL script in Listing 9.3 appends one student record to tblStudent.

Listing 9.3: INSERT a Record

```
INSERT INTO tblStudent
VALUES ('01234567', 'John', '285 Westport', 2016);
```

UPDATE is used to change the value(s) of the record with a certain key value. The SQL script in Listing 9.4 changes the address of the student record with key '01234567'.

Listing 9.4: UPDATE a Record

```
UPDATE tblStudent
SET StudentAddress = '300 Eastport'
WHERE StudentID='01234567';
```

DELETE is used to delete a record with a certain key value. The SQL script in Listing 9.5 deletes the student record with key '01234567'.

Listing 9.5: DELETE a Record

```
DELETE FROM tblStudent
WHERE StudentID='01234567';
```

In the preceding two examples, condition of the query is defined in the WHERE clause, which we will discuss in more detail later.

The preceding SQL commands that we have learned are used for database construction and maintenance. These SQL commands fit in the category of database DDL. The SQL scripts with these commands can be embedded in large computer programs to allow the user to update the database. Apparently, it is not convenient to use these SQL commands to build a database from scratch. Practically, a DBMS can have a user-friendly interface that allows the database designer to create tables and to maintain the tables without using tedious SQL scripts.

Suppose we use the previous SQL commands to create the database as modeled in Figure 9.1, which contains the three tables with their instances as shown in Figure 9.2. We use these data for demonstrating the rest of the examples of SQL scripts that fit in the category of DML or query.

9.4 Query—SELECT

A query is a piece of script that commands the DBMS to retrieve needed data from the database. Queries can generate integrated data from the normalized tables.

In SQL, the SELECT command is used to implement queries. The general structure of SELECT query is

```
SELECT  [attributes] [built-in functions]
FROM    [tables]
WHERE   [conditions]
AND     [conditions];
```

StudentID	StudentName	StudentAddress	StudentEnrolYear
01234567	John	285 Westport	2018
02345678	Anne	287 Eastport	2020
03456789	Robert	324 Northport	2019

CourseID	CourseName	CourseEnroll
ACT211	Financial Accounting	35
ACT212	Cost Accounting	28
MIS315	Information Systems	40
MIS322	Systems Analysis & Design	38
MIS432	Database Design	30
MKT311	Principles of Marketing	25
MGT490	Special Topics	20

StudentID	CourseID	Grade
01234567	ACT211	A+
01234567	ACT212	A
01234567	MIS315	B
02345678	ACT211	B+
02345678	MIS322	C
03456789	ACT212	B
03456789	MIS432	A
03456789	MKT311	A

Figure 9.2 Sample database.

Listing 9.6 is an example of a simple query that *finds the student's name and address of student ID 01234567 from the student table.*

Listing 9.6: Select Specified Data from a Table

```
SELECT StudentName, StudentAddress
FROM tblStudent
WHERE StudentID = '01234567';
```

StudentName	StudentAddress
John	285 Westport

Listing 9.7 is a query that *finds the student's entire record of student ID 01234567 from the student table.* The "*" sign represents all attributes of the table.

Listing 9.7: Select an Entire Record from a Table

```
SELECT *
FROM tblStudent
WHERE StudentID = '01234567';
```

StudentID	StudentName	StudentAddress	StudentEnrolYear
01234567	John	285 Westport	2018

The WHERE clause is used to define the conditions. If it is omitted, the query is to retrieve the entire table.

In some cases, the result of a query may contain duplicated data items. To screen these out, DISTINCT is used. Consider the query *find distinctive student enrollment years from the student table.*

Listing 9.8: DISTINCT Eliminates Duplications

```
SELECT DISTINCT StudentEnrolYear
FROM tblStudent;
```

StudentEnrolYear
2018
2019
2020

9.5 WHERE Clause and Comparison

As shown in the previous examples, the WHERE clause defines the conditions for data selection. In addition to "=" (equal), comparison operations ">" (greater than), "<" (less than), ">=" (greater than or equal to), "<=" (less than or equal to), and "<>" (not equal to) can be applied in the WHERE clause. Listing 9.9 is the query that *lists the names of those students who enroll to the program after 2017.*

Listing 9.9: Comparison—Greater Than

```
SELECT StudentName
FROM tblStudent
WHERE StudentEnrolYear > 2017;
```

StudentName
John
Anne
Robert

A WHERE clause can have a combination of multiple conditions connected through the Boolean operators AND and OR. If the AND operator is applied, the two conditions must be true in order for the combination condition to be true. If the OR operator is applied, at least one of the two conditions must be true in order for the combination condition to be true. When ANDs and ORs are used in the same WHERE clause, ANDs are considered before ORs are considered. To avoid mistakes, it is recommended to use pairs of parentheses to indicate the consideration priorities. Listing 9.10 is a query that *lists the names of those students whose ID numbers are greater than 00234567 and who enroll in the program after 2017 or before 2005.*

Listing 9.10: AND and OR Operators

```
SELECT StudentName
FROM tblStudent
WHERE StudentID > '00234567'
AND (StudentEnrolYear > 2017 OR
     StudentEnrolYear < 2005);
```

StudentName
John
Anne
Robert

Character strings can also be compared using unequal signs because they are represented by internal code (e.g., ASCII code).

For strings of characters (text), the LIKE operator and a "wildcard" are used to test for a pattern match. Listing 9.11 is a query that *finds the student records for those students whose street names contain "Westport."* Here, the percent sign "%" is a wildcard to represent any collection of characters.

Listing 9.11: LIKE Operator and Wildcard "%"

```
SELECT *
FROM tblStudent
WHERE StudentAddress LIKE '%Westport%';
```

StudentID	StudentName	StudentAddress	StudentEnrolYear
01234567	John	285 Westport	2018

Listing 9.12 is a query that *finds the student record for each student whose name has the letter "o" as the second letter of the name.* Here, the wildcard sign "_" represents any one character.

Listing 9.12: LIKE Operator and Wildcard "_"

```
SELECT *
FROM tblStudent
WHERE StudentName LIKE '_o%';
```

StudentID	StudentName	StudentAddress	StudentEnrolYear
01234567	John	285 Westport	2018
03456789	Robert	324 Northport	2019

The IN operator allows you to specify a list of character strings to be included in a search. Listing 9.13 is a query that *finds the student whose ID is "01234567," "00234567," or "00034567."*

Listing 9.13: IN Operator

```
SELECT StudentName
FROM tblStudent
WHERE StudentID IN ('01234567',
        '00234567', '00034567');
```

StudentName
John

9.6 ORDER BY Clause

The ORDER BY clause is used to list the data in a particular order based on the values of an attribute. The default order is ascending. The ASC operator makes ascending explicit. The DESC operator is used to sort data in the descending order. Listing 9.14 is a query that *lists all student records in the reverse alphabetic order by student name.*

Listing 9.14: ORDER BY Clause

```
SELECT *
FROM tblStudent
ORDER BY StudentName DESC;
```

StudentID	StudentName	StudentAddress	StudentEnrolYear
03456789	Robert	324 Northport	2019
01234567	John	285 Westport	2018
02345678	Anne	287 Eastport	2020

9.7 Aggregate Functions

A database stores raw data—not secondary (or processed) data such as average, total, etc.—to avoid data redundancy. One of the important roles of queries is to provide secondary data as information for the user. SQL uses aggregate functions to calculate sums (SUM), averages (AVG), counts (COUNT), maximum values (MAX), and minimum values (MIN). Listing 9.15 is a query that *finds the total number of student records in the student table.* If you want to name the result (e.g., CountOfStudents, you use AS keyword; otherwise, the DBMS uses a default name for the result.

Listing 9.15: COUNT Function

```
SELECT COUNT(*) AS CountOfStudents
FROM tblStudent;
```

CountOfStudents
3

Listing 9.16 answers the query *what are the smallest enrollment number, largest enrollment number, total enrollment number, and average enrollment number in the course table?*

Listing 9.16: MIN, MAX, SUM, and AVG Functions

```
SELECT MIN(CourseEnrollment), MAX(CourseEnrollment),
       SUM(CourseEnrollment), AVG(CourseEnrollment)
FROM tblCourse;
```

Expr1000	Expr1001	Expr1002	Expr1003
20	40	216	30.8571428571429

Note that "aggregate functions" is not allowed to be used in a WHERE clause directly. For instance, a clause such as WHERE COUNT(*)>1000 is not allowed.

9.8 GROUP BY Clause and HAVING Clause

When an aggregate function is used, one might want to find the calculated value for each group. The GROUP BY clause is used to calculate results based on each group. If a condition on the calculated results is needed, the HAVING clause can be added. Listing 9.17 is a query to *find the total number of courses taken by each student, and only include students who have taken at least 2 courses.* Two points are worth noting in this query: First, the query with the GROUP BY clause matches "each" in English. Second, the HAVING clause is different from the condition in the WHERE clause in that the HAVING clause goes with the GROUP BY clause and must use an aggregate function.

Listing 9.17: GROUP BY Clause and HAVING Clause

```
SELECT StudentID, COUNT(*)
FROM tblGrading
GROUP BY StudentID
HAVING COUNT(*) > 1;
```

9.9 Joining Tables

The queries we have examined thus far deal with a single table. If two or more tables are involved in a query, the join operation can be applied. Suppose we are going to *list the names of those students who receive "A" or "A+" in any course.* Apparently, two tables—namely, tblStudent and tblGrading—are involved. To process the query, the query processor merges the two tables into a single large (denormalized) table. Listing 9.18 shows the query.

Listing 9.18: Join Two Tables

```
SELECT DISTINCT tblStudent.StudentName
FROM tblGrading, tblStudent
WHERE tblStudent.StudentID=tblGrading.StudentID
AND (tblGrading.Grade='A+' OR
        tblGrading.Grade='A');
```

StudentName
John
Robert

The SQL script in Listing 9.19 joins the three normalized tables—tblStudent, tblCourse, and tblGrading—to integrate all related data in a denormalized form for the user to view.

Listing 9.19: Join Multiple Tables to Integrate Related Data

```
SELECT *
FROM tblStudent, tblCourse, tblGrading
WHERE tblStudent.StudentID = tblGrading.StudentID
AND tblCourse.CourseID = tblGrading.CourseID;
```

tblStudent.St	StudentNar	StudentAddre	StudentEnr	tblCourse.C	CourseName	CourseEnr	tblGrading.	tblGrading	Grade
01234567	John	285 Westport	2018	ACT211	Financial Accou	35	01234567	ACT211	A+
01234567	John	285 Westport	2018	MIS315	Information Sys	40	01234567	MIS315	B
02345678	Anne	287 Eastport	2020	ACT211	Financial Accou	35	02345678	ACT211	B+
02345678	Anne	287 Eastport	2020	MIS322	Systems Analysi	38	02345678	MIS322	C
03456789	Robert	324 Northport	2019	MIS432	Database Desigr	30	03456789	MIS432	A
03456789	Robert	324 Northport	2019	ACT212	Cost Accountinç	28	03456789	ACT212	B
03456789	Robert	324 Northport	2019	MKT311	Principles of Ma	25	03456789	MKT311	A
01234567	John	285 Westport	2018	ACT212	Cost Accounting	28	01234567	ACT212	A

In the preceding example, tables are joined by using the WHERE clause with conditions. Three general rules are applied in a query with joining tables:

1. The general format of a condition that associates two tables is

[*TableOn-1-Side*].[*PrimaryKey*] = [*TableOn-M-Side*].[*ForeignKey*]

2. If *n* tables are joined in the query, then *n* − 1 conditions are needed. These *n* − 1 conditions are tied by the AND operator.

3. To differentiate the same names in different tables, the table name followed by a period sign is used for an attribute name (e.g., tblStudent.StudentID) to qualify the attribute name. That is, the table name must be quoted as qualifier to specify the table to which the attribute belongs if the query involves multiple tables.

Listing 9.20 shows another example of a query with multiple tables: *Who (student ID and name) receives an "A+" or "A" grade in which course (course ID and course name)? List the results in order of student ID.*

Listing 9.20: Query with Multiple Tables

```
SELECT tblGrading.StudentID, tblStudent.StudentName,
       tblGrading.CourseID, tblCourse.CourseName,
       tblGrading.Grade
FROM tblGrading, tblStudent, tblCourse
WHERE tblStudent.StudentID=tblGrading.StudentID
AND tblCourse.CourseID=tblGrading.CourseID
AND (tblGrading.Grade='A+' OR tblGrading.Grade='A')
ORDER BY tblStudent.StudentID;
```

StudentID	StudentName	CourseID	CourseName	Grade
01234567	John	ACT212	Cost Accounting	A
01234567	John	ACT211	Financial Accounting	A+
03456789	Robert	MKT311	Principles of Marketing	A
03456789	Robert	MIS432	Database Design	A

9.10 Subquery

A SELECT query can embed another SELECT query, which is called subquery. A subquery can have its subquery, and so on. The execution sequence of the query is from inside to outside, which means that the most interior subquery is executed first. There are several reasons for using subquery, as explained next.

9.10.1 Subquery—Reducing Computational Workload of Join Operation

A subquery can be used as an alternative to a join operation in a simple situation when the retrieved data are not integrated. Revisit the query in Listing 9.18, which is to *list all students who receive "A" or "A+" in any course.* One can write a subquery as shown in Listing 9.21.

Listing 9.21: Example of Subquery That Avoids Join Operation

```
SELECT tblStudent.StudentName
FROM tblStudent
WHERE tblStudent.StudentID IN
        (SELECT tblGrading.StudentID
        FROM tblGrading
```

StudentName
John
Robert

```
WHERE(tblGrading.Grade='A+'
    OR tblGrading.Grade='A'));
```

In Listing 9.21, there are two SELECT commands. The second SELECT command finds student IDs that receive "A" or "A+" from tblGrading. The query processor then finds the matched student IDs in tblStudent (by the first WHERE clause). Finally, the top SELECT command finds the corresponding student names.

The SQL query with a subquery in Listing 9.21 finds the same data as the query in Listing 9.18 does, but avoids the join operation, which takes significantly more computation resources than a subquery does. However, in cases where integrated data from two or more tables are going to display concurrently, this type of subquery becomes incapable, and a join operation must be applied.

If the joining tables are large and the needed data from the joining tables do not involve all attributes, a subquery in the FROM clause can reduce the computational workload of the join operation. For example, the query in Listing 9.22 is to *list all student grade records, including only the student numbers, the student names, the course numbers, and the grades.* As StudentAddress, StudentYear, CourseName, and CourseEnrollment are not involved in the query, the tables in the first FROM clause become smaller. Note the new table names in the top-level FROM clause (i.e., tblStudentSmall and tblCourseSmall) and these table names in the WHERE clause for the join operation.

Listing 9.22: Example of Subquery in the FROM Clause

```
SELECT tblStudent.StudentID, tblStudent.StudentName,
        tblCourse.CourseID, tblGrading.Grade
FROM
    (SELECT tblStudent.StudentID, tblStudent.StudentName
    FROM tblStudent) tblStudentSmall,
    (SELECT tblCourse.CourseID
    FROM tblCourse) tblCourseSmall,
    tblGrading
WHERE tblStudentSmall.StudentID=tblGrading.StudentID
AND tblCourseSmall.CourseID=tblGrading.CourseID;
```

StudentID	StudentName	CourseID	Grade
01234567	John	ACT211	A+
01234567	John	MIS315	B
02345678	Anne	ACT211	B+
02345678	Anne	MIS322	C
03456789	Robert	MIS432	A
03456789	Robert	ACT212	B
03456789	Robert	MKT311	A
01234567	John	ACT212	A

9.10.2 *Subquery as an Alternative to* GROUP BY

A subquery can be used as an alternative to the GROUP BY clause. For example, the query in Listing 9.23 is to *show each student's name along with the number of courses she/he has taken* using a subquery.

Listing 9.23: Subquery for Groups

```
SELECT tblStudent.StudentName,
    (SELECT COUNT(*)
    FROM tblGrading
    WHERE tblStudent.StudentID=tblGrading.StudentID)
    AS NumberOfCourses
FROM tblStudent;
```

The use of subquery for groups could cause confusion if the design of the subquery is incorrect. For the beginner, the GROUP BY clause would be better than this type of subquery.

9.10.3 *Subquery—Determining an Uncertain Criterion*

A subquery is used to determine an uncertain criterion. Suppose we want to know *which students with ID numbers greater than "02000000" have the earliest enrollment year of such students.* Beginners of SQL often have the following wrong answer:

```
SELECT StudentName
FROM tblStudent
WHERE StudentID > '02000000'
AND StudentEnrolYear = MIN(StudentEnrolYear);
```

This query does not work. The fact is that SQL does not allow an uncertain term on the right side in the WHERE clause because of its ambiguity. In the preceding wrong SQL, the WHERE clause is equivalent to

```
WHERE StudentEnrolYear=?
```

because MIN(StudentEnrolYear) is unknown in terms of its specific condition. To make a correct WHERE clause, you need to put either a certain value or a subquery on the right side of the WHERE clause. Thus, the correct SQL for the preceding query is Listing 9.24.

Listing 9.24: Example of Subquery for Uncertain Condition

```
SELECT StudentName
FROM tblStudent
WHERE StudentID > '02000000'
AND StudentEnrolYear=
        (SELECT MIN(StudentEnrolYear)
        FROM tblStudent
        WHERE StudentID > '02000000');
```

StudentName
Robert

Two points in writing subquery that determine uncertain criteria in the WHERE clause are worth noting:

1. When the right side of the WHERE clause is uncertain (e.g., MIN, MAX, SUM, AVG, COUNT), you must use a subquery to replace the uncertain condition.
2. In Listing 9.24, you can see that the condition StudentID>'02000000' in the host WHERE clause repeats in the condition in the subquery WHERE clause. If this condition is not repeated in the two WHERE clauses, then the meaning of the query is quite different. For example, if the first WHERE clause is omitted, the query represents *which students (in the entire population) have the earliest enrollment year of those students with ID number greater than '02000000.'* On the other hand, if the second WHERE clause is omitted, the query represents *which students with ID numbers greater than '02000000' have the earliest enrollment year of all students.*

9.11 Tactics for Writing Queries

The following are general tactics for writing SQL scripts in SELECT statements:

1. Read the query carefully. Determine which data are to be retrieved and which attributes are to be included in the SELECT command.
2. If a variable is needed, use a subquery as the variable.
3. Determine which tables will be used in the FROM clause.
4. If two or more tables are involved, use join operation(s) (match the primary key in one table with the foreign key in another table) in the WHERE clause.
5. Construct the WHERE clause by including all conditions that are linked by AND or OR. Never use any aggregate function in the WHERE clause directly.
6. If a condition has an uncertain criterion (MAX, MIN, AVG, SUM, COUNT) on the right side of the condition, use a subquery.
7. Consider GROUP BY (for each group) with HAVING condition, ORDER BY clauses, and other operators (e.g., DISTINCT) if needed.
8. For hands-on practices, you may construct test tables with a limited number of test samples to test the SQL script to see if it generates the expected result.

9.12 SQL Embedded in Host Computer Programming Languages

Computer application programs in large languages (e.g., C++, PHP, and .NET) often host SQL scripts to deal with relational databases directly. These programs, typically called middleware, implement the user interface, retrieve the needed data through the SQL scripts, and then perform manipulations on the retrieved data for the business applications.

To make a connection to the databases and to process the embedded SQL in the host language, specific database connection software must be integrated into the system, as discussed in the ASP.NET and PHP chapters. The format of SQL scripts in a host computer programming language depends on the syntax of the host language. Generally, a SQL script is a text string and is placed between the double quotation mark pairs linked by the "&" signs. Note that an unnecessary space in the SQL script string could cause problems in compiling the program. Also, each cycle of database connections open and close can execute only one SQL script. In other words, if there are multiple SQL scripts in a program, the server must open and close the database connection multiple times.

Chapter 9 Exercises

Consider the following tables of a database:

HOUSE

*HouseAddress	HouseOwner	Insurance

HEATING UNIT

*HeatingUnitID	UnitName		UnitType		Manufactory	
		DateOfBuilt		Capacity		HouseAddress

TECHNICIAN

*EmployeeNumber	EmployeeName	Title	YearHired

SERVICE

*HeatingUnitID	*EmployeeNumber	ServiceType	*Date	*Time

a. Find the owner of the house at 285 Westport Rd.

b. List the heating unit names and numbers of the gas heating units built in the 285 Westport Rd. house.

c. The types of heating units include gas, electric, solar, and many models of hybrid. List the heating unit number, date built, and manufacturer of all heating units other than hybrid models with capacity between 3000 and 4000 cubic feet from largest to smallest.

d. List the names of technicians who maintained a heating unit in 285 Westport Rd. along with the service type performed.

e. Find the name and number of the largest gas heating unit.

f. What percent is the total capacity of gas heating units out of the total capacity of all types of heating units?

Index